Wingshooter's Guide to™

Arizona

Upland Birds and Waterfowl

Hunting Titles Available
from Wilderness Adventures Press, Inc.™

Big Game Hunter's Guide to™

Big Game Hunter's Guide to Colorado

Big Game Hunter's Guide to Idaho

Big Game Hunter's Guide to Montana

Big Game Hunter's Guide to Wyoming

Wingshooter's Guide to™

Wingshooter's Guide to Arizona

Wingshooter's Guide to Idaho

Wingshooter's Guide to Iowa

Wingshooter's Guide to Kansas

Wingshooter's Guide to Michigan

Wingshooter's Guide to Minnesota

Wingshooter's Guide to Montana

Wingshooter's Guide to North Dakota

Wingshooter's Guide to Oregon

Wingshooter's Guide to South Dakota

Wingshooter's Guide to Washington

Wingshooter's Guide to Wisconsin

Great Places™

Great Places Montana

Great Places Washington

Great Places Colorado

Field Guide to™

Field Guide to Fishing Knots

Field Guide to Upland Birds and Waterfowl

Field Guide to Dog First Aid

Field Guide to Retriever Drills

Training the Versatile Hunting Dog

Chuck and Blanche Johnson's Cookbook®

Wilderness Adventures Wild Game Cookbook

Wingshooter's Guide to™

Arizona

Upland Birds and Waterfowl

William "Web" S. Parton

Wingshooter's Guide to™ Series

Wilderness
Adventures
Press, Inc.™

Belgrade, Montana

Published by Wilderness Adventures Press
45 Buckskin Road
Belgrade, MT 59714
866-400-2012
Website: www.wildadvpress.com
email: books@wildadvpress.com

Second Edition 2012

Printed in the United States of America

ISBN 978-1-932098-60-0 (1-932098-60-7)

To my wife, Nicole,
who has walked with me through the best and worst of it
and can still run with the setters.

Table of Contents

Foreword
by Bill Tarrant

No one else could have written this book this well because Web Parton is a hunter. Know what a hunter is? I used to say it was a man who wore his mud well, but that characterization had more color than content.

A hunter is that guy (or gal) you'd want to be with if you were trapped by an avalanche, washed away by a flood, broke a leg, got black water malaria, came down with pneumonia, or fell off a cliff.

A hunter would mend you, comfort you, feed you, and save you. That's what a hunter is. I've gone to field with thousands of hunters all over the world. That's my business: to go with them and write their stories. Among that lot—which was the best on earth or I wouldn't have been with them—I can count on one hand the number of hunters I've met.

Web Parton is on that list. Plus, Web's left a toenail under every rock in Arizona, which is his subject. I've hunted with Web or, at least, I've trailed him. Web puts on eight quarts of water, gathers his dogs by making that sound in your cheek to call horses, and takes off straight up mountains. Know what eight quarts of water weigh? And by the way, that water is for his dogs. Well, it weighs 16 pounds, and the guy's going straight up mountains.

If you could keep up with Web, you'd learn what the vegetation is, what the dogs are doing and why, where the birds are and when they'll appear, the advantages of elevation, and everything there is to know about nature that is pertinent to your particular hunt. I've hunted both big game and birds with Web. Heck, I've been with him hunting small game, too, for I recall all the squirrel we rousted. No matter the quest, Web serves his harvest on the table that night.

I've had duck and quail and squirrel and deer and what-all-else done up as fajitas on Web's groaning board, because he wouldn't hunt except to eat what he seeks. The one exception would be to train his gun dogs on wild birds.

But don't think Web is only a hunter. He apprenticed as a taxidermist in his teens. He is accomplished in wood carving and sculpting. He can paint and handle all sorts of exotic molding materials and make things come to life in them. Web is the quintessential man who hunts and trains dogs. Most of all, I'd say Web is a good conversationalist. He talks from the heart and writes the same way. No counterfeit ever.

I've written some award-winning stories in *Field & Stream* magazine about Web. Not because of any ability on my part to write, but because of the inspiration this guy stirs up in me. I can tell you this: Web could have written a book of poetry as well as a game hunter's guide. Either would have soothed your fretted brow and gentled your galloping heart while it told you just how the world you seek is put together.

Whatever Web tells you in this book, it's the gospel.

Bill Tarrant
Sedona, Arizona

Acknowledgements

First, let me thank Bill Tarrant and Nicole Poissant, without whom this book would not exist. In addition, Don Prentice did double duty as friend and proof reader. Also, Chuck and Blanche Johnson for their trust and patience. Thank you.

Some dear friends allowed me to tag along with a camera and, in general, muck up what could have been perfectly good hunts. Special thanks to Don Prentice, Troy Hawks, Jay Smith, Jim Gross, Mike Merry, Al Peevey, Harold Snyder, John Sherman and Darrell Kincaid.

A book like this doesn't get written by just one person. Many people have been very helpful in sharing their experiences and time. I would like to thank: Dr. Gerry Ault, Randy Babb, Bill Berlat, Tom Body, Dave Brown, Dr. Kevin Carmichael, Earl Carrico, Tim Dooley, George Ferenz, Bill Gaddy, Bill Gilchrist, Dave Hackman, Jonathan Hanson, Roseann Beggy Hanson, Jim Heffelfinger, Gene Hill, John Holt, Suzellen Holt, Bill Kuvlesky, Jim Levy, Sandy McClure, Bob Miller, Burt Miller, Brian Murray, Denise Murray, Ron Olding, Sophie and Wil Poissant, Jack Redeman, Eric Rhicard, Dr. Carol Rowe, Glen Seal, Ron Spomer, General Jim Trail, Rick Wilson.

Also, a special thanks to the Arizona Game and Fish Department personnel who were gracious in sharing their knowledge and expertise, in particular Jerry Perry and Phil Smith.

Introduction

The first time I came to Arizona was in 1974 and 1975. I was fresh out of high school and working in a taxidermy shop in California. Another kid who worked at the shop was a refugee from Tucson, and he and I became friends. Since reading the words of Jack O'Connor as a boy, I had dreamed of Arizona. My friend and I made several trips to hunt quail and ducks and javelina.

I have an old 3½ by 3½ snapshot from one of those hunts. We were somewhere in the Oracle Junction area, and the picture shows a rather wild looking quail hunter with an equally wild setter sitting along side. In the photo I am holding a single bedraggled male Gambel's quail up for the camera. Looking at the picture now, I am impressed by two things. First, photography has improved immensely, and second, my father was right. I did need a hair cut.

Arizona was the real thing. Country forever and all of it for hunting! Twenty years later, Arizona is still arguably the best location in the country for an upland bird shooter.

The amount of public land in Arizona is beyond the frame of reference of most American bird hunters, many of whom take closed access and no trespassing signs as a matter of course. There is a total of 72.6 million acres in the state, with only 13.1 million held in private hands. The rest of the state's area is held principally in National Forest, Bureau of Land Management, Arizona State trust lands, Indian Reservation, military lands and national parks, monuments and wildlife refuges. Most of Arizona is open to hunting; closed land is the exception.

The sheer amount of land can produce tremendous numbers of birds. Arizona's two mainstays, Gambel's quail and mourning doves, have unlimited habitat in the lower two-thirds of the state. The spice of scaled and Mearns' Quail, and white-winged dove sweeten the pot. High bird numbers in conjunction with the state's liberal bag limits offer extraordinary hunting opportunities. While an East Coast grouse hunter goes through two boxes of shells in a season, an Arizona shooter can do the same in a single morning hunt.

Most of the nation's bird hunters stow their gear when winter bites hard in December. Arizona quail seasons run through the middle of February, and spring turkey season stretches from late April into May. Dove season opens September 1st. That's almost half the calendar year.

In addition, Arizona has mild winter weather that allows a hunter to stay in the field for the entire six months that an upland bird season is open. Seasonally, winter visits the state's southern half for a few days somewhere around the first of the year and then it leaves us alone. Hunters often strip down to tee shirts during mid-day on late January and February quail hunts.

Last, Arizona is unique. The state's diversity makes it one of the most beautiful places on earth. All four types of North American deserts are found here: Sonoran, Chihuahuan, Mojave and Great Basin. This is a claim that no other state in the union can make. Elevation starts at 70 feet above sea level in the low creosote brush near

Don Prentice hunting Gambel's quail near Tucson, Arizona.

Yuma and rises to the alpine zone at 12,633 feet elevation on top of Mount Humphries, north of Flagstaff. The state is bordered on the west by the Colorado River, one of the country's great river drainages. Arizona has stunning mountain ranges and beautiful sunsets.

All of these things combine to make Arizona an upland bird hunter's holiday. This book was written to help the resident bird hunter and those who travel from other parts of the country and who want to sample some of the splendors of the state. I have tried my best to be simple and thorough, a balance not easy to achieve in writing, as well as life. I hope I came close a time or two.

Welcome to Arizona. Bird hunters are a small fraternity that grows gregarious in wild, lonesome places. We cherish the comfort of a few moments spent sitting on a tailgate, sipping a cold soft drink and seeing a put-up dog taken out so everyone can look him over.

So, when you're out on the flats with birds calling in the distance, and the dogs are working slow into a stiff wind with their tails whipping figure eights, keep an eye on the horizon. I'll be out there with you somewhere.

Tips on Using This Book

- The state of Arizona is split between two area codes. The Phoenix metropolitan area falls in the state's old area code of 602. The rest of the state was changed in 1995 to the new 520 area code. Be aware that the phone company will not make any allowances for dialing the wrong area code. If, while dialing a call, a recorded voice announces that the number has been disconnected or is no longer in service, or that the number cannot be completed as dialed, be sure you are using the right area code. As a point of reference, the 602 area code applies to the entire Maricopa county, which includes the Phoenix metropolitan area.
- For the purpose of organization, the state is broken down into the six Game and Fish Department regions.
- Each of the six sections includes distribution maps for all species of upland birds found in that section. These general distribution maps are only an approximation and may change due to weather conditions, habitat alteration, and farming practices.
- Although I have tried to be as accurate as possible, please note that this information is current only for 1996. Ownership of hotels, restaurants, etc., may change. I cannot guarantee the quality of the services they provide.
- Always check with the Arizona Game and Fish Department or tribal wildlife departments for the most recent hunting regulations. Prices, season dates, and regulations can change from year to year.
- Motel cost key:

  $ — less than $40 per night
  $$ — between $40 and $65 per night
  $$$ — $65 per night and up

Major Roads and Rivers of Arizona

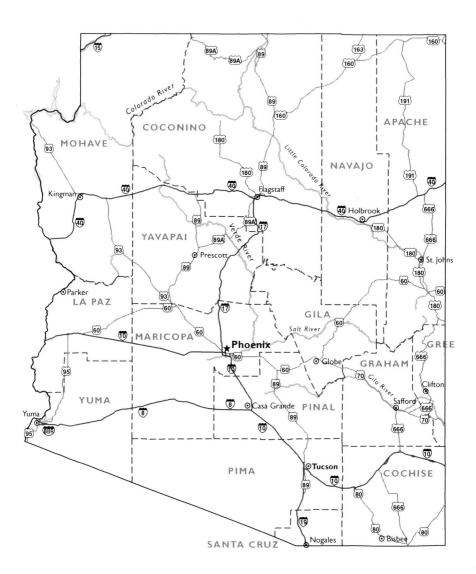

Arizona Facts

6th largest state in the union
113,900 square miles
72,964,480 acres
337 miles across
389 miles north to south
13.1 million acres of private land
15% Forest Service
16% Bureau of Land Management
13% Arizona State Trust Lands
28% Indian Reservations

Elevations: 70 feet near Yuma to 12,633 feet on Mt. Humphries near Flagstaff
Counties: 15
Towns and Cities: 587
Population (2006 estimate): 6,482,505

20 Indian Reservations
2 National Parks
13 National Monuments
6 National Forests
85 Wilderness Areas
24 State Parks

Nicknames: "The Copper State", "The Grand Canyon State"
State Motto: Ditat Deus (God Enriches)
Official Neckwear: The Bola tie
Official State Colors: Blue and Gold
Primary Industries: Mining, Agriculture, Tourism
Capital: Phoenix
Bird: Cactus Wren
Reptile: Ridgenose Rattlesnake
Flower: Saguaro Cactus Blossom
Tree: Palo Verde
Gemstone: Turquoise

Don Prentice with a male Gambel's, scaled, and Mearns' quail.

The Three Species Quest

Arizona bird hunting means quail. In a land of plenty, it is easy to settle into a contented state of bliss. We go to the mesquite-choked, broken ground washes and concentrate on outsmarting the handsome top-knotted Gambel's or work the flats and try to outmaneuver the white-topped scalies. Some days both species turn up in the bag and we appreciate the smorgasbord.

Then, a few times each season, our gaze turns toward the oaks dappling the foothills of the surrounding sky island mountain ranges, and we head for Mearns' country. We go because they are there and we must. We go because it's been long enough since the last Mearns' hunt death march to not quite remember how heavy your feet felt carrying your two-bird take the last mile back to the truck.

The hunting is good and each hunter relishes his day's piece of the pie. But just once, a shooter thinks about having the whole thing. Like Don Quixote scamming on windmills, it becomes an Arizona quail hunter's rite of passage. If a shooter could take all three species in one day, then he would have had the best that Arizona has to offer. It was with the spirit of that challenge that Don Prentice and I set out to take all three in one day.

We headed south of Tucson, to an area where all three species were within walking distance of each other. If this was to be done, then it had to be done clean. No frantic car rides to disjointed pieces of habitat. Don Quixote did not tilt his lance from out of the window of a Ford F150. For the accomplishment to have value it had to be done fairly, on foot.

We parked at the halfway point, above the valley's yellow grass flats, which glowed in the casts of a new dawn. The scalies were down there, just moving off their ground-level roosts, beginning to feed among the yuccas and leaving scent. We parked level with the mesquite. As I stepped from the truck, I heard the nervous "putt, putt, putt" of a Gambel's hen. A covey was leaving. They had been roosting in the mesquite trees and were annoyed at our intrusion. A thousand feet above us the desert folded into a mountain range. I saw the line drawn on the side of the range where the band of oak trees defended the slope from the grassland vegetation below. Under those oaks is where we would find our Mearns' quail.

The strategy was to work low first and pick up the two species that were early risers—Gambel's and scaled. The Gambel's should come easy. We would target them first as we worked down toward the valley. Scaled coveys were often found well above the grass flats interspersed with the Gambel's coveys. If we got lucky we could have both desert birds by 9:30 and begin swinging up toward Mearns' country. Mearns' don't generally move much before 10 A.M., and the hunting is best from noon to 3 P.M., so we would hit the right elevation just about the time that the birds began cooperating.

The weather was cool but I knew that we would be asking a lot of the dogs. We were looking at a possible seven-hour hunt. The dogs had been hunted through the first two-thirds of the season and were hard. There were several stock tanks over the course we planned to follow, and we carried extra water. I also had food to keep their energy up.

I started swinging crate doors open and releasing dogs as Don shuffled gear. My two setters, Belle and Rose, hit the ground running. Don's wirehaired, Tab, dropped off the back of the truck and disappeared into the brush after them. I filled a water bucket for the dogs to leave at the truck, and then got into my own vest and canteen belt. By the time I had put my shotgun together, the dogs had looped back in and were at the water. Don and I stood off to the side, ready to go while the dogs drank, we wanted them good and tanked up. From here on out, water was going to get precious.

I let out a sharp whistle to give the dogs a line. The wind cut on a diagonal to the face of the mountains. We swung around to face it and stepped off into the wind.

The dogs made scent one hundred yards out. Tab worked in close with her nose to the ground while the two setters pushed forward. I saw Belle flash point and then charge forward. Rose saw Belle running and circled wide to the side of her. Belle covered 30 yards and then slammed on point. As Rose came around through the low grass and spotted the find, she cat walked into a solid back. Tab came in behind Belle and froze.

I motioned over toward Don, but it wasn't necessary. He was already moving into position for any birds that broke his way. I came in from the side and got to within 45 yards when the covey jumped. I needed another 10 yards to clear a screen of mesquite and the only shot I had was one single that broke out, straight at me over the tops of the trees. I snapped shot a two-barrel salute and watched the single fly away.

The main covey had flushed across the front of Don and he knocked down a double. Belle came in carrying a bird as I walked over to Don. Tab was busy sorting through a patch of brush. I took the dead bird from Belle and threw it across to Don. He pouched the bird just in time to watch Tab take off on a wild chase with a running cripple six inches off her nose. The Gambel rooster made it ten feet before being scooped up and delivered to hand to Don.

Don and I lined out 15 yards apart and moved in the direction the bulk of the covey had gone. Rose was nowhere to be seen, but when we had gone 50 yards I saw a still, white patch showing through some vegetation, and Belle confirmed it when she slid into a back behind it. Don motioned Tab over to him and told me to take the shot, and then he admonished me not to embarrass him. I walked around the line of low cover and spotted Rose locked up with her eyes fixed on a prickly pear patch ten feet in front of her. I moved forward to close the gap, and as I stepped around a bush, a single blasted out the other side. By the time I could get turned, the bird was past me and I watched Don fold it neatly. Tab rocketed off after the downed bird, and I turned around to see Rose still intent on her cactus with Belle backing. I closed another 10 feet when another single pulled the same trick and Don powdered it with his second barrel. He took the first bird from Tab and she wheeled around to recover the second. I shouted over to remind him that there was a 15-bird limit in place and at this rate he would be out of luck before we could get to any scalies. Don, ever the gentleman, smiled broadly and politely asked me not to move until he had finished reloading.

Then he added insult to injury when he shouted "pull" after he closed the action on his side by side.

I turned back toward the setters and they were still in place, so I made a direct march straight to them. Ten yards out, three Gambel's sprung up out of the cactus. Two of the birds went back low over the dogs barring a shot, but one male swung wide and I touched the first trigger as the barrel swung past his folded back top-knot. The quail cartwheeled and both dogs broke toward the fall. As the dogs went past me, they bumped another single, and I watched it turn end over end into the ground at the sound of my second shot. As I stood there with an empty gun, more birds boiled up in a classic Arizona "popcorn" rise. With another dozen birds in the air going in all directions, Don didn't waste any time. He slapped down another bird with two shots, and then we both watched the show.

After sorting out the carnage, recovering the downed birds, and listening to Don's offer to sell me some of his magic reloads, we lined off for scalie cover. There were another three covey points with assorted singles, but we restricted our shots to one bird per contact so we would not fill out our limits. By the time we hit cover likely to hold both species, Don was at nine and I was at eight Gambel's in the bag.

Yuccas were starting to show up on the grass-covered hills and the mesquites had thinned out and were only thick down along the edges of the washes. I watched the setters drift out onto a grass ridge and start the slow deliberate walk of a dog trailing a running covey. Their legs were moving and their tails weren't, held straight back and stiff to indicate birds in front of them.

Don and I ran to catch up with the dogs. We took up outrigger positions, off to the sides and slightly in front, to be in position for a shot if the covey broke either way at the flush. It took a half run to stay in position and out in front. The dogs trailed for 200 yards with no sighting of birds, only a flowing scent trail. Finally, I caught sight of movement 60 yards ahead of us. Then I made out the shapes of quail running. A few seconds later, the setters spotted them and broke into a dead run. Rose came at them from one side and Belle from the other. Tab brought up the rear, right up the middle. Don called "Can you tell…?" and the covey went. Thirty yards out, 40 birds lifted into the air. The covey had run like scalies, but they were too far out to know for sure whether they were, in fact, scaled or Gambel's. I looked for the softer buff grey of a scalie or the black color on the head of a male Gambel's. They were just too far.

Then, as I brought up my shotgun, I saw them lofting. Instead of following the roll of the ground at six feet, they lifted 20 feet into the air and I figured there was a good chance they were scalies. I covered a bird and fired. When it wobbled but didn't fold, I shot it again. At the second shot, the bird pitched sideways into the ground. Down but not dead, and I was glad to see both setters tearing through the grass after it. I ran right at the melee in case I needed to follow up the runner with a shot on the ground. Gratefully, when I reached the area, both dogs were returning and Rose had a quail in her mouth. I couldn't make out the bird clearly until she released it, and then I knew we were two-thirds of the way there.

I had not heard Don shooting, but when I got back to him, he held up a bird with one hand and a thumb pointing skyward with the other. We had the covey spread out, so we tried to pin a few singles. Tab struck a solid point in some featureless grass and Don rewarded her with a clean kill. Belle had another point that she broke and relocated several times until Rose, who was backing, ran forward and came in from the other side and stopped the bird from running. With the two setters locked up and pointing each other, I stepped in the middle and took an easy, going away single. That was all we found of that covey and really, with scalies, four out of 40 isn't a bad ratio.

Don and I parleyed. The dogs had been on the ground for two and a half hours. They were still in good shape, but it was time to get going and see about those Mearns'. We were a stiff one-hour's walk away from the lowest oaks. We were 15 minutes from a stock tank. Though we had kept them watered, nothing reinvigorates a dog like a belly soaking in a cow tank. We decided to get to the tank, water, feed and rest the dogs, and have lunch.

We took off back through Gambel's country and pressed for the tank. As is always the case when you've filled out your limit or are out of shells, birds were popping everywhere. We kept the dogs close and didn't slow down. At the tank, we got the dogs watered, refilled plastic water bottles, and broke out the canned gourmet cat food. I gave each dog a 4.4 ounce can and then we sat down in the shade of a mesquite and let the dogs sleep while we ate our lunch. We gave them a 20-minute siesta and then began heading uphill.

The mesquite trees thinned out when we got to the base of the mountains. Instead of the soaptree yucca that we found on the low end of the mesquites, other types of yucca took over here. Lechuguilla and bear grass yucca dotted the hillsides above us. The oaks started appearing along the bottoms of the slopes where rain water ran off the mountain. Manzanita and catclaw filled in the understory.

We picked a wide canyon mouth, where two ridges spilled out onto the desert grasslands. During good Mearns' years, surplus coveys are sometimes found below traditional Mearns' habitat. This wasn't a good year, but the higher we got the better our chances were of finding a covey.

We were near to the bird's traditional range when the canyon walls narrowed down. The elevation started pitching up sharply and what had been a hike became a climb. We scrambled over a rimrock step and the valley floor leveled off for 200 yards in front of us. Mature oak trees shaded the thick yellow grass that carpeted the bottom and sides of the canyon. In the cool shadows below the oaks, the grass gave way to a layer of dead oak leaves. We walked to the base of a large oak to take a breather and let the dogs drink from a small trickle that flowed out of a side canyon. Don was the first to spot the diggings among the clumps of grass, small rocks, and oak duff. He held his shotgun out towards the ground, like a pointer. "Today's", he said. I walked over to him and we looked around at the steep slope and tight side canyons. The little rascals were here somewhere.

Tab started it off by walking a tight circle with her nose glued to the ground, 20 yards off to the side of us. The setters had piled up in the shade and were resting when they spotted the wirehaired. They raised up their heads and stopped panting as they watched her body language. When Tab lined out in the trough that ran up the edge of the valley, along the bottom of the slope, both setters leaped to their feet and followed her. I whistled and gave the setters an over, up slope. They veered off of Tab and scrambled uphill. I took off after them. Don fell in on the valley side of Tab and we started up the valley. I kept my position on the side hill about 40 yards above them. The Mearns' covey was probably feeding somewhere in front of us on the bottom end of the slope. I kept the setters working the high ground in case the covey had gone high. This was Tab's specialty, and she didn't need a white dog streaking in front of her.

Tab trailed the covey until the slope gave way to a side canyon. In the open flat, where the two pieces of bottom ground met, Tab quickened her pace. Her stubby tail started spinning in fast figure eights. I heard Don caution her and then I watched her step into a classic point. You could tell by her intensity that the birds were right off her nose and not going anywhere.

Don called point and motioned for me to join him. From my perch on the slope, I could see there was no clear way down. Once I gave up my elevation and dropped into the thick strip of vegetation that lined the valley's edge, there would be no way to see, let alone shoot, when the birds flushed. I called back to Don and told him to take it. I couldn't get to him. Mearns' almost always flush uphill and maybe one would come my way.

I whoaed the two setters when they came down to me to investigate why I had stopped. The three of us watched the show. Don stepped into the point and seven quail jumped in front of Tab. I watched Don's barrels track through a bird and explode a shower of oak leaves at the first shot, as the bird put a tree between itself and the gun. The barrels kept swinging and when the bird came out the other side, a second shot puffed the bird and slapped it to the ground. Don, who had done this before, didn't move after the shot. He calmly reloaded, took a breath, and then took a step. Two more birds rocketed out. He killed both on a side by side, straightaway going uphill. He held his step and reloaded. One step. Two steps. Three steps. No more birds. I shouted my congratulations down to him as he turned to release Tab to retrieve. She went after the first downed bird, and I cut the setters loose to search for the last two birds that had fallen even with us on the slope.

As Don stepped forward to take the retrieved bird from Tab, a last holdout broke for the atmosphere. The single curved back over Don in a high arch and bored uphill straight at me. All I could hear was the roar of the quail's wings as it went over the top of me. There was no time to think. It was just twirl, point and fire. I kept spinning after the shot and was lucky not to roll down the hill. I had no idea if I had connected. I yelled, "Did I hit it?" Don shouted back, "I couldn't tell." I went uphill in the direction of the potential fall and was glad to see Rose coming downhill with an adult male Mearns' in her mouth. I took the bird from Rose and shouted downhill to Don, "We've done it."

It took a few minutes to collect the other two birds, and then I came downslope to Don. It was time to head home. We had taken four Mearns' out of a 10-bird family group. That was enough. The dogs were ready to go home. We started on the return trip back out the canyon. When we got to the rimrocks, the grasslands spread out in a huge vista below us. The Gambel's and scalies were out there, and several miles away, a speck of a truck shown like a jewel in the afternoon sun.

It had been a grand adventure. My knees hurt. My feet hurt, and I knew this would be one of the premiere memories of my life. Don said, "It doesn't get any better than this," and I agreed with him. Then I told him, "It could never mean as much a second time."

Arizona Bird Hunting Regulations

Licenses

Arizona offers four classes of licenses, one of which will be required by those hunting birds in the state, the one exception being that children under the age of 14 may hunt wildlife, other than big game, without a license when accompanied by a properly licensed person of 18 years or older. No more than two unlicensed children may accompany any license holder. The license is valid for the calendar year, from January 1 through December 31.

2012-14 Fees	Resident	Nonresident
Class G, general hunting	$32.25	$151.25
Class F, combination hunt & fish	$54.00	$225.75
Class F, youth combination hunt & fish (under 20 years of age)	$26.50	$26.50
Class H, 3-day nonresident only hunting (not valid when applying for big game hunts; valid for sandhill cranes)	N/A	$61.25
Turkey permits (includes a $3 non-refundable application fee)	$25.50	$77.75

As required by A.R.S. 17-333.03 and R12-4-203, dove hunters age 16 and older shall have in their possession an Arizona Migratory Bird Stamp which will validate their license for the federal Harvest Information program. The Arizona Migratory Bird Stamp may be obtained, for a cost of $4.50 on or after July 1, from any Arizona Game and Fish Department office or wherever hunting licenses are sold.

Persons 16 years of age or older must have in their possession a valid Federal Migratory Bird Hunting Stamp when taking ducks and geese, and a valid, signed Arizona Waterfowl Stamp attached to their hunting license or printed privileges on their license when taking ducks and geese. This stamp or privilege will automatically register the holder for the federal Harvest Information Program for the taking of ducks and geese. Persons 16 years of age and older must have in their possession a valid Arizona Migratory Bird Stamp or privilege when taking coots and common moorhens pursuant to A.R.S. 17-333.03 and R12-4-203.

Hunter Education   A hunter safety education course is available and encouraged in Arizona, but not required.

Shooting Hours   "Legal shooting time is during daylight hours, see individual Commission Orders. Weather can alter times. In general, if you can see well enough to shoot safely, you are legal. Taking wild animals or birds by moonlight or artificial light is illegal, except for raccoons, reptiles and other mammals as prescribed in R12-4-304, page 61(A.G.F.D. 96/97 hunt proclamation). Other time requirements apply for migratory birds (see Migratory Bird Regulations)." (A.G.F.D. 96/97 hunt proclamation).

Motor Vehicles and Firearms   "No person may knowingly discharge any firearm or shoot any other device upon, from, across or into a road or railway," (A.G.F.D. 96/97 hunt proclamation). A person must be off of the roadway before discharging a weapon. There is no legal minimum measured distance.

With the exception of challenged hunter access/mobility permits, it is considered illegal to hunt from a motor vehicle in the state of Arizona. Vehicles may be used only as conveyances to take a hunter to and from the field. There is some latitude for field personnel in enforcing this law. If an area wildlife manager sees a vehicle pull over and begin hunting, thirty yards past where a quail covey ran across the front of the vehicle, it could be interpreted that they intended to stop there all along. If that same wildlife manager witnesses a slam on the brakes, flinging the doors open, and a high speed, armed, bail-out, then he could very well interpret it as road hunting and issue a citation. This is not the way to have a quality hunting experience, and the sad thing is that I sometimes see young children in these vehicles, being taught the wrong things.

Landowner Permission   In Arizona, land is considered legally posted when it is signed at any access points. Basically, that means that if a no trespassing sign is present, then the area is legally posted and closed to entry. Permission to trespass may be verbal or written.

Nontoxic Shot   Nontoxic shot is required statewide for the taking of waterfowl as mandated by federal law. This law effectively eliminates combination bird hunts that included jump shooting tanks for waterfowl, unless only nontoxic shot is used for everything. The law prohibits any person hunting waterfowl from having lead shot in their possession in the field. Before the restriction, it was common in a day's hunt to shoot remote tanks for ducks and doves, and hunt quail on the way in and out.

In order to comply with the law, a hunter must now segregate shot at his vehicle, and if walking into a tank to hunt ducks, only have nontoxic shot in his possession.

Magazine and Gauge Restrictions   Shotguns used for the taking of upland game and waterfowl may be no larger than 10 gauge. Shotguns must be "capable of holding no more than two shells in the magazine, unless plugged with a one-piece filler limiting the magazine capacity to two shells, incapable of removal without disassembling the gun." (A.G.F.D. 96/97 hunt proclamation.)

SEASON DATES

Gambel's, Scaled, California and Mearns' Quail

- **08-09 Statewide Season Dates**: Oct. 3– Feb. 8 (Gambel's, Scaled and California); Nov. 28 - Feb. 8 (Mearns')
- **Bag Limit**: Fifteen (15) quail per day in the aggregate of which no more than eight (8) may be Mearns' quail
- **Possession Limit**: Thirty (30) quail in the aggregate after opening day of which no more than fifteen (15) Gambel's, Scaled, or California quail in the aggregate may be taken in one day. After Nov. 28, the 30 quail possession limit may include Mearns' quail of which no more than eight (8) may be taken in any one day.
- Quail cleaned in the field must retain one leg as proof of species

Mourning and White-wing Dove

- **08-09 Statewide Season Dates**: Sept. 1-15 (Mourning or White-wing); Nov. 21 - Jan. 4 (Mourning); Sept. 1, 2008-Aug. 31, 2009 (Eurasion collared dove)
- **Bag Limit**: Ten (10) Mourning and White-winged Doves per day in the aggregate, of which no more than six (6) may be Whitewinged Doves.
- **Possession Limit**: Twenty (20) Mourning and White-winged Doves in the aggregate after opening day, of which no more than twelve (12) may be White-winged Doves. No more than ten (10) doves in the aggregate, of which no more than six (6) may be White-winged Doves, may be taken in any one day.

Band-tailed Pigeon

- **08-09 Statewide Season Dates**: Sept. 12–Oct. 5
- **Bag Limit**: Five (5) Band-tailed pigeons per day.
- **Possession Limit**: Ten (10) Band-tailed pigeons after opening day, of which no more than five (5) may be taken in any one day.

Blue Grouse

- **08-09 Statewide Season Dates**: Sept. 12–Nov. 17
- **Bag Limit**: Three (3) blue grouse per day
- **Possession Limit**: Six (6) blue grouse of which no more than three (3) may be taken in any one day

Merriam's Turkey

Hunters are restricted to their permitted game management unit.

- **08-09 Fall Statewide Season Dates**: Oct. 3-9
- **Bag Limit**: 1 turkey per calendar year

Sandhill Crane

Crane permits are awarded through a limited permit drawing for four separate hunts.

- **2008 Season Dates**: Hunt #9001: Nov. 22–24; Hunt #9002: Nov. 26–28; Hunt #9003, Nov. 30–Dec. 2; Hunt #9004, Dec. 4-6
- **Bag Limit**: 2 sandhill cranes per calendar year
- **Lawful Taking Devices:** Shotgun, crossbow or bow and arrow as prescribed in R12-4-304.
- **License Required**: Any valid hunting license and Sandhill Crane Hunt Permit-tag.
- **Shooting Hours**: One-half hour before sunrise until sunset.

Waterfowl

- **Lawful Taking Device:** Shotgun, crossbow, bow and arrow or falconry as prescribed in R12-4-304.
- **License Required:** Any valid hunting license plus a valid Arizona Waterfowl Stamp and Federal Migratory Bird Hunting Stamp (i.e., federal Duck Stamp).
- **Shooting Hours**: One-half hour before sunrise until sunset.
- **Bag Limit:** The daily bag limit of ducks, including mergansers: Seven (7) per day not to include more than: two (2) redheads; one (1) pintail; two (2) canvasbacks; seven (7) mallards, no more than two (2) of which may be female or Mexican-like ducks; and three (3) scaup. Coots and common moorhens (gallinules): Twenty-five (25) per day, singly or in the aggregate. Geese: Four (4) white geese (snow, including blue and Ross' geese) per day and three (3) dark geese (Canada and white-fronted) per day.
- **Possession Limit:** The possession limit of ducks including mergansers: Fourteen (14) after opening day, only seven (7) of which may be taken any oneday, but no more than:
    - a. four (4) redheads
    - b. four (4) female mallards or Mexican-like ducks
    - c. two (2) pintails
    - d. six (6) scaup
    - e. four (4) canvasbacks.
- **Coots and common moorhens (gallinules):** Twenty-five (25) singly or in the aggregate.
- **Geese:** Eight (8) white geese (snow, including blue and Ross' geese) and six (6) dark geese (Canada and white-fronted).

GENERAL WATERFOWL

Open Areas do not include any area closed to hunting under A.R.S. Sections 17-303 and 17-304 or Commission Rules R12-4-301, R12-4-801, R12-4-802 and R12-4-803.

Season dates	Notes	Open Areas	Legal wildlife
Oct 17, 2012 - Jan 25, 2013	(1,3,4,5)	Desert Zone: those portions of Units 6 and 8 within Yavapai County and Units 10 and 12B through 45	Ducks including mergansers, coots, and common moorhens (gallinules)
Nov.1 , 2012 - Jan 25, 2013	(1,3,4,5)	Desert Zone: those portions of Units 6 and 8 within Yavapai County and Units 10 and 12B through 45	Scaup
Oct 17, 2012 - Jan 25, 2013	(1,3,4,5)	Desert Zone: those portions of Units 6 and 8 within Yavapai County and Units 10 and 12B through 45 EXCEPT Units 22, 23 and 27	White geese (snow, blue and Ross') and dark geese (Canada and white-fronted)
Oct 3, 20012- Jan 11, 2013	(2,3,4)	Mountain Zone: Units 1-5, 7, 11M, 9, 12A and those portions of Units 6 and 8 within Coconino County	Ducks including mergansers, coots, and common moorhens (gallinules)
Oct. 18, 2012 - Jan. 7, 2013	(2,3,4)	Mountain Zone: Units 1-5, 7, 11M, 9, 12A and those portions of Units 6 and 8 within Coconino County	Scaup
Oct 3, 2012 - Jan 11, 2013	(2, 3,4)	Mountain Zone: Units 2-5, 7, 11M, 9, 12A and those portions of Units 6 and 8 within Coconino County	White geese (snow, blue and Ross') and dark geese (Canada and white-fronted)
Nov 15, 2012- Jan 11, 2013	(3,4)	Special Goose Seasons: Units 1 and 27	White geese (snow, blue and Ross') and dark geese (Canada and white-fronted)
Nov 15, 2012 - Jan 25, 2013	(3,4)	Special Goose Seasons: Units 22 and 23	White geese (snow, blue and Ross') and dark geese (Canada and white-fronted)

GAMBEL'S QUAIL DISTRIBUTION

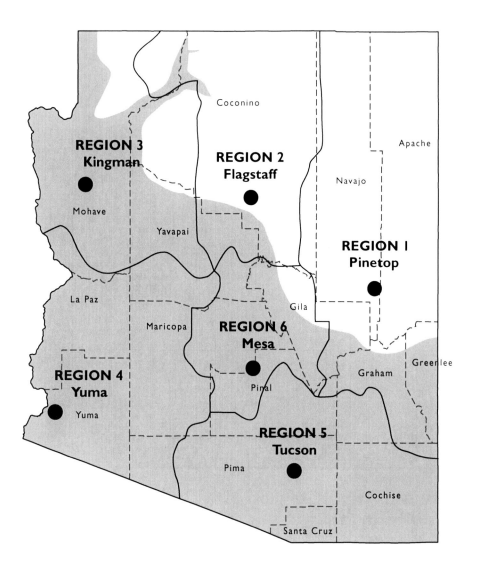

Gambel's Quail

Lophortyx Gambelii

QUICK FACTS

Local Name
Gambel's, Desert Quail, Arizona Quail, Common Quail, Topknot Quail

Spanish Name
Codorniz de Gambel, Codorniz Comun

Size

10-11.5 inches (25.4-29.2cm) in length, 6 ounce average weight

Identification in Flight
Gambel's quail appears as a small grey bird in flight. At close range, the buff-white breast, black belly, white dart-shaped lines on the side coverts, and white-lined black face mask are evident. Adult males sport a distinctive black topknot. The wings of flushing birds make a loud "whirring" sound.

- Gambel's quail make up approximately 90% of the quail hunter's bag.
- Gambel's quail can be very vocal in the mornings and evenings.
- Much of the Gambel's activity centers around desert sand washes.
- Mesquite thickets are important as roosting sites and cover from airborne predators.
- Gambel's quail will use standing water but are not dependent on it.

Color
Both male and female are predominantly grey when observed from a distance. When viewed in hand, however, there is a distinct contrast between the sexes. The male Gambel's quail has a distinctive black throat mask and black belly patch. The male also has a sienna brown cap on its head. Both the cap and throat patch are highlighted with white lines. Both sexes carry a teardrop shaped topknot plume, although it is much smaller on the female. Gambel's quail also have russet side coverts highlighted with white dart-shaped lines. The lower breast is cream white.

Sound and Flight Patterns
Gambel's quail are extremely vocal. The male's four note "Chi-ca-ca-go" call is synonymous with the desert Southwest. Barring wind, this call can carry as far as a quarter of a mile and is most often heard in the morning and evening. It is used as

a rally and regrouping call for coveys. Walking up calls is a very productive method used by hunters to locate birds. Once a hunter locates and approaches a covey, the hens often emit a soft continuous "put-put-put-put-put-put" cackle. This indicates that the birds are aware of the hunter's presence and that they are running and/or about to flush. During early morning feeding and while going to roost in the evening, hens use a similar cackle that is more raucous and animated. While hunting, I have heard the sound from this cackle carry a hundred yards.

At the flush, Gambel's wings make a whirring sound that combines into a roar when an entire covey lifts off a hillside. Gambel's won't lift any higher off the ground than necessary. Typically at the flush, quail will clear the brush by two to three feet and follow the contour of the cover like a cruise missile. They aim for the nearest cover and put it between them and the gun. Once the danger zone is cleared, the bird stops flapping and coasts, stiff-winged, one to two hundred yards before pitching in. Rather than holding at the landing area, they often run to another location.

A word of caution for hunters: because Gambel's quail fly so low to the ground, dogs are in danger of being struck by the shot pattern. Be sure that you know where your dog is before you shoot.

Similar Game Birds

It is very difficult, even for the experienced eye, to distinguish between Gambel's, scaled, and California quail on the wing. If a gunner concentrates on looking for the black topknot and dark face, he can eliminate the scaled, however, the differences between the Gambel's and California are subtle color hues. The base color of the side coverts on the Gambel's is brown, while the California's is grey. The breast on a Gambel's is a solid color. The California quail's breast carries a scaled pattern.

Hunters should note that California quail in Arizona are a remnant population of introduced birds. As such, they are very few and rarely seen.

Flock or Covey Habits

Gambel's quail are covey birds. A home range averages from 19 to 95 acres. Between the months of August and February, the birds will generally be found in groups of 25 to 50. During the latter part of the season, January and February, coveys are sometimes encountered numbering a hundred birds or more. Some of these groups may actually be a single covey. Others are created when a hunter pushes several smaller coveys together and the birds all jump at the same time. I have had both Gambel's and scaled quail rise from the same large "covey."

During good years, beginning as early as February 1, adult birds start pairing off. Hunters in the field at that time will hear males "caw calling" and encounter pairs of birds independent of any coveys. My experience with these early bonding pairs is that they are difficult to work with dogs. They don't leave much scent and that affords them some protection. The fact that the males are calling does betray their position, but hunters walking them up without a dog won't locate many. A good dog, given time, can eventually pin these birds. Hunters attempting to take them should be aware that they are removing next year's stock. By late March, the coveys are disbanded.

Successful hunter with pair of Gambel's quail.

Reproduction and Life Span

"Caw calling" in the early spring announces the beginning of the yearly reproductive cycle. Male Gambel's take up small breeding territories, go to the top of a high vantage point, and advertise for a mate. Males are commonly seen on large boulders or perched at the top of ocotillo, mesquite or palo verde trees. If something on a grander scale presents itself, so much the better. I have seen quail calling from the top of telephone poles and radio towers. Birds pair for the season and raise their young together. Both sexes take turns incubating the eggs. Nesting activity peaks in early April but can continue into August.

There has been much debate about Gambel's bringing off two or three clutches of young a year. There isn't any scientific evidence to support this, and young chicks observed late in the year are more than likely the repeat attempt of an earlier failed nesting. If multiple broods occur, it is a rare and isolated incident. The pair form a loose nest on the ground within protective brush or cactus. Clutch size averages around a dozen off-white eggs. Incubation takes 21 to 23 days. Young chicks run a gambit of predators, while adverse weather, both hot and cold, also takes a toll. In some years, mortality can be very high.

Arizona Game and Fish biologists have discovered a correlation between the amount of vitamin A stored in a quail's liver during the winter months and nesting success the following spring. By collecting samples and charting the data, game managers have a reliable indicator with which to predict hunter success the following season. If there is adequate rain during the critical period from October through March, the desert will respond with a verdant green carpet of filaree. The quail rely heavily on this annual grass as a primary food source. In the process, they take on large deposits of vitamin A that gears their systems up in preparation for breeding. The new vegetation also provides cover and excellent insect reproduction for the chicks when they are hatched in midspring. This provides optimum survival conditions for the young. In years with very little moisture, and consequently no filaree, it may be that no breeding activity will be triggered at all. Without the vitamin A reserve, adult birds will not engage in the risky business of nesting as their offspring would have little chance of survival.

As with Arizona's other quail, Gambel's are thought to have the potential to live to five years of age.

Feeding Habits and Patterns

Gambel's feed in the morning and evening. Look for them on open hillsides and elevated flats along mesquite-lined washes. During midday, they retreat to the heavy vegetation that choke the sand washes. Birds are easiest to locate while feeding. They are vocalizing and leaving scent trails that a dog can key in on. The best singles work comes when a covey spreads out in grass and low brush away from the wash's protective cover. Quail use the washes as escape routes. Birds from a disrupted covey that make it back to the wash will not be relocated.

Birds are quick to exploit seasonal food sources as they become available. In September and October, the heads of quail are stained pink from eating the fruit of prickly pear cactus. During midseason, small seeds and mesquite beans are taken. In late winter and early spring, if there has been sufficient rain, the birds prepare for breeding by filling their craws with delicate, green filaree grass.

Preferred Habitat and Cover

Gambel's quail can be found from the salt cedars near sea level along the Colorado River, to 6000-foot piñon pine slopes on the Mogollon Rim. They utilize all available habitat types found in most of the lower two-thirds of Arizona with the exception of the lower desert creosote brush community, in which they are largely absent.

Stands of dense roosting cover are Gambel's one universal requirement. In the majority of their range, mesquite and its accompanying understory (including catclaw, elderberry, and hackberry) provide this. In the lower desert, salt cedar thickets along watercourses are used heavily. Juniper trees and low oak brush make ideal cover in the higher elevations of Gambel's range.

Gambel's will utilize standing water but are not dependent on it. Early in the season, the area around water tanks may hold higher densities of birds. Rain spreads available water and can disperse bird numbers. To locate early quail, hunters can use tanks as a starting point and work out from there. Once the heat dissipates, supplemental standing water is not as important, and the bird's water requirements are met by the food they ingest while feeding.

Harold Snyder's setter, Casey, delivers a Gambel's quail to him.

Locating Hunting Areas

Gambel's quail are almost everywhere. Most of Arizona is a vast unbroken strip of Gambel's habitat.

1. Hunt topography and vegetation types. Use a topo map to pick ground and cover that will maximize your success. If available in your area, concentrate your efforts between 3000 and 4500 feet.
2. When scouting a prospective hunting area, get out of your vehicle and listen for calling.
3. Follow mesquite-lined sand washes and look for concentrations of birds.
4. In the early season, hunt the area around water sources.
5. Ranchers can be a wealth of information regarding bird populations in their area.

Looking for Sign

Gambel's quail tracks are easily seen in the fine sand at the bottom of mesquite washes. Dusting areas are also easy to spot and a sign of covey activity. When you locate concentrations of tracks, work the surrounding areas thoroughly. Early and late, listen for birds calling. Sometimes quail will respond to a quail call.

Hunting Methods

Bird hunting in Arizona means Gambel's quail. A lot has been said about the difficulty of hunting desert birds and many days, it's true. There are those days, however, when everything works and the birds are cooperative. It's hard to predict Gambel's quail, and I've made it a point not to try. All things considered, they are one of our most interesting and challenging game birds. Many bird hunters have been converted into Arizona desert quail aficionados as a result of the vast amount of huntable public land, the four-month-long season, mild winter weather, generous bag limits, and the large populations a good season can offer.

There is nothing straightforward about hunting Gambel's quail. Most game birds follow a reasoned strategy for evading a hunter. Gambel's, however, have their own bag of tricks. One day they hold for the gun, and the next they leave a hunter dazed and confused, wondering at what point he wore through the bottom of his boots.

Desert quail country is very big, giving a Gambel's covey a lot of room to maneuver. A covey's preferred response to an approaching hunter is to start a straight line run as an intact covey, leave little or no scent for the dog to follow, and hook off their straight line to hold as singles. Gambel's will generally hook within 100 yards. In rare instances, I have seen them still running at 400 yards.

At 200 yards, the inexperienced hunter starts wondering why he hasn't caught up with the birds yet. One of the things a hunter quickly learns is that he can't run fast enough to catch a running quail. Back trailing to locate them doesn't work because the birds are holding somewhere off to the side of the original line. Then, even when a dog does get a point, the bird will probably run out and jump wild at 40 yards.

On a typical day, coveys will generally flush out of shotgun range. They will fly as one group, and a hunter may mark them down and walk them up. The technique here is to try to force the birds to hold as singles. After two to three repeated flushes, the covey should break up and hold. Some days, they hold the first time.

Learning to hunt Gambel's quail takes some time. It's like sitting down to a boxed jigsaw puzzle. Each hunt helps a hunter put together a few pieces. With experience, a bigger picture begins to take shape.

I had an experience that showed me just how Gambel's can evade a hunter. It was the last day of one of my first quail seasons in Arizona. Bandita, my English setter, and I were hunting a large, cactus-covered flat in the bottom of the Verde River Valley. Many birds had made it to the end of the season, but they had been shot over and weren't making any mistakes. By the way Bandita was working, I could tell we were going through birds most of the afternoon. However, she had not been able to move, let alone hold, a single one of them.

Again, Bandita made scent and dropped into the bottom of a shallow canyon, as I walked the ridge above her. She flash pointed and I saw a covey of birds 30 yards in front of her line out and begin running. She didn't see them, but she took off at a fast walk following their scent stream. Over the next 150 yards, I watched the running quail covey dwindle as birds peeled off in ones and twos. Bandita traveled right over the paths of the escaping singles and never smelled them. It was as if the only birds

Hunter surveying Gambel's quail habitat.

leaving any scent were those still in the covey. At the end of the chase, Bandita locked up. I dropped into the bottom and flushed and killed the last remaining bird in the group—a juvenile male. I can't tell you why he had enough scent to allow a point and the 30-odd birds before him didn't. I do know that those birds were moving from the very beginning and there wasn't any time to draw straws to determine who was going to be the last in line. We worked that entire canyon bottom back up and never found another bird. That was the only bird I killed that day.

The above story illustrates how difficult it can be to work Gambel's. On other days, Gambel's quail are relatively easy to work. If a hunter persists, Gambel's can provide some of the finest shooting in North America.

In an even fight, the birds are going to have a decided advantage. However, there *are* things that a hunter can do to shift the balance. For example, pick areas with dense ground cover (Gambel's quail run in thin ground cover). I am referring specifically to grass growing at ground level, although thick prickly pear cactus growth also applies. Hunt the yellow grass. The low vegetation will stop the birds and hold them.

Somewhere around early December, hunting success will improve dramatically. Scenting conditions, which were abysmal during the early portion of the quail season, are now improved and allow the dog work to become much more consistent. Snake danger diminishes as well. At the same time mesquite leaves start dropping, and areas

Troy Hawks and Jake discussing strategy.

that were previously too thick to track birds in are now shootable. The best months for quail hunting in Arizona are December and January.

Let weather work in your favor. Cool temperatures allow a hunter to work all day. Hunting on the days after rain should improve scenting conditions. On the rare days when a light snow blankets the desert, the birds are at a decided disadvantage and will hold very well for a dog.

As a hunter moves into the field, success can be improved by anticipating the bird's behaviors. Random as their actions may appear, they are predictable. Here are some tricks to use that give the hunter an advantage.

When approaching a covey, try to flush quail toward open hillsides. Mark the singles and push them toward shallow ravines and erosion cuts. Any geographic feature that has a sharp edge and a dropoff will stop birds from running. Singles will hold at the edge rather than risk crossing it.

Listen for calling quail and use a quail call to locate coveys. At times, birds can be extremely vocal. Mimic the "Chi-ca-ca-go" call. Using your ears can save your feet a lot of walking.

If a hunter breaks up a covey and has trouble locating singles, an effective method is to sit quietly and wait for the birds to regroup. They will start calling to each other about 15 minutes after they think the hunter has left. In late afternoon, they start calling

Erosion cuts such as this often stop running quail and allow them to be held by pointing dogs.

almost immediately. Give them a few minutes to converge in one area, and then go at them quietly. This will generally work once with a regrouping covey.

Gambel's use "safe" areas where singles regroup after a covey is broken up. I have seen half of a covey hold as singles in a 50-yard circle. They collect in an area near the site of the original covey rise. An experienced Gambel's hunter will develop a sixth sense about locating these sites. I mark the flushed birds down and follow a short distance, then double back and hunt the original contact area thoroughly, searching for a concentration of holding birds. Several spots may "feel" right. Sometimes I get lucky the first time.

Birds that have received a lot of pressure may forego the covey rise altogether. At a hunter's approach, quail simply spread out and hold. Birds literally must be stepped on before they will flush. The hunter without a dog won't know that he has just walked through a covey. An often heard complaint regards the small size of coveys. A hunter will report finding "coveys" of three or five or ten. I am always suspicious of unattached birds bumping wild in an otherwise birdless area. Depending on scenting conditions, a hunter may or may not find the others, but they are there somewhere.

Hunting Dogs

From what I have written, a person may come to the conclusion that Gambel's quail hunters can face a few challenges in the field. The average hunter/dog team arriving from out of state can find enjoyable hunting despite these challenges. However, there are some hunters who qualify as specialists. Most dogs will adapt quite well to Gambel's hunting and make serviceable dogs. However, like the desert quail hunting specialist, some dogs also become equally as specialized.

Much of what is considered "normal" dog work is counterproductive with Gambel's quail. Polished manners, such as holding steady to shot and not relocating until released, are detrimental in Gambel's cover. A great Gambel's dog bumps running coveys with the daring of Errol Flynn flashing a sword. He catwalks with impunity, his right eye roving for runners and his left ear cocked, listening for their scurrying. And then, when the birds cooperate, he does everything right. The partnership of gunner and dog transcends control with Gambel's quail hunting.

I finish my dogs steady to wing and shot before we start on Gambel's. It gives them a certain polish and maturity. Within two weeks of turning them loose on desert quail, they know more about working quail than I do.

The dog decides that a lot of the high points of training are counterproductive. A dog that isn't allowed to abandon a point and relocate is going to spend most of his time stopped, while the quail will spend all of their time running. A good dog can differentiate between a covey that will hold and one that won't. If a cautious approach won't hold the birds, the most productive thing a dog can do is to run in and flush so that they aren't able to leave as one group. The dog learns that scattered birds can be worked as singles.

A dog needs to break at shot in order to be under the birds when they fall. This is covered at length in the section on the "Arizona Gun Dog," but it bears mentioning again. If you hold your dog back and release him to retrieve, he is going to lose a lot of birds.

All of this can make for a pretty wild dog. In Gambel's hunting, there is a wide latitude of acceptable behavior. A hunter has to trust the dog to make the right decisions.

Many conflicts between hunter and dog arise because of poor scenting conditions. I am not saying that there aren't times when a dog goes into business for himself, but a hunter needs to be circumspect before passing judgment. A dog can't work what it can't smell.

I can't make this point strongly enough. There are times when a dog can't smell desert quail. During the breeding season and normally lasting through the middle of November, quail often leave no scent. I think that the quail themselves have some control over this, and I think the heat and dryness of the country also contribute in some way. Time of day is also a big factor. On some days, I find that only the early morning and the last couple of hours of the afternoon offer productive scenting conditions. I don't understand it and I cannot predict it. It's a very effective survival strategy for the quail, while also being extremely frustrating for hunters attempting to get dog work.

I once had a pair of quail nest in some stacked logs near an outside working area. From my angle, as I worked, I could look down and see the hen or rooster setting

Ken Stevens moves in to flush a single Gambel's pointed by Emma.

the eggs. On a typical day, I would be working outside for four to five hours. Two setters and a Chesapeake Bay Retriever loafed and slept within three to five feet of the nest, in a variety of wind and weather conditions, and never smelled the birds. This experience left me impressed with the effectiveness of their scent controlling ability.

The following is a story to illustrate this point. I loaded Rose, a brash three-year-old female English setter, and headed out to hunt the last three hours of the afternoon. It was December, and the conditions looked promising: mid-50s with a soft breeze. I parked the truck on a hill overlooking a large flat choked with mesquite and catclaw. The area had been safe from early season hunters because the green foliage was too thick to shoot through. The green cover was gone now, and the area was all mine. I released Rose and put on my gear. We dropped off the hill and waded into the catclaw. Rose tore through the cover. She hunted hard for two hours with marginal results and produced no birds. I had a couple of wild flushed birds in the bag. The quail weren't giving her much and, as a result, her performances didn't look very good. I decided to cut our losses and save it for another day. We had walked a pretty big loop out on the flat. We eventually hit our dirt, two-track road, well over a mile below the truck and back along the edge of the country we had already covered. I unloaded my shotgun and carried it broken open over my shoulder. Rose lined off up the road and we started the long march back to the truck.

She had gone a couple of hundred yards when her head went up and she left the road and drifted into the wind. She pointed and held a covey 50 yards into the catclaw. I killed a couple of birds on the rise, and we harassed the singles for a time. I figured it was a nice ending, and we returned to the road. She did it six more times and never put a foot down wrong. I finally had to put a lead on her to get her to stop pointing coveys. We were at a limit and running out of light. Every hundred yards or so she would raise her head, tug on the lead and try to drift off the road.

Her marginal performance early in the hunt was not her fault. The change in scenting conditions made it possible for Rose to pin the birds. I would have been the one in error if I had held her responsible for her early poor showing. A dog can't work what she can't smell.

Field Preparations

Gambel's quail are excellent eating. They can smell a little strong if not eviscerated quickly because many are shot at close range and receive shot damage. A popular cleaning method is to breast the birds at the end of the hunt. As they are not a large bird, it takes several to make a meal.

Shot and Choke Suggestions

- **Thick Cover:** skeet /improved cylinder 7½ shot
- **Open Cover:** improved cylinder/modified 7½ first shot, 6 shot back-up (the larger shot helps reduce lost cripples).

Scaled Quail Distribution

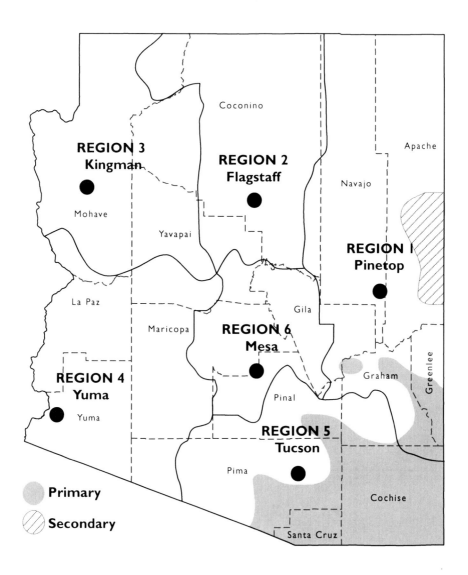

Scaled Quail

Callipepla squamata

QUICK FACTS

Local Name
Scaled quail, scalie, cottontop quail, blue quail

Spanish Name
Codorniz Escamosa, Codorniz Azul, Zol'n

Size: 10–11.5 inches (25–29cm) in length, 7 ounce average weight

Identification in Flight
Flushing scaled quail offer no conspicuous markings. The top of their backs and wings are a solid-colored, medium blue grey. They have a buff white breast and head crest. The breast is marked with a heavy scaled pattern, and side coverts are highlighted with white darts similar to a Gambel's quail. In flight, their wings make a "whirring" sound.

- Scaled quail make up approximately 6% of the quail hunter's bag.
- Scaled quail cover is most often characterized by open grassland and soap-tree yucca.
- The most common strategy scaled quail use to initially avoid hunters is to run. After one or two flushes, singles will often hold.
- Early in the season, hunt around water sources to locate bird populations.
- Scalies roost on the ground on open ridges.

Color

Male and female scaled quail are indistinguishable at a distance. Both are a basic blue-grey overall. Upon close examination, the male's throat feathers are a solid cream color, while the hen's are cream with fine, dark streaks. The breast of both sexes is cream white overlaid with a dark scaled pattern. Scaled quail sport a distinctive cream white head crest that is easy to spot as birds on the ground run in front of a hunter. The crest's color glows in a way similar to rabbit ears backlit by the sun.

Sound and Flight Pattern

Scaled quail are vocal but not to the degree of Gambel's quail. The "chuc-ker, chuc-ker, chuc-ker" covey call can be used by the hunter to aid in locating birds, but this call and other scaled quail vocalizations are extremely ventriloquial and makes it difficult to locate the birds.

Unlike Gambel's, which hug the ground contours during flight, scaled quail tend to loft when flushed. Their wings give off the characteristic quail "whirring" sound when flushing.

Similar Game Birds

Scaled quail resemble both Gambel's and California quail. In Arizona, their range overlaps both species. The Gambel's and California carry a black face mask and top knot plume that aid in distinguishing them from scaled quail.

Flock or Covey Habits

Scalies are runners. They will hold for a hunter, but it might take a flush or two to get them in the mood. Like late season Gambel's, end-of-season scaled quail who have received some hunting pressure will at times forgo a covey flush altogether. Upon a hunter's approach, they just spread out and hold as singles. A hunter and dog walk through a spread and holding covey, unaware they are surrounded by birds. One or two birds bump wild, and the hunter assumes they are isolated individuals. When a bird jumps, I call the dogs in and have them search the immediate area thoroughly. There is usually a covey somewhere. The search may take several minutes and only produce two or three contacts, but many hunts are made up of these repeated short contacts. The rule of thumb is, while Gambel's and scaled quail use the same escape strategies, scalies are consistently more successful with them.

Coveys may number from 15 to 60 individuals, with an average covey being about 30. Bird numbers are tied to seasonal conditions. Foraging quail cover 25 to 100 acres in a day. The average home range is under one square mile. I see scaled quail coveys in the same general areas season after season.

In early spring, coveys disband and males take up breeding territories. Cocks climb elevated perches and issue a call similar to a Gambel's quail "caw" calling. The young are raised by both parents. Coveys are reassembled by October.

Reproduction and Life Span

Breeding activity begins in late February and culminates in April and May. Males occupy a breeding territory and, from an elevated perch, broadcast a "squawk" call that is returned by adjacent males. Territories are defended from other males.

Nests are on the ground in dense cover such as prickly pear or cholla. Scaled quail clutches contain nine to 16 eggs, and like other species, chicks can fly within a few days of hatching.

Brace of scaled quail.

Depending on summer rains, nesting can be deferred to late summer. Occasionally, very young birds show up in the bags of opening season hunters.

Life span is thought to be as much as five years.

Feeding Habits and Patterns

Birds begin their day in the grass on open ridges. This gives a hunter a place to begin looking. Scaled quail habitat has a mostly uniform appearance making it difficult to visually separate a "feeding area" from any other. Feeding activity peaks in the morning and evening. Midday, impenetrable cover like mimosa, catclaw, prickly pear, mesquite, and chainfruit cholla are used as loafing areas.

Scalies feed on prickly pear fruit. Birds killed in October often have their faces stained pink from this. They utilize various fruits, leaves, and seeds, including those from mimosa, mesquite, whitethorn acacia and Russian thistle. Scaled quail eat a higher percentage of insects than other quail species. It is reported that scalies will use sorghum fields where available.

Preferred Habitat and Cover

Open country and undisturbed grasslands interspersed with soaptree yucca are the characteristic of scaled quail cover. Even in historically occupied areas that have been invaded by mesquite overstory and populated by Gambel's quail, the remaining scaled quail coveys will cling to remnant grasslands. On the western edge of their range they use chainfruit cholla thickets heavily as escape cover. In these areas, the first thing a covey will do when encountering a hunter and dog is to run them through the worst cholla-carpeted area available.

Scaled quail are essentially a Chihuahuan desert grassland species. Their range is restricted primarily to the southeast quadrant of Arizona between 3,500 and 4,600 feet. The restricted population of the Hargravei subspecies is found north of Springerville and ranges between 5,500 and 7,000 feet elevation.

On the western edge of their range, some coveys have a preference for foothill valleys against desert mountain ranges. A covey flushed from the bottom of such a foothill valley up onto a prickly pear slope will generally hold well. These birds are most often found initially in or around dense chainfruit cholla.

Locating Hunting Areas

Most scaled quail populations are found in southeastern Arizona. They can be found both in the main valley bottoms and up against mountain ranges.

1. For scaled quail, the most common form of scouting is to drive the back roads and look for quail.
2. Birds will respond to a quail call.
3. Early in the season, concentrate on areas around water sources.

Looking for Sign

Scaled and Gambel's quail live in such close proximity that it would be difficult to differentiate the origin species of any quail sign located. Tracks in sand washes and dusting areas could indicate the presence of either or both birds. Listening for calling birds could pinpoint coveys. Sign found in an area devoid of mesquite overstory could probably indicate scaled quail. Short of finding a raptor kill, the only positive identification would be to physically see or hear the quail.

Hunting Methods

Scaled quail do all the things Gambel's quail do, except they do it better. Everything in the Gambel's section on evasion strategies and scent applies to scalies. Most of the time, scaled quail don't make many mistakes. It makes being there, when they do, all the more worthwhile.

Typical scaled quail country is wide open. Coveys will usually flush wild out of range. Flushed birds will usually run when they land. If a hunter can mark flushing coveys down and follow up quickly, it is possible to find singles. Once a single is located, a hunter needs to slow down and work the immediate area thoroughly. There are probably other birds present. A good rule of thumb is that the birds seem to run about a third as far as you think they have. I make it a point to double back and work the ground I had previously covered. Dogs often turn up birds on the second go around.

While associated with grass cover, some scalies are found in typical Gambel's quail habitat. Here, despite inappropriate grass cover, Belle delivers a scaled quail to Dr. John Serman during a Gambel's quail hunt.

Another rule of thumb is that a hunter can expect to locate about one-third the number of singles of a scaled quail covey as that of a Gambel's. On some days, singles come fairly easy. Other days, one or two is an accomplishment.

Unlike Gambel's quail, scalies often loft when they flush. They rocket up 10 feet above any brush and level off before they put any distance between themselves and the gunner. A shooter anticipating this can take advantage of some nice open shots.

Gambel's and scalies make a good combo hunt package. While it is possible to target specific habitat and focus strictly on scaled quail, the most common quail encountered in the majority of southeast Arizona bird cover will be Gambel's. It makes the most sense to take the shots that present themselves. This means that the majority of birds in the bag will be Gambel's.

Hunting Dogs

I have seen some very good dog work on scaled quail. While scalies are difficult, they can be worked successfully by dogs. Everything written in the Gambel's quail Hunting Dog section applies here.

In thick cover, Gambel's and scaled quail respond to a dog in the same manner: they run until they hold. An experienced dog learns to hunt close and slow when singles are present and to push hard when birds are running and not going to hold. Like billiard balls exploding in a fast break, a covey that flushes in all directions is much more likely to hold as singles.

Open grass calls for a big running dog that can locate coveys at a distance. What a man can walk in an hour, a dog can run in 10 minutes. In the bottom of the big valleys in southeastern Arizona, the view is unrestricted. It is possible to watch a dog running at 500 yards. A hunter learns to trust that a dog will hold the coveys it can and bust the ones it can't.

Field Preparations
Scaled quail are slightly larger than Gambel's, but it still takes half a dozen to feed two people. Birds should be cleaned promptly and cooled in an ice chest. Because of the large bags common in Arizona, most local hunters breast birds at the end of a hunt. Scaled quail are as delectable as they are hard earned.

Shot and Choke Suggestions
- **Thick Cover:** skeet/improved cylinder 7½ shot
- **Open Cover:** modified/full 7½ first shot, 6 shot back-up (the larger shot helps reduce lost cripples)

MEARNS' QUAIL DISTRIBUTION

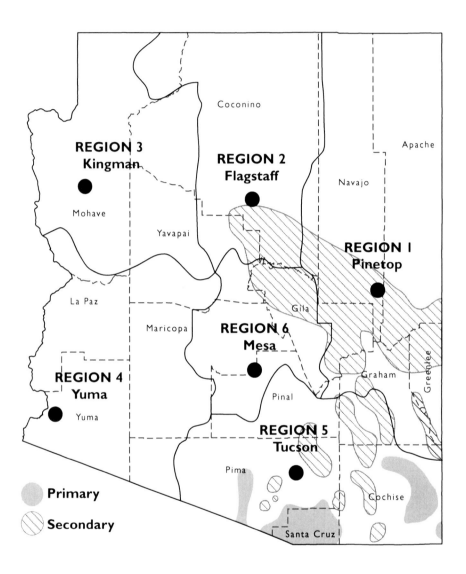

Mearns' Quail

Cyrtonyx montezumae

QUICK FACTS

Local Name
Harlequin quail, Montezuma quail, fool quail, Massena quail, painted quail

Spanish Name
codorniz pinto, cincoreál

Size
8–9.5 inches (20–24 cm) in length, 6.9 ounce for males and 6.2 ounce for females average weight

Identification in Flight
Mearns' quail carry a strikingly bold, distinctive color pattern that is readily discernible in flight. They appear as a large, quail-sized bird. Adult male Mearns' exhibit a vibrant black breast overlaid with white polka-dots, and a solid black rump. The male's face is decorated with a white/black pattern and an olive/russet crest. The back is mottled olive with slight dark barring. The black and white pattern is apparent in a flushing bird. A female Mearns' plumage is colored soft brown and white. The sexes are readily distinguished in flight. On the wing, both sexes show hardly any tail feathers. Their wings are startlingly loud in flight.

- Mearns' quail make up approximately 4% of the Arizona quail hunter's bag.
- Mearns' season runs the last Friday of November and ends the second Monday in February. The limit is 8 per day and 16 in possession.
- The average daily kill, as indicated by Game and Fish surveys, is about two birds per day.
- Summer monsoon rains dictate breeding success.
- A bird dog is a necessity for productive Mearns' quail hunting.
- Mearns' require an oak tree overstory and a 40% grass ground cover.
- Mearns' are generally hunted after 10 a.m., with the most productive time often being between noon and 3 o'clock.
- Mearns' quail live in some of the prettiest dog country in North America.
- Birds feed predominantly on tubers, which they dig from the ground. Find fresh "diggings" and a covey should be feeding nearby.
- Because of the thickness of oak trees, many hunters equip their dog with beeper collars while pursuing Mearns'.

Mearns' quail are one of North America's most beautiful birds.

Color

Mearns' quail vie with wood ducks and ringnecked pheasants as being North America's most brilliantly colored game bird. The first time a hunter holds an adult male Mearns' quail, it is hard to believe it is real.

The predominant feature of the male is a jet black breast covered with white polka-dots. A black and white pattern extends over the face, while the back is a green/grey base color blending to russet at the nape. The green/grey is covered with gold darts and black polka-dots. The male's head carries a russet/gold crest. The beak and legs are highlighted with powder blue.

Female Mearns' are covered with a mottled pattern of browns and golds, with some white blends across the lower breast and face. They are very similar in color and pattern to a female bobwhite quail.

Mearns' quail have evolved long, heavy claws for digging their preferred food: tubers.

Jim Morehouse of Arizona Quail Hunts prepares to strap a Tri-Tronics beeper collar on his GSP male, Danny.

Sound and Flight Patterns

A flushing Mearns' quail covey explodes like a hand grenade, throwing brightly colored shrapnel in all directions. Their wings give off the characteristic "whirring" sound. Because Mearns' covey home range is associated with oak-covered hillsides, most flushes are directed uphill. Flushing birds quickly put some vegetation between themselves and the gun.

Before present day gunning pressure, most Mearns' coveys would only travel a short distance at flush, land, and hold. While hunting Coues deer in remote canyons, it is still possible to bump birds that fly 40 yards and pitch in. Unfortunately, if a road is in reasonable walking distance, coveys are found by hunters and educated to fly like hell and disappear.

My experience with Mearns' is that coveys hold well and flushed singles run like jackrabbits. Although a hunter marks flushed birds down on the hillside above him, the birds won't hold until they reach open grass on the top of a hill. Birds that flush out of sight over the hill can generally be found at the bottom of the next canyon. A hunter will do well to relocate a third of the number of birds that come up in the original covey rise. While at times it may be possible to kill more, hunters generally restrict their take to two or three birds and then move on to another covey.

Some hunters, in an effort to locate singles, wait for a broken covey to start calling while regrouping. The call is best described as a wavering, ventriloquistic wolf whistle. Coveys will start regrouping 15–30 minutes after they feel the hunter has left.

Similar Gamebirds

Both Gambel's and scaled quail can overlap Mearns' quail range. Even in flight, it is not difficult to distinguish Mearns' quail from the two desert species. Mearns' are appreciably larger, display more color, have very short tails, and their wings are louder in flight.

Flock or Covey Habits

Mearns' coveys are made up of single family groups. They average in number between five and eight. On rare occasions, a hunter may find a group of a dozen or more. Their average home range size is 15 acres.

Much has been written about how well Mearns' quail hold. In the case of coveys this is often true, although this last season I saw several groups bump wild off dogs that were 30 to 40 yards away. A prospective hunter should know that they also can run very well. The old literature mistakenly states that because Mearns' have evolved legs set far back on their bodies for digging, they don't have the ability to run effectively. This is not the case. I've watched singles outrun a trailing setter.

Mearns' quail spend their life on oak-covered hillsides. They are found at different altitudes on these hillsides, depending on the availability of food and time of day. They roost on the ground in open grass away from any tree cover. Roosting birds, such as bobwhite quail, form in a circle with tails touching. Hunters sometimes locate these roosting sites consisting of a circle of quail feces. Mearns' are not early risers. When they do leave the roost in the morning, they start feeding. Starting somewhere between 10 a.m. and noon, I often find them in the trough at the bottom of a canyon. They loaf and feed there until about 3 p.m., at which time they may again start to move back uphill.

Hunters trying to locate quail need to take their feeding movements on the slope into account. Early morning hunters should work the flat tops of the hills and open valley floors at the edge of the trees for roosting birds. If no birds are found, hunt the trough where the valley floor meets the slope. If those areas prove unproductive, search at another level on the hillside. If birds aren't in the bottoms at midday, work the midslopes.

An approach some hunters use is to hang a beeper collar on a wide-ranging dog and let the dog cover all of it. The dog checks back intermittently, and the hunter walks along the valley floor waiting for the point beep sound. I have been on some of these hunts, and the method can be productive. The problem comes when the dog points on midslope. If the cover is thin enough to get through, the slopes are often so steep that a shooter straightening up for the shot falls over backwards. But, of course, if it was easy everyone would do it.

My personal preference is to work the canyon bottom between 10 a.m. and 3 p.m. And, as new Mearns' hunters learn, do a lot of walking.

Reproduction and Life Span

Pairing begins in late February and early March. Like Arizona's other quail species, males stake out breeding territories and call to attract a mate. Their nesting territories are established by June.

Mearns' quail nest later than Gambel's. Also, Mearns' breading success depends on summer monsoon rains, unlike Gambel's, which depends on winter rains.

Birds nest from late June through early August. It is not uncommon for very young birds to turn up in the bags of early season hunters. Nests are constructed of woven grass and leaves on the ground. Clutch size averages 11 eggs and incubation takes about 25 days. The young hatch between late July and late September. Chicks are raised by both parents. Unsuccessful hens may renest, but there are no second hatches.

No longevity records are available, but it would be safe to assume that Mearns' quail are capable of living at least four years.

Feeding Habits and Patterns

Observant hunters walking through Mearns' country will notice "diggings" unobtrusively clustered in the grass and fallen oak leaves. Fresh diggings means a covey is nearby.

The primary food source for Mearns' from October through June are oxalis bulbs and sedge tubers. They prefer oxalis to sedge. Birds scour the oak duff accumulated below oak overstory and dig these two foods. In heavily populated areas, hillsides can appear terraced from feeding activity. Diggings are about 3 inches long and fan shaped. They can be very extensive in some areas. Skunks, *Coati mundis*, turkeys and small rodents make similar markings that are sometimes confused with Mearns' feeding areas. Javelina also root during feeding, but their excavations are heavier, with hoofed tracks present, making them easily distinguishable from Mearns'.

During good years, birds also utilize acorns. They supplement their diet with forb and grass seeds. Birds also take insects when available during the fall and winter and feed on beetles extensively while nesting and raising young in the spring and summer.

There are accounts from years past that on rare occasions, Mearns' quail congregated en masse and exploited a bumper food source. Observers reported these quail concentrations feeding in an area for several days to a week, exhausting the food supply and then dispersing.

Mearns' quail habitat is some of the prettiest dog country on earth.

Preferred Habitat and Cover

Mearns' quail country has a distinctive look to it. Birds live under the oaks at 4,000 to 6,000 feet elevation. Hunters prospecting for Mearns' will see the dark green trees dappled on the surrounding mountains like a wide sedimentation band on a multicolored cliff face. At times, random coveys are found in the mesquite/grass valleys below 4,000 feet and up into the pines and spruce to 9,500 feet. A hunter looking for huntable populations should concentrate his efforts in the oaks between 4,800 and 5,100 feet.

Birds need an oak overstory (canopy) of at least 20 percent, with 30 percent being optimum. They also require a heavy grass understory. Most Mearns' country is grazed by cattle and overgrazing has in the past, and in some areas continues, to be a problem. Even with all other conditions being ideal, if an area is overgrazed there will be no birds present.

Locating Hunting Areas

While Mearns' have a fairly large secondary range, Arizona's primary hunting areas are the southeastern mountain ranges above 4,000 feet, primarily the northernmost

Mearns' quail hunting means "the uphill charge." Two hunters chase a flushed covey upslope.

extension of the Mexican Sierra Madre range that crosses over into southeastern Arizona and the extreme southwest corner of New Mexico. They have very specific habitat needs that pinpoint their potential whereabouts.

1. Mearns' have two essential habitat requirements: oak overstory of at least 20 percent and a thick grass understory.
2. The majority of Mearns' range is on National Forest lands. Begin scouting where public access roads cross the 4,000-foot mark.
3. Walk the lower edge of the hillsides in the bottoms of canyons and look for diggings. They are most easily spotted in the moist soil and oak duff below mature oak trees.
4. Standing water is not a habitat requirement.
5. Concentrate hunting efforts on the heavily oak-covered north slope.

Looking for Sign

As discussed earlier in this section, fresh diggings are a sure indicator that a Mearns' covey is nearby. These shallow, 3-inch wide, cone-shaped depressions are found in the grass below oak overstory. I judge the freshness of diggings by the amount of moisture left in the soil. Fresh diggings appear darker and moist, while the excavated earth of old diggings is dry.

Hunting Methods

Of the six quail species found in the United States, Mearns' quail is the most exquisite and unique. While they are generally at the top of a visiting hunter's wish list, they are also the most difficult to hunt successfully. Well-trained dogs are a necessity. Their habitat and characteristics aren't similar to any other gamebird species. Only Arizona and New Mexico currently allow a Mearns' season.

Mearns' quail are found on oak-covered, north-facing slopes in appropriate range. Some hunters feel that the birds have a predictable timetable for their position on the slope. Either the birds roost in the bottoms and feed uphill, or roost on the tops and feed down. I have never noted a predictable pattern. I have had the most success searching the slopes at different elevations until I find birds and then working that elevation. It takes an experienced dog and a lot of walking.

Mearns' coveys can hold very tight. Half the time they don't come up as one group. After firing at the birds in the initial flush, reload immediately before taking another step. The next footfall could raise birds. I have seen coveys spread out while feeding on a hillside come up in five separate groups over a 40-yard area.

Another trick is to not watch for a pointed covey to raise from the ground. It wreaks havoc with the shell-to-bird ratio. Instead, watch the open space 6 feet above the point area and when the birds appear, pick one.

Many shots are through screens of oak leaves. Copperplated shot keeps more pellets in the pattern and kills more birds. Mearns' quail are not very tenacious of life, and one pellet will anchor a bird.

Singles can be very difficult to locate. Sometimes they disappear altogether. Mark them down and go after them immediately. A hunter that relocates a third of the birds in the covey is doing well. Contrary to the popular misconception, single Mearns' run like jackrabbits.

Hunting Dogs

I have heard others say that they thought Mearns' gave off a strong scent for a dog. This hasn't been my impression. Dogs new to Mearns' hunting don't seem to take the scent seriously on the first contact. They half-heartedly stop, flag, take a step, and then look silly when a covey gets up. My best Gambel's dog never did take enough of an interest in Mearns' to point them. She always regarded them with disdain, as trash birds.

Some dogs get to liking Mearns' to the exclusion of other birds. A hunter can finish dogs steady to wing and shot and keep them there if he restricts their hunting only to Mearns'. This can't be said about our other desert quail.

A dog's working range is an oftheard debate among Mearns' hunters. One school wants a close-working, versatile breed that will stay tight and slow and not stir up any birds. The other school hangs a beeper on a dog that will tear up the topography, says a silent prayer, and sends them on. Both work, one better on some days than the other.

English setter holding a Mearns' covey on the edge of the trees.

Field Preparation

Mearns' are excellent eating. Their breasts are longer and larger than Arizona's other quail species.

Shot and Choke Suggestions

- **Shot:** No. 7½ shot. Copperplated shot is preferred because many shots are through trees.
- **Chokes:** open as most shots are over points.

Arizona Dove

MORNINGS AND AFTERNOONS

A distilled image of Arizona is the muted fireball sun crowding the horizon, with a pair of doves blazing across its face. It reflects the rhythm and the heat of the state and begins a wingshooter's season.

September dove hunting is hot. It begins with swirls of motion: finding gear put away for the season's hiatus and feverishly assembled the night before the opener; the dog, who picked up your cues days before, now rests her front feet on the gear pile while her tail blocks the door—all things being carried outside must submit to her inspection. Damn! Where are those 8s? You bought them two weeks ago so you would be ready, and now they're not where you remember leaving them. Such is the pace of September doves.

The wake-up alarm goes off; the khakis go on; grab your gear, breakfast, and a gun and find the dog sitting in the driver's seat. She looks at you, letting you know that she isn't the one who isn't ready to go. Arriving at the prearranged shooting spot, you recognize other vehicles with friends standing alongside them. You swing the door open and the dog is gone. At the tailgate, you cinch the shell bag tight—wasn't there more belt left dangling at the end of last season? You pour a box of 20s into a side pouch and then heft another. Is one box enough? It's the same question every opening morning, and at seven birds, you're back at the truck for another box. You balance the load by dropping another box worth on the other side. A whistle brings the dog to heel, and the two of you take up your place in the skirmish line.

Orange sunlight splinters the horizon, and you call over to the gun next to you, "When is shoot time?"

Down the line you hear a pop. Then, on the other side, another shooter echoes it and adds a second for good measure. Overhead you hear the whistle of wings, and you raise your shotgun and pivot wildly, searching the sky for the bird. By the time you find it, the opportunity is gone and your neighbor folds the dove neatly. The dog breaks to make the retrieve, and you stop him with a whistle blast. It's not our bird. Not yet.

The first groups of dove swarm out of the desert and assault the line of guns. Pop. Pop. Pop, pop. Birds fall three shooters down. Then you catch the dog intent on something in front of you, and you see them. Two birds coming low over the mesquites. The dove hits the edge of the tree line and flairs upward over the top. You swing the 20-gauge past the first bird and into the second. Wheel. Pivot. The bead swings through the head of the bird, the shotgun sees air and thump! On its own volition, it slams into your shoulder. Another season has begun.

Too soon, it is the afternoon of the last day. The mid-January sun feels warm. In 30 days, quail will also end and the long wait begin. It's been a relaxing shoot with good friends who now wait on the road at the truck for you to take your last bird.

The dove start flying a little before 4 p.m. and funnel into the milo for 45 minutes. They come in high with a stiff wind until they're over the field and then the birds

Sadie, a Chesapeake Bay Retriever, with a late season limit of mourning doves.

fold and settle into the grain to feed. It took the modified barrel to reach them, and there were several missed shots before you found the lead. Like the tide trickling to a standstill and then slowly reversing, the birds start coming back out. They leave low, fighting the wind, and with one more shot, it's over for another year. The old dog is tired but looks like she has the heart for one more retrieve before six months of rest.

A hawk comes across the adjoining cotton field and floats out over the milo. Clouds of mourning dove boil up in waves and roll off the hawk's shadow like water cut by a shark's fin. One, two, three hundred birds in the air and part of the cloud swings toward you. The dog stiffens and stares at their coming, and you pick a bird.

MOURNING DOVE DISTRIBUTION

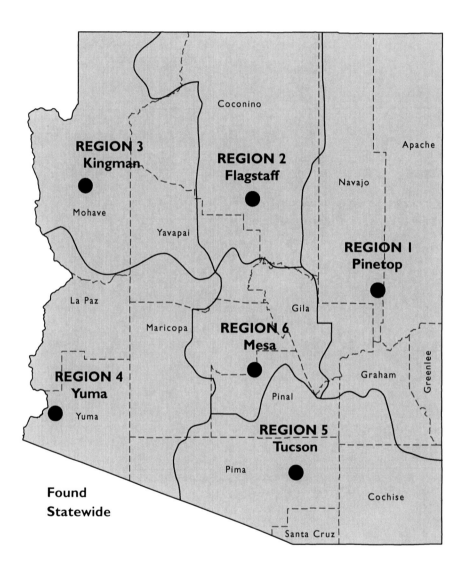

REGION 3
Kingman

Coconino

REGION 2
Flagstaff

Apache

Mohave

Navajo

Yavapai

REGION 1
Pinetop

La Paz

Gila

Maricopa

REGION 6
Mesa

Greenlee

REGION 4
Yuma

Graham

Yuma

Pinal

REGION 5
Tucson

Found
Statewide

Pima

Cochise

Santa Cruz

Mourning Dove

Zenaida macroura

QUICK FACTS

Local Name
Mourning Dove, Common Dove

Spanish Name
Huilota, Tórtola, Tiuta

Size
11–13 inches (27–33 cm) in length, 5-ounce average weight

Identification in Flight
Mourning doves in flight appear as medium-sized, fast moving, pigeon shaped birds. They are grey overall with a buff colored breast. Their tails come to a conspicuous sharp-pointed end. Dove's wings make a rhythmic whistling sound in flight.

- The daily bag limit for mourning dove is 10 per day.
- Mourning dove are found statewide.
- Mourning doves are very prolific and have a very high reproductive potential.
- Early season doves are best hunted on desert water tanks and weed fields.
- In summer, doves drink approximately 7% of their body weight in water.
- Late season doves are best hunted in grain fields in agricultural areas.
- Early season doves respond to cold weather by heading south into Mexico.

Color

Both males and females are nearly identical in appearance. Overall plumage is a grayish brown. Their chest and belly soften to a light tawny brown. The bottom of the tips of the tail feathers are highlighted with white. On close inspection, the bird has small black ear marks and several small black spots on the scapulars and upper wing coverts. The top of the dove's head is capped with a blue-grey crown, and the unfeathered skin around the eye is powder blue. The sides of the nape of the neck shimmer with a translucent purple iridescence. Legs and feet are red.

Al Peevy prepares to take a dove out of a flock leaving standing cotton.

Sound and Flight Pattern

In flight mourning doves are swift and direct, resorting to acrobatics only when eluding predators or gunfire. Their wings make a distinctive whistling sound. On opening day, birds fly at treetop level. Hunted doves respond to shooting pressure by flying at 30 to 40 yards elevation or higher.

Birds fly in the morning and evening. Their morning feeding flight begins at full light, typically 10 minutes after sunrise. They are active for two hours and are back on their midday roosts by 9:30 to 10:00 A.M. Hunters might shoot an active feeding area

A limit of late season mourning doves.

for the first half of the morning, then relocate and intercept birds returning to their mesquite bosque roosting areas. Doves need water daily in hot weather and will fly long distances to get it. Birds coming to water in the mornings do so after having fed. Hunters waiting in ambush on water tanks should not expect to see incoming birds until 8:00 A.M.

Afternoon shooting is prohibited in the early season. During the second season, shooting the evening feeding flight over agricultural fields can be very productive, but water tanks seldom produce. Also in the second season, large concentrations of newly arrived migrating birds are sometimes located feeding and loafing in the desert. Although these concentrations are occasional and sporadic, they make for several days of fine shooting when located.

Similar Game Birds

White-winged doves are sometimes confused with mourning doves, however their differences are readily apparent in flight. Whitewings have a broad white line on their upper wing, fly later in the morning, are larger, fly slower, and have a slower wing beat. A whitewing's tail is square while a mourning dove's comes to a sharp point.

American kestrels are also occasionally mistaken for mourning doves. In flight, kestrels lack the strong downstroke of a flying dove. Kestrels also have a heavier head and shoulder, and a rounded tail.

Don Prentice and his German wirehaired pointer, Fritzel, wait for a shot as mourning doves swarm overhead.

There are two species of small doves (Inca doves and ground doves) that are sometimes mistaken for the larger mourning dove. They have a silver cast to their bodies and their wings flash russet in flight. These smaller doves are half the size of a mourning and fly close to the ground. An observant shooter shouldn't have any problem discerning the difference.

Flock or Covey Habits

Mourning doves congregate in large numbers to exploit a food source. Rather than moving in one large flock, feeding doves come in sporadic singles and small groups. Once the birds have massed for feeding, large flocks can lift up and swing over a field in response to an overhead raptor or as a prelude to returning to their roosting areas. By studying the bird's approaches as they enter a field, a hunter can be positioned

Typical desert stock tank that provides early season dove shooting for Arizona hunters.

under their flight pattern. It will generally remain consistent as long as the birds use the field.

Flying birds follow canals and tree lines. Early season hunters park on access roads that parallel agricultural canals and take birds as they fly the waterways. The most productive areas are where canals divide natural desert and crop land. By planning shots, a hunter can drop birds on the dirt canal bank and access road as the birds fly out of the mesquites. Dead birds are easily recovered when lying in the open. Without a dog, as many as half the birds dropped in mesquite/brush cover can be lost. Also, tramping around during the early season in thick brush after downed birds is a good way for both hunter or dog to find a rattlesnake.

When dove season opens on September 1, many resident birds have already begun their migration and are in Mexico. September hunters will notice a significant reduction in mourning dove population after the season's first few days. Additional migrating birds arriving from northern Arizona and the intermountain states boost resident bird numbers. However, from the middle of September until the second season ends in January, all locally fledged birds are gone and shooting is made up of birds raised in Utah, Nevada, Idaho, eastern California, eastern Oregon and eastern Washington.

Reproduction and Life Span

I see mourning dove nesting everywhere: little random assemblies of twigs that don't look as if they could make it through a 10 mph breeze stuck on the side of the eaves at the post office, in short palm trees at the shopping mall parking lot, wedged into the bracing of a dilapidated windmill tower on a remote desert water tank. To say mourning doves are prolific is an understatement. In some areas of Arizona, doves have been observed nesting every month of the year. Arizona gunners take one to two million mourning doves per season.

Courtship activities begin in late February, when pairs perform grand swooping courtship flights. Males can be heard broadcasting their soft cooing courtship call. Breeding activities peak in April and May.

Mourning doves return to their hatching area to breed and raise their young. Nearly 95% of returned dove bands are recovered within one degree of their original banding site.

After two white eggs are laid, incubation duties are shared by both parents. Fledglings appear in 14 to 15 days. Squabs grow very rapidly and are ready to leave the nest in 12 to 14 days. A new clutch of eggs is laid and incubation begins anew. On average, mourning doves bring off four nests a season, with seven being the record. Mourning doves are thought to live as long as six or seven years.

Feeding Habits and Patterns

Mourning doves feed both early and late on small seeds they glean from the ground. Once a food source is located, birds will continually return until forced by hunting pressure or weather to move elsewhere. Early season birds work fallow agricultural fields for weed seeds and congregate on rare sources of grain like cattle feedlots and dairies. The preferred food for late season doves is grain. By November and December, milo is ripening and attracting hungry flocks. Most fields are planted in cotton, so successful dove hunting requires prospecting for shootable milo fields. Scout early and locate several fields, then monitor them before opening day to see which will afford the best shooting.

Preferred Habitat and Cover

Mourning doves are found statewide and utilize all available habitats to some extent. Their preferred range is lower elevation deserts covering the bottom two-thirds of the state. The largest nesting concentrations were once found in extensive mesquite bosques along permanent river courses. Sadly, these densely vegetated dove factories have been cleared down to a minute fraction of their original size. Birds still rely heavily on dense stands of natural desert near water. These roosting areas consistently produce good shooting for dove hunters.

Darrell Kincaid tracks across the front of a fast-moving mourning dove as Abigail tries to mark the fall.

Locating Hunting Areas

Opening day, early dove season, sounds like a war—literally. Arizona dove hot spots are the state's worst kept secrets. Historically, birds are found in the same general areas year after year. Ask any three people and you'll end up with a detailed map. After locating an area, here are some tips to pinpoint a spot:

1. Look for water—birds follow canals, river courses, and especially the thick mesquite and salt cedar strips that line river canals.
2. Watch for doves congregating on power lines midmorning and late afternoon.
3. Look for likely agricultural and weed fields and, during shooting hours, hunter's vehicles grouped around those fields.
4. Cattle feed lots and dairies attract birds that glean waste grain.

Chesapeake Bay Retriever with a limit of mourning doves at the edge of a desert tank.

Looking for Sign

Large flocks of feeding doves are readily apparent. Drive rural roads and follow trading doves. Watch for concentrations of birds on power lines near agricultural fields from 8 to 9:30 in the morning and again in the late afternoon. Use binoculars and glass for doves feeding on the ground or boiling above vegetation in promising fields. Sitting on a tank before the opener will tell you if dove are watering there.

Hunting Methods

Dove hunting means pass shooting. It's all pretty straightforward: find a spot with ample birds; study how the birds travel; get underneath their flight pattern and ambush them as they trade back and forth. I suppose a person could embellish it with a dove call and decoys set up on a tall high line wire or tree, but the shooting is so good here that I have never seen anyone do it.

MOURNING DOVE — 55

The September 1 dove opener brings to an end the long night of darkness and despair that befalls an Arizona wingshooter when the quail season ended the previous February. Opening day dove is a social event complete with shooting stools and ice chests. There are ample birds and amplified heat radiating down from the summer sun, both of which make for a short, early morning shoot. Dove fields can accommodate enough guns to keep the birds moving and leave a volunteer or two at the shoot's end to count up the empty hulls in your bird bucket and compute your bird-to-shell ratio. The first couple of days the shooting's pretty easy. Arizona dove hunting begins about the third day.

A few days into the season, the birds are flying higher and with a noticeable reduction in numbers flying. The remaining hunters are concentrated in those areas where doves are working the best. Opening day dove hordes have been replaced by a sporadic trickle, and a limit is much harder to scratch down. If a good, out-of-the-way field or flyway can be located, it could produce all the way through the first season which runs 10 or 11 days. Mostly though, continued hunting will depend on looking for new areas.

If one knows other hunters in the area, get on the phone and start asking them where they're finding birds. The Game and Fish Department is always a reliable source of mostly generic information, but it will point a person in the right direction. Local area game managers can be very specific about their particular units.

When all else fails, there is the whore's last recourse: drive to a likely area an hour after shooting time, roll down your vehicle window and steer toward the sound of gunfire.

Hunting Dogs

Retrievers will get a real workout on a dove shoot. With the daily bag at 10 birds per day, a dog retrieving for two or three guns has got some nonstop fetching to do. All breeds are used with many versatile and pointing breed quail dogs serving double duty.

As it is the season's first hurrah, dogs generally aren't in good enough physical shape to handle an extensive workout. Early season dove hunting is a very hot affair. Temperatures often exceed 100 degrees by 10 o'clock in the morning. Dogs need plenty of water. If at all possible, I hunt beside a water source like a canal or tank. A dog that can get into water and swim will stay cool. If I'm field shooting, I carry a 3-gallon covered bucket full of water that I set on the ground beside me and leave available at all times for the dog.

The loose feathers that build up on a frothing dog's mouth while retrieving doves cause some retrievers to swear off doves. The water bucket cools them down and helps keep their mouth free of feathers. Also, this water is readily available for the hunter to soak down the dog's belly periodically, helping to lower body temperature.

A short tie-out cable or Jaeger lead is a handy way to control a slipping, nonslip retriever. The sheer numbers of birds overhead and constant shooting can temporarily derail a steady young dog's resolve. Rather than add frustration to what is supposed to be an enjoyable outing for both of you, cable a runner to a fence post, truck bumper, tree trunk, or what have you. Release him when there is something to fetch.

Remember to be very careful during the early season regarding rattlesnakes. Sending dogs into heavy cover to search for downed birds is an invitation for a frantic ride to the emergency vets. Pick your shots so that birds fall in the open. If one gets by and makes the treeline, go with your dog and watch for snakes.

Field Preparations

Dove meat is dark and similar to duck. It has provided the main course for many a beginning-of-season feast. Hunters carry ice chests for cooling out cleaned birds and breast out doves by twisting off the head and wing and pushing their thumbs up under the bird's sternum. One good pull and the breast rips free. Remember, federal law requires that one fully feathered wing remain attached for identification.

Shot and Choke Suggestions

- **Low fliers:** skeet/improved cylinder 8, 7½ shot
- **High fliers:** modified/full 7½, 6 shot

White-winged Dove Distribution

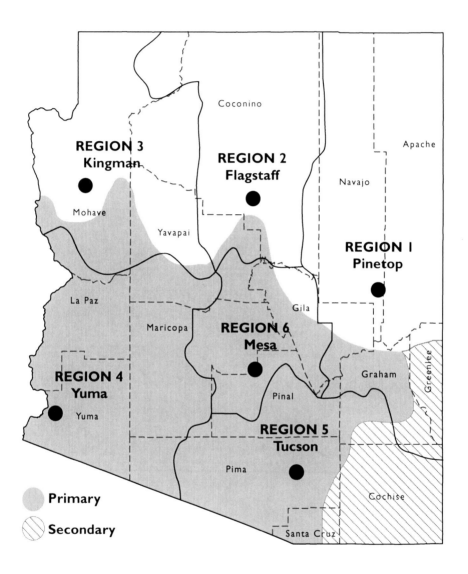

REGION 3
Kingman

REGION 2
Flagstaff

REGION 1
Pinetop

REGION 6
Mesa

REGION 4
Yuma

REGION 5
Tucson

Coconino

Apache

Navajo

Mohave

Yavapai

La Paz

Gila

Maricopa

Graham

Greenlee

Pinal

Yuma

Pima

Cochise

Santa Cruz

Primary

Secondary

White-winged Dove

Zenaidia asiatica

QUICK FACTS

Local Name
Whitewing, Sonoran dove, Sonoran pigeon, Mexican dove

Spanish Name
Paloma con alas Blancas, Torcáz, Torcaza

Size
11–12½ inches (28–32 cm) in length, 5.5 ounce average weight

Identification in Flight
The most obvious field marking on a whitewing is the brilliant flash of white on the wing's upper surface as a bird flies. A whitewing's tail is square. Its wing beats are slow and its flight steady and direct. At a distance, the dove's body is an overall grey color with a dark band midway on the bottom of the tail and white feathers at the tip.

- Hunters are allowed 10 doves per day, of which 6 may be whitewings.
- The glory days of Arizona white-wing shooting are over. Mourning doves make the shooting.
- White-winged dove and saguaro cactus range overlap.
- Migration into Arizona is timed to coincide with the flowering of saguaro, one of their primary food sources.
- Most of Arizona's whitewings have left for Mexico when the September 1 dove season opens.
- Whitewings fly later in the morning than mourning doves.
- Most of the birds in an opening day hunter's bag will be very young birds.

Color

Whitewings are predominantly a varying shade of olive grey, darker on the back and top of the neck and head, and softening in hue on the breast and face. Its primary flight feathers on the wings are a deep grey-black. The lower edge of the upper wing coverts are marked with a brilliant white line that gives the bird its name and primary field mark. The lower tip of the square tail is highlighted in white. Their legs and feet are red. An adult bird's iris is orange-red, and the eye is surrounded with a patch of unfeathered powder blue skin. There is a short, linear, black "ear mark" on the side of the face. A translucent purple-green iridescence covers the sides of the neck directly behind the "ear mark."

Geoffrey and Brent Barstow score on a double of whitewings.

Sound and Flight Pattern

Whitewings are present in Arizona from March through September. During their courtship and breeding periods, birds are very vocal, their cueing floating among the saguaro. The call is a distinctive "who cooks for you" with the heaviest accent on the last note.

A whitewing's flight is slow and direct. They favor traveling over heavy lines of vegetation along or near watercourses. While mourning doves are moving shortly after dawn, whitewings don't begin flying in earnest until 7:45 or 8:00 A.M. Historically, birds utilized grain fields before their August/September departure from Arizona. However, due to the shift to cotton as the state's primary crop, early grain is as scarce as concentrations of whitewings.

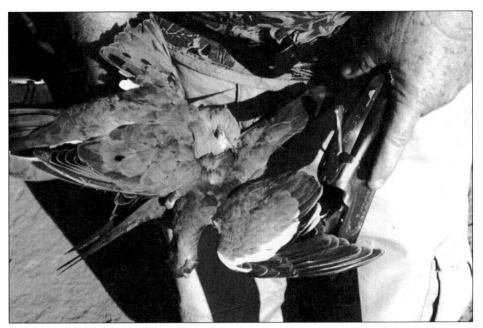

Comparison photo of white-winged and mourning doves. The white bar on the upper wing is very conspicuous in flight on a white-winged dove.

Similar Game Birds

The flash of white, the slower wing beat, and the square tail signal that a white-wing is among the mourning doves approaching. In the thick of a shoot with birds flashing by, an occasional whitewing gets dropped, only to be identified when brought to hand. If a person slows down, it is not difficult to differentiate between the two species.

First, whitewings fly later in the morning, often well after shooters have filled their limits on mourning doves and left the field. They are bigger, slower in flight with slower wing beats, have a semisquare tail, and flash white on their upper wing surfaces while flying. They are found in or near the thick mesquite/salt cedar ribbons that grow along permanent water. Often, small populations of whitewings fly overgrown canals between roost sites and food.

Two other species of miniature dove share whitewing range: ground doves and Inca doves. They are half a whitewing's size, have a body color of silver grey as opposed to olive grey, and flash russet wing primaries in flight. The two smaller doves fly low to the ground and are difficult to confuse with the larger whitewing.

Flock or Covey Habits

The glory days of whitewing hunting in Arizona ran from the mid-1950s to the early 1960s. Shooters filled their 25-bird-a-day limits from flocks of thousands of

White-winged dove travel north to Arizona during the nesting season specifically to feed on the fruit of the organ pipe and saguaro cactus.

white-wings streaming overhead. Sadly, along with the river-fed, mesquite bosque nurseries that propagated them and the grain that supported them, these legions of birds are gone.

During the open season, I don't find flocks of whitewings so I am reticent to write about flock habits. Occasionally in some areas, I see sporadic small groups numbering from several individuals to several dozen. One field in early September, which has been in standing grain for several years running, holds a few hundred birds. This large field is swarmed by thousands of mourning doves from all sides and used uniformly across its entire area by the feeding mourning doves. The only place in this field where whitewings can be found is an overgrown creek channel with running water in the bottom that touches one side of the field. The whitewings congregate in a small group of trees that line the water.

For the average gunner in southern Arizona, a couple of whitewings showing up in the bag for three days of shooting (30 birds) would be about right. The rare white wing flies by and a g s it's presented. Many of the birds brought to bag are newly fledged youngsters, still too young to leave for Sonora.

When shooters hunting with me from out-of-state ask specifically to target whitewings, we go to areas that have water and appropriate vegetation and hope for the best. If we get lucky, they pick up two or three and fill out the rest of their bag with mourning doves.

Ross Leggett and his GWP waiting during a lull in the morning flight.

Reproduction and Life Span

Migrating whitewings return from Mexico from mid-April through mid-May. Pair selection begins immediately, with males advertising for a mate by calling and engaging in stiff-wing, soaring courtship flights. The female lays two creamy white eggs in a rather poorly constructed nest, and incubation chores are tended to by both parents. Depending on temperature and elevation, eggs hatch in 13 to 19 days, with the first young showing up around the end of June. Chicks fledge the nest in late June and July. In areas of abundant food, a second nesting can take place, although the norm is for parent birds to return to Mexico as soon as the young leave the nest. By as early as mid-July, adult whitewings are en route to Mexico, with the majority of birds departing by August 15th. Birds winter along the west coast of mainland Mexico from extreme southern Sonora and Sinaloa south.

    White-wings can live up to five years.

Feeding Habits and Patterns

Large concentrations of whitewings have generally been associated with cultivated fields of grain. This is still true in Mexico where birds are hunted into February and March of the year. Arizona gunners, however, have a narrow window of opportunity running from September 1 through September 10 or 11. When grain is not readily available, it is rare to see any concentrations of white-winged doves. Whitewings come north across the border in late April and early May to raise their young and feed on the pollen and fruit of saguaro and organ-pipe cactus. They also forage for desert plant seeds such as ocotillo, jojoba, prickle poppy and dove weed. Most adult birds have left for Mexico before the season opens.

Whitewings feed later in the morning than mourning doves, typically beginning their feeding flights a full hour to an hour and a half after dawn. Birds tend to follow vegetation-lined water courses as they travel to feeding areas. A hunter willing to wait and pass up the earlier arriving mourning doves can work a known whitewing route for trading birds.

Preferred Habitat and Cover

Whitewings are birds of the Sonoran desert. Smaller populations are found in the state's southeastern section and along the Colorado River, but the main stronghold is the saguaro cactus region that fills the state's central and south central parts. Dense mesquite bosques that once lined river courses provided sheltered nesting colonies, producing tremendous hatches of young. Birds still use similar habitat where available.

Locating Hunting Areas

Most whitewings that are taken are random individuals falling to mourning dove shooters. It is difficult to specifically target whitewings. Short of knowing an area that whitewings historically frequent, here are some tips that might help:

1. Ask someone. Most area hunters, who are approached in a polite, respectful manner, will go out of their way to help a person unfamiliar with the area.
2. Remember that whitewings have specific habitat needs and will use the same area yearly. Even an old lead is worth checking out.
3. Look for concentrations of birds along permanent watercourses. Whitewings nest in mesquite trees that line water, and while most have left for Mexico by mid-August, some late nesters and birds of the year may still be present.
4. Scout in July and early August while numbers of whitewings are still present.
5. Look for grain.

Looking for Sign

Scout dove areas with a pair of binoculars and look for white on the wings. While mourning doves are more conspicuous while loafing and traveling to feed, white-wings fly later in the morning and stick to heavy belts of vegetation where they are more difficult to see.

As grain fields are scarce, it is easiest to start there. If birds are present, they will be using available grain. Locate the grain in your hunting area well before opening day and watch the feeding habits of any whitewings using the fields. Watch how they approach and from where. Pick a good ambush spot underneath the flight lane, and then say a prayer that no weather front pushes them south before opening morning.

Hunting Methods

Like mourning dove shoots, white-wing hunting is a pass-shooting affair. Find a concentration of birds and pick a spot below their flight lane. With Arizona's current daily bag limit of 10 doves per day, six of which may be whitewings, it's not a bad idea to take four mourning doves early and then wait for the whitewings to arrive. A shooter's resolve can be sorely tested while mourning doves tantalizingly whistle by. When I go out specifically for whitewings, my resolve probably averages eight mournings to two whitewings.

Hunting Dogs

Certainly, everything mentioned in the mourning dove, hunting dog section applies to whitewings. As whitewings fly later in the morning, dogs will be out in the rising heat longer. Keep retrievers cooled down and, if possible, periodically submerged in water. When the temperature is pushing 100 degrees, an active dog can get in trouble fast. Watch out for snakes.

Field Preparations

Adult whitewings are slightly larger than mourning doves, but most of the doves taken will be birds of the year and smaller than a mourning dove. Also, like mourning doves, whitewings are excellent eating.

Most hunters clean doves by pulling the breasts, leaving one wing attached in order to satisfy legal requirements. Cool the meat in an ice chest on the drive home.

Shot and Choke Suggestions
- Low fliers: skeet/improved cylinder 8, 7½ shot
- High fliers: modified/full 7½, 6

BAND-TAILED PIGEON DISTRIBUTION

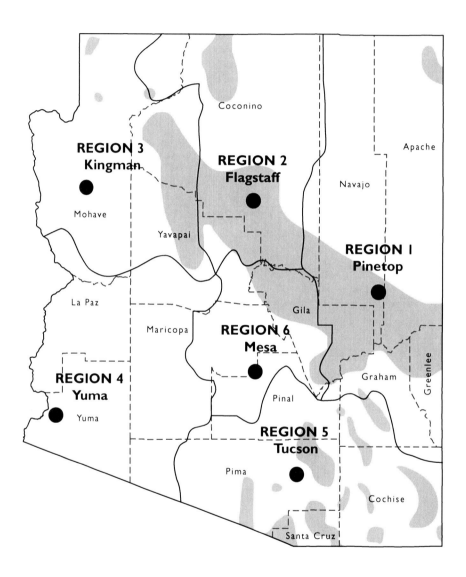

Band-tailed Pigeon

Columba fasciata fasciata

Quick Facts

Local Name
Bandtail, pigeon

Spanish Name
Paloma de Collar, Pichón Grande, yaz, Cuauhpaloma (Mayan)

Size
14–15½ inches (35.6–39.4 cm) in length, 12 ounces average weight

Identification in Flight
Bandtails are a large, dark blue-grey, pigeon-shaped bird. They have a square, slightly rounded tail, and a strong, steady wing beat. Pigeons are seen in groups of five to 40 or more. Their flight is silent except when leaving a perch. Then, their wings make a loud "flap, flap, flap" sound or, as large groups, combine their flight sounds into a roar. Gliding birds coast stiff-winged with their wings held at a 45-degree dihedral angle.

- The 95/96 season ran October 18–27. The daily limit was 5, the possession limit was 10.
- Bandtail hunters are required to have a special bird permit issued free of charge by the department.
- Tree squirrel season runs concurrently and makes for a good combo hunt.
- During the season, bandtails are found between 4500- and 7000-foot elevation, in mountainous terrain where oak and/or pine trees are present.
- Bandtails lay one egg per nesting, but may nest up to three times per season.

Color

For a bird that appears drab at a distance, bandtails when viewed in hand are beautifully colored. The upper surface of a bandtail is a blue cast, slate-grey. Its breast lightens in color to take on a violet cast and turns to a pale buff on the belly. Primary flight feathers are dark grey. The upper surface of the slightly rounded tail is divided horizontally at the halfway point by a narrow dark-grey band. The lower half of the tail's upper surface is a soft light-grey, while the bottom below the band is nearly grey.

Adults have a metallic green nape highlighted at the top with a white crescent that forms a thin dividing line between the base of the skull and the neck. Eyes are dark brown with red eyelids, and its beak is yellow with a black tip. Legs and feet are also yellow, with feathering coming one-third of the way down the front of the tarsus.

Sexes can be differentiated by the vividness of color, with males having the most striking coloring while females show a much-muted plumage with only faint traces of iridescence. Juveniles are easily identified by buff-tipped greater wing coverts and a near or totally absent white collar and metallic green nape.

Sound and Flight Pattern

Bandtails are highly migratory. A hundred pigeons might be sighted one day and by the next day there will be none at the same location. In the state's central regions, populations are present up to midseason. In mountain ranges along the Mexican border, birds may be found through closing day. A typical flock would contain five or six individuals, with groups of 40 or more seen occasionally.

Pigeons coming into water or a feeding area do not do a lot of circling. Instead, they fly in and light onto a tall dead snag or large mature ponderosa pine. Like a Gambel's quail covey, one bird takes sentry position in the upper reaches of the tree. Feeding flights begin about a half hour after daylight and continue until 9:30 or 10:00 A.M., when birds retire to loafing areas to wait out the midday. Birds feed first and then water, so hunters waiting on water should not expect to see birds until later in the morning.

Similar Game Birds

A bandtail looks very much like a domestic pigeon and could be easily confused for one. Feral domestic pigeons are found around urban and agricultural areas. Bandtails inhabit slopes and higher elevation, so there is not much crossover in terms of range, eliminating most chances for misidentification.

Bandtails are sometimes mistaken for blue grouse when they explode off a limb, their wings clapping a "flap, flap, flap." The dark silhouette of a perched bandtail taking refuge in thick evergreen tree boughs during midday also looks very much like a hiding blue and could initially lead to their misidentification.

Flock or Covey Habits

Bandtails are gregarious birds that have been observed on rare occasions in flocks of a hundred or more. Average group size would be around five birds with a large flock numbering up to 40 or more. As stated earlier, birds travel to food and water in the morning, loaf during midday on large dead snags and mature trees, and fly again in the evening.

Reproduction and Life Span

Arizona's bandtail population winter in Mexico in highlands that divide the states of Sinaloa and Durango and south into Nayarit. Birds return in March to take up breeding

Band-tailed pigeons are beautifully marked birds. (Randall D. Babb, Arizona Game & Fish Department)

territories throughout suitable mountain ranges in the central and southeast areas of the state. Like other Arizona dove species, male pigeons "coo" and engage in ritual display flights as a precursor to breeding.

Nests are constructed by both parents, with a typical clutch containing one glossy, white egg. Chicks begin hatching in May. In years of adequate forage, most pairs will nest twice, some three times. During poor years, some birds may decline nesting all together.

Eggs hatch in 18 to 22 days. Young leave the nest in 24 to 26 days. Feeding females and fledged young form small daytime loafing and feeding flights until September, when nesting activity has ceased and birds travel more broadly in preparation for the migration south.

Bandtails that nest in Utah, Colorado, and New Mexico funnel down through Arizona during migration. While Arizona native birds may leave before hunting season, these later migrants repopulate bandtail haunts and provide shooting.

Bandtails are thought to have the potential to live to 6 years of age.

Feeding Habits and Patterns

During the summer and up through the beginning of September, pigeons feed on elderberries, mulberries, currants, pine seeds, acorns and, where available, cultivated grain. As the birds ready for their trip south, they concentrate on Gambel oak acorns, piñon nuts, and mountain elderberries. Bandtail will hang upside down like parrots and feed on clusters of elderberries.

Bandtails also use salt and other minerals. I have not personally seen this, nor was I able to locate another hunter who had located such an area, but it is well represented in the literature. Along with the Pacific Coast population, interior bandtails supplement their diet at salt licks and by drinking at mineral springs.

Preferred Habitat and Cover

Bandtails are mountain birds, where they prefer precipitous slopes and jagged ridges. They are dependent on such food sources as mountain berries, acorns, and piñon nuts. Pigeons frequent large, dead snags and mature ponderosa trees as roosting areas.

In summer, birds range as high as 9,100 feet in the spruce zone, but hunters looking for birds during the 10-day late October season will find birds in oaks and pines from 4500 to 7000 feet in elevation.

Locating Hunting Areas

Because of the bandtail's preferred habitat, most of Arizona's pigeon range is on National Forest land open to hunting. The secret to finding birds is familiarity with an area and scouting just prior to the season opening in order to pinpoint populations. Even after much hard work, if a storm blows in just prior to the season, birds can leave and everything changes overnight.

Arizona's national forests are transected with an extensive network of logging roads that allow scouting hunters to cover a lot of ground. It is probably best to start by glassing ridge lines and slopes at midday. Look for flocks of bandtails loafing on exposed dead snags. Glassing hunters will pick up sentry birds high in the trees and then, after closer observation, the rest of the flock tucked in tight on lower branches. I have come across groups using ponderosa pines on the flat ground above canyons. Some of these flocks were spread over a hundred-yard area. Generally, groups were betrayed by one or two individual birds I spotted while driving down a forest service road.

Once birds are found in an area, check tanks to locate where birds are watering. Look for tracks and feathers at the water's edge. If a tank looks promising, sit it one morning and see if your suspicions are well founded. Birds will often light in one particular tree before dropping down to water. Make a note of their patterns and pick an ambush spot near their beacon tree.

Looking for Sign

Glassing slopes and ridges will let you know that birds are in the area. On water, look for tracks and feathers. Pigeon feet are larger than a dove's and slightly heavier. Mourning doves are also migrating through pigeon range at the same time, so a person who is scouting will have to be conscious of their differences. Many mourning doves in these areas are on water at midday and early afternoon, while pigeons prefer morning up until 10:00 A.M.

Hunting Methods

October is a beautiful time to be in Arizona's high country. Tree squirrel season is open during the bandtail hunt. Both species are found in the same areas, and squirrels make for a great consolation prize. A hunter may not find pigeons, but most years there are a bunch of bushytails.

As with most hunting, the hard part is finding them. Much energy is spent in locating huntable populations of birds. Earlier in this section, I discussed scouting methods and habitat requirements. Once birds are located, then a hunter can work on putting them in the game bag.

Loafing flocks spotted roosting, while glassing or traveling forest service roads, can be stalked like a bedded, big game animal. Hunters can usually slip in within shotgun range on a flock. I find that birds are not terribly spooky initially, and if I'm cautious, they will let me get within 25 yards. Give them a reason and that changes. Different shooters coming in from several sides can cover various escape lanes that run through the trees, and someone may be able to get in position for a shot.

Take the first bird as it leaves the branch and then try for a second. This is easier said than done. Birds dive from the limb and make twisting turns to put the nearest tree between them and the gun.

In areas with a large population of birds, a hunter may be able to ambush birds as they fly to water or feed. Birds may consistently use a saddle or follow a ridgeline while traveling. Pigeons fly at treetop level or slightly higher, making them just about right for a modified choke.

The most productive method is ambushing them when they come into feed or water. If a hunter can locate an active feeding/watering site, then he can position himself so that he has some control over the shot. Birds often have a "beacon" tree they light on before they drop down and land. Large flocks of pigeons that have been shot at and prevented from coming in will often return in small groups, much like a flock of greenwing teal, repeatedly returning to a desert tank.

Hunting Dogs

Retrievers are a big asset when hunting bandtails. Many pigeon areas are very steep, and the best mark a hunter has on a bird falling downslope is obscured by trees. Even with a dog, a bird that makes it into a canyon can be difficult to find. Because of thick cover, a dog is quickly lost to sight and cannot be handled into a fall. Over water, a retriever again comes in handy.

My experience is that pigeons tolerate the presence of a dog reasonably well, but a dog that stays still will not spook incomers and can observe difficult marks more effectively. Bandtail country has an abundance of trees, and rather than struggle with a dog breaking at shot, tethering a moving dog to a tree trunk will eliminate any frustration.

Field Preparations

Pigeons have dark meat and, when cleaned, look to all appearances like a large dove. Bandtails can be breasted like doves or plucked and prepared whole for a more formal presentation. Some hunters draw and hang their birds before cleaning.

Shot and Choke Suggestions

- **Close range:** skeet/improved cylinder 7½ shot
- **Long range:** modified/full 7½ and 6 shot

BLUE GROUSE DISTRIBUTION

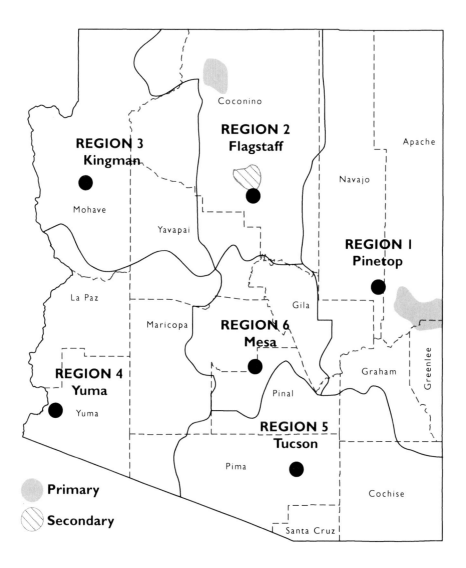

Blue Grouse

Dendragapus obscurus obscurus

QUICK FACTS

Local Name
Grouse, mountain grouse, blues

Spanish Name
Blue grouse are not found in Mexico.

Size
15–21 inches (38–53 cm) in length, males up to three pounds, females 1¾ to 2 pounds

Identification in Flight
Often the first glimpse a hunter has of a blue grouse is a large, square-tailed, blue-grey bird jumping from the ground to thick overhead pine or spruce cover. The second contact is the nerve-rattling sound of the same large bird exploding from overhead branches and offering no possibility for a shot.

- In Arizona, available blue grouse habitat is very limited, and hunt success is best described as spotty. Hunters whose primary interest is in hunting blues would be best advised to go elsewhere.
- Blue grouse season runs from early September through mid-November.
- During the 1995 season, the bag was three per day and six in possession.
- Blue grouse hunters are required to obtain a special game bird stamp, issued free of charge by the department.
- Early September grouse hunts are popular with gun dog owners because, during that time of year, the grouse's high altitude habitat areas are the only place in Arizona cool enough to comfortably work a bird dog.
- Arizona blues are of the "dusky grouse" subspecies.
- Blue grouse range above 8,500 feet.

Color

In terms of color, blue grouse are not visually demonstrative birds. Male plumage is an overall dark blue-grey. Feathers on the back, sides, and upper wing coverts are highlighted with a pattern of sooty white vermiculation. Side coverts are lined with off-white darts, similar to a Gambel's quail. Its large, square fantail is slightly darker than the body and nondescript with the exception of a slight grey terminal band. The entire tarsus is feathered on a grouse. Eye color is brown. Adult males have a reddish-orange patch of skin above the eye. Two similar, large oval skin patches on the sides of the chest are visible during strutting displays. Females and juveniles are a mottled brown with dark tail feathers.

Sound and Flight Pattern

During breeding season male grouse make a hooting sound to announce their strutting territories. For this reason, in the Pacific Northwest, one of their colloquial names is hooter. During hunting season birds are silent.

Grouse encountered on the ground, when approached, usually flush into a nearby tree. They tend to light in the thickest section, between the lower third and the midsection of a mature conifer. Some fly into the forest and are impossible to relocate. Marked birds are often very difficult to spot secreted among evergreen boughs. Blues may flush when a hunter closes to around 20 yards. Some birds are lost completely when they refuse to show themselves, and a hunter is not able to get the bird to flush. It is similar to locating a tree squirrel hiding in a tree. Blue grouse are strong fliers. Once they decide to bail off a limb, they flat leave. Birds launch into adjacent tree cover and are exceedingly hard to hit as they flash through the trees.

Similar Game Birds

Bandtail pigeons are sometimes mistaken for blue grouse as they launch from overhead limbs. The loud flapping of a pigeon's wings tends to startle and confuse a hunter intent on being prepared for a flushing grouse.

There are no other birds that resemble blue grouse in Arizona's high country.

Flock and Covey Habits

Early season flocks of four to six birds typically are made up of a hen and her brood. Occasionally two hens with broods combine to form groups of a dozen or so birds.

Adult male birds are solitary and are encountered less frequently, partially because they restrict much of their activity to heavier, dense tree cover. When adult males are located, it is often along steep canyon rims where their slope sanctuaries are a jump away.

Flocks roost in trees as family units. Blue grouse flock behavior is similar to turkeys. Birds feed along the edges of forest openings and overgrown logging roads. Where available, new growth in burns attract foraging birds. Birds loaf at midday under heavy cover on the ground. They feed again in the late afternoon and return to roost at sunset.

Reproduction and Life Span

Like other North American grouse species, adult male blue grouse establish breeding territories and strut to attract females. Territories range up to two acres in size. Males engage in elaborate displays with fanned tails and stiff wings cupped downward. They typically select a small opening or clearing and post themselves on a stump or deadfall. Inflated air sacks in their necks emit the soft "hoot" sound that give the bird its colloquial name. Mating activity peaks during the last week of May and the first week of June.

Hens are intercepted as they travel through a male's breeding territory. After mating, the male has no further contact with the hen and she sets up housekeeping alone. Males remain on their strutting grounds and breed other available females.

Hens nest in underbrush and debris on the ground. The nest is lined with grass and conceals five to 10 eggs. Chicks hatch after 26 days. Most young appear in the 30-day period running from June 15 through July 15. Chicks feed heavily on insects and, at two weeks of age, clutch size runs from 4 to 6 young. Chicks are said to be capable of short flights by the time they are seven days old.

When winter comes to the high country, surviving groups break up and find roosting sites in dense conifer trees. They survive by eating spruce needles until spring, when the cycle begins again.

Blue grouse are thought to be capable of living 10 to 15 years.

Feeding Habits and Patterns

Early season blue grouse, taken while feeding along meadow edges, have crops that contain dandelions and young grass shoots. Birds search out seasonal food sources, with raspberries being one of the most frequently used. Birds also forage on gooseberries, elderberries, blackberries and other currants, aspen leaves, and Douglas fir needles.

Birds forage early and late along the meadow edges and forest openings. Adult males tend to stick to thicker timber and, as a result, feed more heavily on aspen leaves, grasses, and Douglas fir needles.

In winter, grouse roost in dense conifer trees and subsist principally on a diet of conifer needles. One reliable observer told me of seeing a tree, singled out by a solitary grouse as a winter roost, circled at the base with a winter's buildup of droppings. His rationale for the prodigious amount of droppings was that conifer needles have such a low nutritional value that it required a large intake to sustain the bird.

Preferred Habitat and Cover

Blue grouse are citizens of the high spruce/alpine zones above 8,500 feet elevation. These areas are found in the White Mountains, the Chuska Mountains, and on the north Kaibab Plateau. An additional transplanted population was started on the San Francisco peaks near Flagstaff in 1975. This is the sum total of the limited grouse habitat available in Arizona.

Birds rely on Douglas fir and aspen as food sources during the year. Male blue grouse frequent thick stands of timber and steep slopes. Solitary adult males are found in established territories on the cinder cones that lift up above the forest horizon. Hens with broods prefer meadow edges, logged areas, and forest openings. Successional growth in burns and logged areas promotes berry bushes and an abundance of grass cover and insects for chicks.

Research in other states has shown blue grouse to have a reverse migration, with birds going to higher elevations in winter. This apparently is not the case with Arizona blue grouse, since there isn't sufficient higher elevation for them to travel to (Brown, 1989, p. 58). Summer and winter ranges are the same.

Locating Hunting Areas

Grouse need a mixture of subalpine meadows and dense stands of conifers. Males prefer steep slopes. Elevation is the first indicator to use when trying to locate grouse populations. Study topo maps and pinpoint the few areas that rise to sufficient height to support blues. In the White Mountains, this makes for a short list.

Flyfishermen working White Mountain trout streams or those traveling to high country lakes may see hens with chicks in August. Those areas bear close examination when the season opens in September.

Once a suitable area is located, search for available food sources. Look for birds using available berries and hens with broods feeding along the edges of meadows, overgrown logging roads, burns, and areas opened up by logging.

Looking for Sign

Grouse leave a dropping similar to that of a small turkey. Found in the field, they could indicate a roosting or feeding area.

Blues do not appear to use open water, apparently receiving adequate water from rain, the plants they eat, and dew that collects in the mornings. As a result, there is no value in scouting tanks for tracks and feathers. Similarly, birds are silent and make no sounds that would betray their presence in the field.

Hunting Methods

Blue grouse in Arizona could best be described as a trophy bird. I think that it's a fair bet that as hunting birds with gun dogs continues to gain popularity in Arizona, more hunters will make September treks to the high country. Grouse hunting offers a chance at cool weather to run dogs and maybe a bird or two.

Most birds are taken in meadows and forest openings early in the season while hens with broods are still together feeding on berries. Most birds taken are hens and birds of the year. Males are solitary, seldom leaving the safety of steep slopes and heavy timber. By October, all grouse are very difficult to locate.

Hunt early and late. The first three hours in the morning and from 3:30 P.M. until dusk are the most productive. Also, periods after a weather disturbance, common in the September high country, may stimulate the birds into feeding. Walk likely looking country and search for food sources.

Grouse, when first approached, will often fly into the nearest tree and attempt to hide from the approaching gun. When these birds leave the safety of the tree, they can be very difficult to hit. For this reason some hunters take the birds, if they can spot them, as they first flush or while still sitting on the limb. I've had the experience of flushing two blues into a tree, marking them, and killing one bird on approach. Then I spent the next half hour trying to see, spook, intimidate and finally out-wait the other, only to eventually give up and walk away.

Flocks caught on the ground can act much like Mearns' quail, staggering their flushes so that several shots are presented instead of one mass covey rise. If a bird flies out of sight, uninjured, into the trees or down a canyon, consider it lost. More than likely, no amount of follow-up will allow a hunter to relocate the bird.

Adult males are large, impressive birds and would make for an impressive mount if it weren't for the fact that through October, the birds have pin feathers. This renders them, depending on the degree of pin feathers, very poor mounting candidates. Grouse season is open through mid-November and, by that time, males should be mountable. It is on my list of things to do, to take a "trophy" late season male at the close of the season when the bird is at his best and the taking is the most difficult. Maybe next year!

Hunting Dogs

I've hunted blues with a setter/Chesapeake Bay retriever team that worked well. The setter pushed a few birds that a retriever walking at heel wouldn't have, but without the setter assistance, we wouldn't have known they were there at all. On the Chessie's side of the ledger, the retriever found a couple of over-the-edge-of-the-canyon sailers that were beyond a setter's retrieving frame of reality.

Blue grouse caught on the ground will hold for a point. A pointing dog that is cautious and deliberate around birds is what's called for. Some of the larger meadows are well suited for a pointing breed that can cover a little ground. The bird's habit of walking around in plain sight, or other distractions such as tree squirrels, would preclude the use of a young dog who hasn't yet matured to the hunt. A retriever working as a close-range flush dog or a versatile breed working at the same range could be a real assist.

Field Preparations

Blue grouse is excellent eating. Early season birds feed on raspberries, gooseberries, blackberries and other currants. When the season ends in November, birds have started feeding on Douglas fir and spruce needles, but I've been told by those who have eaten late season Arizona birds that it did not affect the flavor.

Grouse can be plucked or skinned according to individual preference. A blue grouse breast is similar to a pheasant, differing only in being slightly larger in width.

Shot and Choke Suggestions

- Improved cylinder/modified 7½ / 6 shot
- Blues leave very quickly and a shotgun that points quickly is needed to stop them.

MERRIAM'S WILD TURKEY DISTRIBUTION

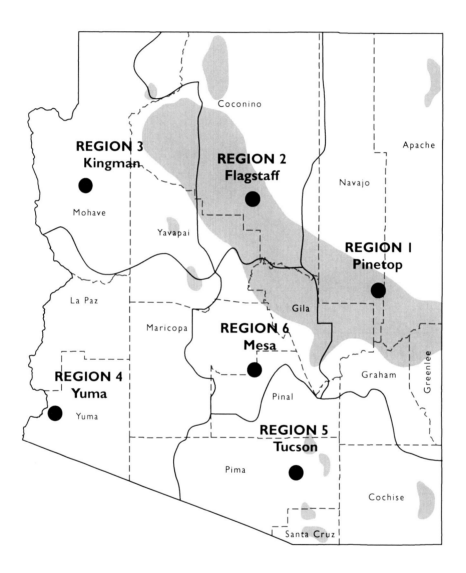

Merriam's Wild Turkey

Meleagris gallopavo

QUICK FACTS

Local Name
Turkey, wild turkey, gobbler

Spanish Name
Guajalote Silvestre, Cócono

Size
Male 30–36 inches (76.2–91.4 cm), female 21–25 inches (53.3–63.5 cm), 5 ft. wing span

Identification in Flight
On the wing, turkeys look huge. Their body and tail is a dark, iridescent bronze-brown. Primary flight feathers are light grey with black barring, and tails are square. The heads of adult male turkeys are colored in bright vivid shades of white, red, and powder blue. The overall impression is that of a large dark shape sailing.

Turkeys take wing with a thunderous commotion. Once airborne, they flap their wings for a distance and then coast out of sight on stiff wings. I'm always taken aback when I flush a group of turkeys in the pines. How could something so big leave so quickly?

- In Arizona, turkey is classified as a big game animal, and permits are allocated through a limited permit drawing.
- Arizona hunters are allowed one turkey per calendar year.
- Both spring and fall hunts are offered.
- Only bearded birds are legally taken during the spring season.
- Any turkey is legal game during the fall hunt.
- In Arizona, Merriam's turkeys are generally associated with slopes containing ponderosa pine and Gambel oak.

Color

A turkey ghosting through the shadows looks dark and nondescript until the sunlight hits it. The dark brown feathers of the chest and back simmer with a purple iridescence. Arizona birds have tan edges highlighting the ends of the rump coverts. The color appears like blonde frosting on rump. There is also a wide blonde, terminal band that runs on the edge of the bird's large square tail. The head of hens and poults is partially feathered and dark. Gobbler's heads are arrayed in a striking blend of white, blue, and red. Turkey flight feathers are light grey with dark grey accent bands.

Sound and Flight Pattern

Turkey vocalizations are extensive and better addressed as the subject of an entire book rather than a few short paragraphs here. It is important to learn how to use a turkey call if a person intends to kill a turkey. I am not a good turkey caller, but I have spent some time chasing elk with a diaphragm and bugle tube. The same type of diaphragm is used for calling turkeys.

When I first started bugling elk, state-of-the-art calls were awful sounding whistles. When diaphragm calls first hit the market, they sounded good but were hard to master, with a cassette tape as a student's only guide. Videotapes were the teaching aid that allowed the masses to learn how to work elk bulls into a bugle.

If I wanted to become deadly with a turkey call, I would buy several different types of turkey calls, check out every turkey hunting/calling video available, and practice like hell to get proficient. Then I would go into the woods and spend a lot of time with the real thing.

No amount of quotation-marked, bird vocalization pronunciations I could write would bring a strutting gobbler within shotgun range for you.

For such a large bird, turkeys can take to wing easily. A turkey's escape pattern is to wheel and run. Birds often do not take to wing, but instead run for the cover of dense forest. Birds caught in the open will take to flight to reach heavy cover quickly. Their flight is more in line with a diving duck that runs and becomes airborne, as opposed to a puddler that springs straight into flight.

Similar Game Birds

Blue grouse are sometimes confused with turkeys. This generally happens with groups of early season grouse hens and juveniles seen feeding on the edge of heavy cover. Blues have much shorter legs that are fully feathered. Turkey's legs are thin and visible at a distance. Their legs have the appearance of stilts lifting the turkey off the ground.

Flock or Covey Habits

In Arizona, turkeys are hunted during both a spring and fall season. Hunters patterning birds will see different flock patterns according to the time of the year.

In the fall, hens with poults and gobblers do not associate. Most turkey flocks encountered in the field consist of a hen with partially grown birds of the year or a communal grouping of two or more hens with young. These maternal flocks are very active as the young poults search out the food energy they need to grow. Hens and chicks work the open edges of meadows and old logging roads, feeding on insects and greens. As a result, they are the most exposed and most commonly seen turkey flock during the fall.

Groups of "jakes," young first-year males, are seen feeding separately from females. Adult male bachelor groups, on the other hand, are more secretive during the fall and tend to stick to heavier cover, becoming very difficult to find.

Bill Berlat and his daughter, Kim, with an Arizona Merriam's turkey. (Bill Berlat)

During spring mating season, gobblers actively seek the company of hens. Males stake out strutting territories and do their best to attract hens. Both males and females are found in the same areas at this time of year. Birds spend the night roosting in trees on timbered slopes and fly down at first light. By locating an evening roosting site, a hunter can be in a good position at first light the following morning to intercept a gobbler.

Reproduction and Life Span

The image of a strutting tom turkey is an American icon. The Thanksgiving trilogy of Pilgrim, blunderbuss, and fantailed turkey are learned by every school-aged child in the country. Ask any child what sound a turkey makes and she will tell you.

Starting in April, mating season begins in earnest. Adult gobblers engage in elaborate strutting displays where they slowly step, stiff-legged and tail fanned, all body feathers fluffed out and wingtips quivering. Gobblers attract and hold harems of hens through strutting and calling. Males vigorously defend their strutting ground from other males.

After mating, hens construct nests in dense vegetation and lay 8 to 15 eggs. Eggs hatch in 26 to 28 days, with chicks arriving in late May through early June. Males take no part in the hatching or rearing of the young. Poults are reared by the hens and stay in maternal flocks through the October hunting season.

In the wild, average life span is 8 years of age. Turkeys are capable of reaching 12 years of age or more.

Feeding Habits and Patterns

Turkeys feed in a loose flock formation. Bird tend to sweep into an area and move fairly quickly as they feed. The birds I have watched feeding were wary and perpetually moving. The flock has many eyes and one warning "pert" can freeze every bird stone still or send them exploding for cover. They often work the edges of meadows and openings so that, if needed, escape cover is just a few steps away.

Hens with chicks concentrate their feeding efforts in open clearings and along water where they feed on greens and insects. Adult males restrict their feeding activity to more heavily wooded areas. During fall, both sexes use mast crops heavily, depending on availability. Birds eat pine seeds and, when pushed to lower elevations by snow, juniper berries and grass seeds.

Preferred Habitat and Cover

Merriam's turkeys are generally associated with slopes having both ponderosa pine and Gambel oaks. Many of northern Arizona's turkeys are found in the country along the edges of the Mogollon Rim and canyons that come in from the rim. I've often seen turkeys on the open floor of mature ponderosa forests, but they were always within a quarter mile of a slope or canyon. Most of those turkeys were in immediate proximity to stands of Gambel's oak tree.

In the southern part of the state I've seen turkeys along riparian water courses at 4,000 feet elevation in the Catalina Mountains. These birds were well below the ponderosa pines but were in canyons that rose up in elevation and were crowned with thick stands of ponderosa. Turkeys roosted in mature sycamore and cottonwood trees that lined permanent water. I observed the turkeys at 4,000 feet during Coues deer hunts in November and December. When I returned with a spring turkey tag in April, the birds had left the area and were in the pines at 7,000 feet.

Turkeys need open water. Researchers have found that most nests and roosts are located within one and a half miles of water. Turkeys use the many stock tanks spread throughout Arizona's high country for both water and to feed on the grass and insects found along their banks.

Locating Hunting Areas

Most of Arizona's turkey country is in national forest or Indian reservation: all of it accessible to hunting.
1. Start with maps of the areas you are interested in hunting.
2. Using the maps, concentrate on areas above 6,500 feet in elevation.
3. Make note of the high ground that follows canyons, edges of mesas, and permanent water courses.
4. Go to the areas you noted and start at water sources. Look for tracks and droppings of birds coming in to drink. Confirm that birds are, in fact, in the area.
5. After locating an area with sufficient signs of turkey use, look for roosting sites. Walk the mature stands of roosting trees and dead snags early and late and listen for birds. Try to elicit gobbles from males by owl hoots, howling, yelling, crow calling, etc. Try to get them to betray their positions.
6. The night before the hunt, be sure birds are still in the area and, if possible, pinpoint their evening roosting site. Be in place before first light the following morning and call to the birds as they come off the roost.

Looking for Sign

Turkeys have a large, distinctive track that, because of its size, can't be mistaken for another type of bird. They also leave large droppings that are hard to confuse with any other birds and are indicative as to gender. Male droppings are a long semi-straight segment that is rounded on the thickest end and pulled to a thin sharp point on the other. Hen droppings are smaller and deposited in tight coils. The color is olive with white frosting on the end.

Begin searching the edges of watering areas and look for tracks in the mud at the water line. Search for droppings and feathers. Walk the edges of possible feeding areas and again, look for droppings and feathers.

Listen for turkey vocalizations. Even the sound of a turkey flying onto, or out of, a roosting tree is very distinctive and, at that still time of the day, can be heard from a long way off.

Hunting Methods

Turkeys, under Arizona Game and Fish statutes, are big game,and have been hunted that way since the time of European settlement. Hunters still-hunted likely turkey country and, using a rifle, took any shot that presented itself out to 200 yards or more.

At the April 1996 Game and Fish Commission meeting, the law was amended to restrict turkey hunters to shotgun only. My understanding is that this restriction will take effect with the 1997 spring season. Now, hunters must rely on a call to bring birds to within shotgun range.

Turkey hunting is broken down into spring and fall seasons. During the fall hunt, the most productive method of hunting is to still-hunt through likely turkey habitat and try to ambush flocks. Most of the birds encountered will be groups of hens and poults. If a good shot is not available or if a hunter is interested in only taking called birds, a person can flush the group and then set up and recall the birds with a "kee, kee, run" call series. After the flock breaks up, pick out a good concealment spot and wait silently for a few minutes and then begin calling.

In spring hunting, gobblers are the only legal bird. The first trick is to be in an area that contains birds. Once in an area that is holding turkeys, locate their roosting sites. It is counterproductive to go exploring while the season is under way. This will more than likely scare birds and should have been done during preseason scouting. Instead, try to get the Toms to gobble from their roosts and let you know where they are. There are many tricks used to elicit a gobble. An owl hooter, crow call, coyote howl, siren, and loud shrieking yell are some of the ones I've heard used. In the old days, a simple gobble from a turkey call used to work.

Once a Tom responds, work into the bird and set up an ambush. Two people work better than one. Have the gunner out front and the caller in the rear. That way, as the bird works in, he will have to walk past the shooter's position on his way to the caller. Some hunters have had good success using hen decoys or hen and jake decoys. The caller needs to know just the right words to say, and the shooter should hold for the base of the neck.

Arizona's spring turkey season is timed to coincide with the second peak of strutting activity. The management objective is to allow the primary breeding period to go off unimpeded. The majority of hens are bred and retire to nesting areas to set up housekeeping. Later, when the season opens and males are removed from breeding activity, the loss does not impact future recruitment.

Ideally, gobblers are still supposed to be as receptive to calling during the hunting season as at the height of the preseason primary breeding period. Many turkey hunters take exception to this and feel that during the later breeding period, gobblers are much less interested in coming in to a call. Weather and other factors come into play also. Some years the breeding period comes in earlier than others, and the hunt season can open well after the second breeding cycle has peaked. In those years, working birds can be very difficult.

Arizona turkey numbers have been declining for the last decade. In my opinion, a conservative approach to managing the state's turkey population is the best course of action.

Hunting Dogs

Turkeys are classified as big game in Arizona. The use of dogs in hunting big game, with the exception of hounds to run bears and lions, is illegal.

Field Preparations

Birds should be eviscerated immediately after being taken and allowed to cool. A turkey that has been plucked makes the best presentation for the table, but birds can be skinned and/or boned out, according to an individual's personal preference.

Shot and Choke Suggestions

The stories of shot-dead turkeys getting up and running are legend; arrow-shot birds, especially. Shotgunners have expressed a broad range of opinions regarding the kind of load that is most effective on a turkey. Let me offer you a consensus of what I've heard.

- **Close range, called birds:** 10 & 12 gauge, full choke, shooting 3 and 3½ inch, 4 or 6 shot.
- **Longer range, still-hunted birds:** 10 & 12 gauge, full choke, 3 and 3½ inch, 2 or bb shot.
- **Archery:** The most effective killing broadhead I've seen is a Vortex.

SANDHILL CRANE DISTRIBUTION

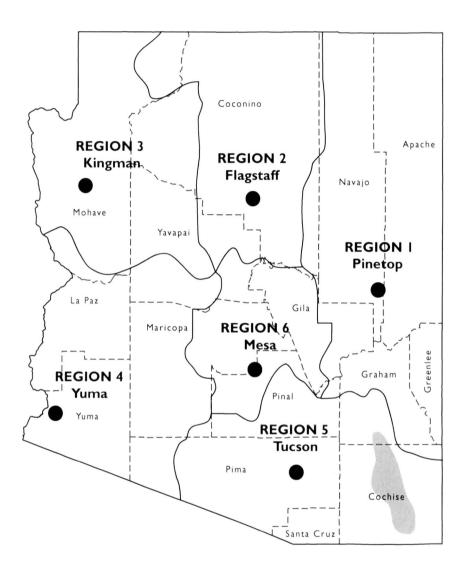

Sandhill Crane

Grus canadensis canadensis (lesser)
Grus canadensis tabida (greater)

QUICK FACTS

Local Name
Sandhill crane

Spanish Name
Grulla, Grulla Cenicienta

Size
34–48 inches (86.4–121.9 cm) in length
Greater sandhill 10.8–14.8 pounds; lesser sandhill 5.4–8.2 pounds, wingspan of up to 7 feet

Identification in Flight
Sandhill cranes are huge and impressive in flight and, once seen, not easily mistaken or forgotten. Birds are an overall grey with a very large wingspan that darkens on the outside primary feathers. They have a long neck, the head carries a red cap from the eyes forward, and they have a white chin. In flight, a crane's long, stilt legs trail straight behind and readily distinguish them from a juvenile swan. While flying, birds are very vocal, announcing their continuous "pu th th th th th th th th th th th ut."

- Arizona sandhill permits are awarded through a limited permit drawing.
- Permit holders are allowed two cranes per year.
- Four 3-day seasons are held in November.
- The open hunt area is adjacent to the Willcox playa in southeastern Arizona's Sulfur Springs Valley.
- Cranes feed principally in cultivated grain fields.
- Greaters fly later in the morning than lessers.
- Cranes prefer wide shallow water, sand bars, and mud flats as roosting areas.
- Cranes are thought to mate for life.
- 20% to 40% of Sulfur Springs Valley's wintering cranes are greaters.
- 60% of Arizona's crane harvest are greaters.

Colors

Arizona has a huntable population of both lesser and greater sandhills. While adults of both subspecies are predominately grey, the lesser is nearly half the size and darker overall. Birds may have a varying degree of yellow/rust-stained breast feathers and tertials. A limited number of the Canadian subspecies are also present. The birds have a white chin and a skull cap that is bright red on adult birds and rust brown on juveniles. Eyes are straw colored, and their long, stilt legs are black. As seen from below while flying, the outside edges of the bottom of the bird's primary wing feathers are darker grey then the rest of the bird. Juveniles are a mottled brown.

Sound and Flight Pattern

Sandhills begin leaving their roost area shortly after first light. Hunters waiting in the fields around the Wilcox playa will hear the cranes calling, working themselves up to begin their morning feeding flights. Occasionally, small groups of birds will temporarily take wing and boil up over the playa only to settle back in.

As the birds leave in earnest, long strings of lessers form in ragged lines and head out to their feeding areas. Lessers travel in large groups of 15 to 40 or more. Greaters begin flying later in the morning, and travel in smaller flocks of one to eight. While the lesser's flight is generally high and toward a seemingly predetermined area, greaters fly lower to the ground and are more susceptible to working into decoys. At times, individuals and small groups of greaters are found traveling in larger flocks of lessers. On the wing, the two subspecies can be differentiated from each other by a slight flip of the greater sandhill's wing tip as it is fully extended on the down stroke. The movement is subtle but evident after comparing both types on the wing.

The sandhill's call is very distinctive and heard as a floating lilt above the wind when the birds are mere specks on the horizon. Their "pu th th th th th th ut" call is an easy call to mimic with the human voice, and with a little practice a hunter can mouth call to prospecting flocks. Cranes have myriad other vocalizations consisting of croaks and pertts, to long trills that they use to communicate from overhead to birds on the ground.

By midmorning, flocks have fed and are returning to the playa's safety to loaf through the day. Later afternoon feeding flights are sporadic, high and direct, and very few birds are taken. Some hunters have had the rare group drop into their decoy spreads in the late afternoon, but by 10:30 in the morning, a day's crane hunting is generally considered over.

Similar Game Birds

Sandhill crane hunts are closely monitored because of their visual similarity and close association with whooping cranes (an endangered species). Adult whoopers are white and easy to distinguish from sandhills. Juvenile whoopers still carry white on the belly and chest but are mottled overall and more difficult to differentiate. Whooping cranes winter on the Gulf Coast and along the Rio Grande River in New Mexico. Whooping cranes are not normally present in Arizona.

Sandhill crane. (Randall D. Babb, Arizona Game and Fish Department)

Great blue herons are sometimes identified as a sandhill by novice hunters. Herons are much smaller, multi-colored, and fly with their necks tucked in. Juvenile swans are the right size but carry some white, have longer necks, and don't trail long stilt legs.

As a result of the crane's large size, long neck, and long trailing stilt legs, they are seldom confused with any other types of birds.

A "V" of sandhill cranes fly overhead. (Randall D. Babb, Arizona Game & Fish Department)

Flock or Covey Habits

As mentioned earlier, cranes travel in flocks of several to dozens on their daily feeding flights. Birds use communal roosting areas where up to thousands of birds congregate to spend the night on shallow water pans, mud flats, and wide river sand bars. The principal roosting area in the Sulfur Springs Valley is the southern end of Willcox Playa. Sandhill cranes begin leaving shortly after sunrise to forage and return to the safety of the roost by midmorning to loaf through the afternoon. Birds do feed in the evening, but most hunters concede that the afternoon hunt is generally nonproductive.

Reproduction and Life Span

Lesser sandhills found in Arizona breed far north in Alaska and Canada. Greater sandhill populations breed in the intermountain West. By mid-March, Arizona's crane populations have left the state and begun their northward migration to nesting areas. Cranes have a strong allegiance to these areas and return annually. Sandhills are not given to nesting in new areas and will continue to use less than ideal nesting sites rather than abandon historic use areas. Some mated pairs have been seen to use the same nest year after year.

Don Prentice waits for sandhill flights to begin.

Birds are sexually mature by their fourth year. Cranes mate for life. Mate selection begins on wintering grounds and escalates through the spring migration. Birds engage in elaborate strutting displays and courtship dancing. Sandhills construct a raised mound of vegetation as a nesting platform and stake out a nesting territory of 40 to 90 acres that they defend vigorously. Two eggs are laid, one of which generally survives. Both parents incubate the eggs. Chicks appear in 28 to 32 days.

Young sandhills rely almost entirely on insects for food. Within three months, youngsters are flying with their parents to feed in grain fields. By the end of August, sandhills have begun their migration southward.

The life span of a sandhill crane in the wild is thought to be 12 to 15 years.

Feeding Habits and Patterns

Sandhill crane's food of choice is corn. The Sulfur Springs Valley is an important agricultural area with, among other crops, corn commonly grown under center-pivot irrigation. Area cranes have also been observed using oats, alfalfa (occasionally), and cotton stubble (where the observer thought the cranes were feeding on nut grass tubers). Cranes also land in plowed dirt, tumble weed, and fallow fields where they feed on grasshoppers or simply loaf.

Preferred Habitat and Cover

Sandhill cranes have specific habitat requirements that, when absent, preclude using the area. Foremost, cranes need a large shallow water area such as a pan, mud flat or sand bar as a nonviolated roosting site. Second, they need nearby agriculture fields for feeding, preferably corn. Finally, birds seek out midday loafing areas such as fallow and dirt fields. Fortunately, the Willcox Playa is an ideal roost site, and the surrounding Sulfur Springs Valley provides the rest.

Locating Hunting Areas

The secret to successful field hunting is knowing which field the birds are going to feed in before the fact. Then, be there and set up a convincing decoy spread so you control where the birds will land in the field. Finally, shoot straight so that your efforts don't go for naught.

Those hunters fortunate enough to draw crane permits need to arrive in the hunting area at least a full day before their hunt begins. This is so they can be there the preceding dawn to follow the birds out from the roost and locate the particular field they are using. It is best to locate several fields in order to have alternates should a problem develop, such as showing up on opening morning and finding another group already setting up or not getting permission to hunt in that field. It is not always possible to locate more than one or two fields in a morning scouting run, so a hunter might consider budgeting more than one day.

Looking for Sign

The most productive means of locating feeding fields is to physically see the cranes in the field. Then you know how many and where. Take binoculars and a good map so you can mark promising fields. Ask local farmers where they are seeing birds. They know which fields are planted in corn and who owns them. The real search sometimes comes after a hot field is located and then finding the owner to obtain permission to hunt.

Hunting Methods

Sandhill cranes are most successfully hunted in feeding fields over decoys. Unlike ducks and geese, where the more decoys used the better, cranes respond well to small groups of dekes. Hunters have good success with spreads of four to a dozen. There is only one commercially made crane decoy currently on the market, a standing sentry bird. A hunter needs a spread composed of mostly head down feeders. Therefore, out of necessity, crane hunters make their own dekes.

Silhouettes are popular and easy to make. I have seen birds work to simple cardboard cutouts held up by wood stakes, as well as much more elaborate wood/goose shell composites. Some hunters fabricate standing, full-bodied decoys that look very convincing. As with any decoying, some days anything works and other days nothing.

Successful crane hunter with the Arizona season limit of two sandhill cranes. (Randall D. Babb, Arizona Game & Fish Department)

Blind construction is very important. Cranes respond best to spreads placed in the open, in the middle of a field away from anything that could conceal a hunter. Some types of cover lend themselves to easy concealment, such as corn stubble, the edge of standing corn, or a tumbleweed field. Laying out in the ruts caused by center pivot wheels or covering up against the wheels also work well. Large obtrusive blinds made of vegetation not native to the field should be avoided. Shallow pits dug with the owner's permission can be deadly on birds.

Flagging trading flocks works very well on cranes and can turn wavering groups.

Kites should work very well also, although I have taken them on several hunts but never had enough wind to keep them airborne. Voice calling to an overhead group helps to convince wary birds that all is as it seems.

Cranes coming into a decoy setup may not buy it completely and will land off the decoys well out of range. Any new birds that approach the spread will invariably shun the confederates and land near the real birds. It is tempting to leave the blind and put the real birds back into the air, thereby removing any competition. If a hunter will wait it out, when the down birds leave, they or later arriving birds will swing over the decoys for a look-see and offer a shot.

Hunting Dogs

The downside to using a retriever on cranes is the potential for injury to the dog. On the flat, open fields where hunting takes place, a dog really isn't necessary, anyway. I have taken my Chessie on crane hunts, just to take her, and know for certain that her movements have flared incomers and cost us birds. I suppose I felt protected by the belief that she was far too mean to be damaged by a mere mortal crane.

I had a red setter who was a regular on crow shoots when I was young. We killed a ton of crows, and I couldn't begin to guess how many she retrieved in her career. A crow has the same sharp, pointed-type beak as a crane. Early on, she came in from a retrieve with a beak buried half way up her nostrils, a half per side, and a very agitated crow pinching and twisting the hell out of her nose. From that point on, if she came on a down crow and it was still alive, she would stand over it and bark, but she would not pick it up.

I have heard stories from other hunters of how good an account crippled cranes gave of themselves when these hunters walked out to dispatch the wounded birds. I would think that a dog, without the capacity to stand back and fire a finishing shot, could easily end up losing an eye.

Field Preparations

To my mind, a plucked crane minus the long legs, looks and tastes very similar to a Canada goose and can be field-handled in the same way. Some hunters clean birds by removing the leg and breast meat and preparing dishes accordingly.

The Arizona Game and Fish Department operates a check station where all successful hunters must present their birds for examination. The purpose of the exam is to ascertain the subspecies, sex, and age of any cranes taken in order to better manage the population. Unless it is necessary to prevent spoilage, department personnel prefer that birds be brought in before they are cleaned. However, if you want to mount any of your birds, be sure to tell the survey personnel before you produce them, because the first thing Game and Fish personnel do when they examine a crane is pull out the belly feathers, which will ruin the bird for mounting.

Shot and Choke Suggestions

Sandhills have a reputation for being pretty tough customers. The secret to killing cranes clean (as with any large bird) is to wait until the birds are close enough before you pull the trigger. I have seen birds smacked hard at 35 and 40 yards that wobbled all over but didn't fold. The birds locked their wings and started gliding. Some were recovered and some weren't. Out of a 12- gauge, close enough means not much more than 25 yards. I can't speak from personal experience, but those who shoot 10-gauges swear by them. Nontoxic shot is not required for sandhills unless a person is shooting on a federal refuge.

- 12-gauge and 10-gauge, full choke with lead shot, 2s and bb.

ARIZONA WILDLIFE REFUGES

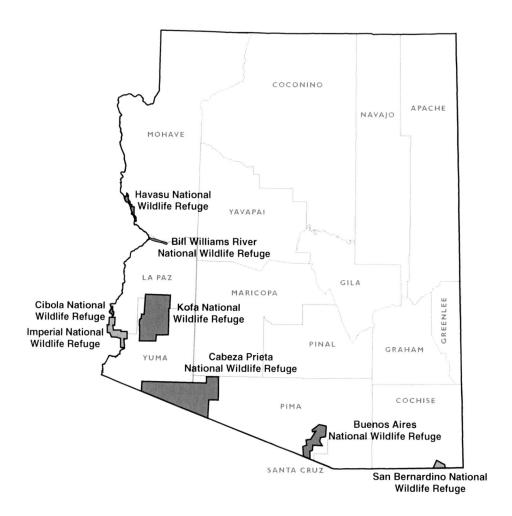

Waterfowl

Most people don't think of Arizona as a waterfowler's destination spot and mostly, they're right. With some exceptions, Arizona's migrating ducks are hunted while they loaf, as random targets of opportunity on small stock ponds. Some transplanted residents use traditional methods learned in their previous waterfowl-rich home states, but Arizona as a rule doesn't have enough standing water to hold the large concentrations of waterfowl necessary to make decoying productive. However, there are some notable exceptions. For those willing to prospect, a duck hunter can do quite well, with the added bonus of having a location not shared with many other shooters.

The secret to finding waterfowl is to go where the water is. In Arizona, this narrows the search down considerably. The most common form of duck hunting here has always been jumpshooting the many stock tanks scattered throughout the backcountry. Hunters develop a route of a dozen or so tanks they can drive in a morning. When the ducks are in, this method can be very productive. When they aren't, it makes for a very slow hunt. Once the route is learned, the hunter knows where the birds tend to sit on a particular tank, how to approach, and just where to come up over the berm. Some tanks are too wide or long for a single shooter and may require more than one gun to cover all the possibilities.

Before the days of steel shot and lead shot possession restrictions, tank jumping made for a wonderful duck/quail/dove combo hunt. Some of the most consistently productive duck/dove tanks were away from any road access and approached at the end of a quail walk. The only legal way to do this now is to use approved nontoxic shot for all bird hunting. If you shoot at waterfowl in the field, you cannot have any lead in your possession. I remember when the California Waterfowl Association was fighting the steel implementation back in the early '80s. We were told that steel was solely a waterfowl issue. Some hunters counseled that this was an open door for nonlegislated federal restrictions. They warned that the feds had bigger fish to fry. Surprise!

There are both permanent and, depending on rain, occasional bodies of water that hold huntable numbers of birds. Start prospecting with a map. When an interesting area is located, check to make sure there are no shooting restrictions and then go exploring. On national forest maps, many of the higher elevation, dry lake beds that are shown hold some water year-round; more water when it has rained. I have had very good early season shooting and seen large numbers of birds on these flooded areas and never had to share them with another gunner. As there is often very little cover on these flood basins, they require a coffin box or small grassed over marsh boat as a layout shooting blind.

Some of the national forest lakes are shallow and have heavy cattail growth. They consistently hold significant numbers of puddle ducks and divers like redheads and ringnecks. These lakes work well for conventional decoy hunters. There are water storage reservoirs that back up a lot of water during wet years. They can be a bonanza for an experienced waterfowler with the proper boat and gear. The Colorado River, though not the mighty ribbon of water it was a century ago, is a major migratory

Red, a German shorthaired pointer, brings in a hen mallard.

corridor for waterfowl heading south into Mexico. The river and adjoining backwaters are Arizona's best waterfowling area.

There are three federal refuges on the Colorado mandated to provide public hunting. One of these refuges, Cibola National Wildlife Refuge, shortstops and holds most of the Canada geese found within the state.

All of Arizona's rivers offer some duck hunting possibilities. Concentrate on the areas near agriculture or those stretches of river near large water impoundments. Birds will fly up and down the river channel to feed and retire to the big water to loaf

A typical southern Arizona stock tank that has been "jumped" successfully.

and roost. The hunting improves at season's end when duck populations have arrived in mass.

Indian reservations offer some excellent waterfowl hunting, the San Carlos, White Mountain, and Navajo reservations in particular.

The Arizona Game and Fish Department currently manages two wildlife areas in the White Mountains (Pintail Lake and Jacques Marsh) that were created with municipal sewage effluent. I would feel a little squeamish about giving the dog a big hug after a retrieve, but birds are there.

Hunting Methods

Jumpshooting is the most common type of duck hunting in Arizona. I mentioned it earlier, but let me add a few more tips. Birds will tend to stack up on adjoining ponds as hunters flush them. Leaving another party member waiting over a small set of decoys on a nearby tank can be productive.

The ballistic limitation of steel is especially evident while jumpshooting. The birds fly straight away from the gun, often at extreme ranges. The only shot offered is up the back. Number 2 steel shot out of a modified choke seems to work best for me. Some shots offered are too far to take.

Coming across a large group of ducks using a tank (60 or more), a hunter with

Goose hunter assembles decoys.

decoys might consider flushing the birds and not shooting, then setting out decoys and waiting for the birds to return in small groups.

With river hunting, finding an access point to get to water is a problem. Most of the land is public, so it is not a trespass issue. Rivers have heavy belts of vegetation lining the banks that can be impossible to get through.

What is called a river in Arizona wouldn't get more than stream or creek designation in another state, but since there isn't much water around the ducks use them. As the rivers are shallow and not very wide, they are easy to hunt. Vegetation for blind material is close at hand, and the birds move along a fairly thin flight corridor.

Since it is necessary to set up on the sand bar along a narrow ribbon of water, I have found that only a few floaters are needed to add movement to the decoy spread. The majority of my setup is mallard field shells. I can comfortably carry a couple dozen, with several floaters thrown in, by myself. Most of Arizona's rivers have few

Canada geese piling into a field. (Randall D. Babb, Arizona Game & Fish Department)

access points and lightweight decoys give me the freedom to move up and down a river looking for just the right spot. If a hunter is willing to make the extra effort, digging a coffin box blind into a sand bar could be deadly on birds.

Big water lake and marsh hunters can set up along the shorelines or use a boat to get out on the water. Hunting Canada geese with field decoys from the shores of the few large reservoirs, where there are populations of geese is also productive.

Ducks

Mallards and teal are the most common types of puddle ducks encountered while hunting tanks in Arizona. Ringneck ducks and occasional redheads are the divers most often seen while jumping tanks. Other puddlers, such as gadwall, widgeon, and pintails, and divers like canvasbacks, lesser scaup, buffleheads, and ruddys are also seen in lesser numbers. Rivers can also hold common mergansers and the rare hooded merganser and wood duck. Goldeneye and redbreasted mergansers are found on large water lakes and the Colorado River.

There is a type of mallard subspecies called a Mexican duck. Both sexes are similar in appearance to a hen mallard with subtle differences in bill coloration and wing speculum. Mexican duck range in Arizona is restricted to the southeastern corner of the state.

Geese

Canada geese are the most common goose found in Arizona. The large moffitti (Western) subspecies being the primary Canada goose type present. Statewide wintering populations peak at 10,000 to 15,000 birds.

Cibola NWR holds the majority of the state's wintering Canadas. There are smaller groups on the adjacent Havasu and Imperial NWR.

In central Arizona, both Roosevelt Lake and San Carlos Reservoir hold consis-tent populations of Canadas. The White Mountains and the northeast quadrant of the state also have Canada geese flocks (units 1 and 27 are closed to the taking of Canada geese). Other areas in the state may hold very small groups or have birds migrating through.

Some Snow geese winter on the Colorado River, and occasional small groups are seen in other parts of the state. Any white-fronted geese migrate through Arizona to Mexico well before the hunting season begins. Ross's geese are rare visitors to the state.

The Hunter Afield
THE ARIZONA GUN DOG

"Almost all of my Gambel's quail hunting was done without a dog, as few dogs can stand the thorns and the thirst of typical Gambel's quail country." (Jack O'Connor, *The Shotgun Book*, 1949)

The use of gun dogs in the Southwest is relatively recent. Until the 1960s, Arizona was thought to be too inhospitable for a working dog. The belief back then was that heat, cactus, snakes, and rocks would destroy a dog. If the dog was able to survive those legions arrayed against him, the next obstacle was a quarry impossible to hold, preferring running to flight over barren ground that held no scent. The only option the desert quail hunter had was to "pot-shoot" them.

Arizona's population growth started after World War II. As a result of Arizona's hospitable weather, it became a center for military aviation and training. Many of the pilots who were stationed here returned after leaving the service. Many of those servicemen had hunted over continental breeds while stationed in Germany during the 1950s. In addition, beginning in 1960, all pilots for the new German Luftwaffe were trained at Luke Air Force Base. Lufthansa pilots were trained at Goodyear Municipal Airport. Many of these men were bird shooters and brought their traditions and dogs with them. They were supported by an established German immigrant community in Glendale and the west side of Phoenix. This would explain the early foothold and long running predominant use of the German Shorthair pointer in southern Arizona.

Today, all breeds are used for Arizona hunting. Which dog works best in the desert? If a person went strictly by the numbers of dogs already in service, the German shorthaired pointer would be the odds-on favorite, with the Brittany following not too far behind. There is also a good showing of English pointers and English setters. In addition, the German wirehaired pointers, griffons, and pudelpointers have a small cadre of loyal followers. Other versatile hunting breeds as well as Irish and Gordon setters are also represented in smaller numbers. Retrieving breeds are used in the uplands as flushing dogs and walked at heel for upland birds and waterfowl as nonslip retrievers. Curiously, I have seen very few flushing spaniels in the field, although they should work very well in some of our cover.

For the average hunter, I think the German shorthair pointer's premier position is well deserved. Arizona is versatile dog country. In a day's hunt, a dog can be called upon to: point and retrieve quail; fetch jump-shot ducks from a stock pond; and calmly sit at heel in a milo field watching for doves to fall. As a general rule, shorthairs are biddable, easily trained, and natural retrievers. They tend to range closer than some of the other breeds. This means that a larger percentage of the birds that bump wild off the dog will be within acceptable shotgun range. In general, this holds true for all the versatile breeds.

Another decided advantage of the versatile dog is their use of ground scent as well as air scent. They will find a crippled Gambel's quail squirreled down a pack

Troy Hawks and his GSP swing on rising Gambel's quail.

rat midden that an English pointer or setter wouldn't have a chance of recovering. I make this point at the risk of jeopardizing my life membership in the "Setter Lovers Society." In the majority of hunting days, a versatile breed dog will put more birds in the bag than a setter or pointer. It all comes down to a personal choice regarding style. My preference is watching a bird dog run full bore 200 yards out. The wide-ranging dog will find coveys on days when a close working dog won't. It's a trade-off that each hunter has to decide for himself.

For the early season hunter, water requirements and how a dog handles heat become a real concern. Lower elevations can be very warm through the end of November. Jim Levy of Tucson, AZ, remembers being one of the first bird hunters to run dogs in southern Arizona. When he and his brother, Seymour, arrived from the Midwest in the early '60s, they ran Weimaraners. After five years, they switched to English pointers because, as Levy says, "A small, fine-boned English pointer can

German shorthaired pointer with a ring-necked duck.

handle the heat a whole hell of a lot better." Large, heavy dogs have a harder time. Light-footed, floating runners use less water. I have heard people express concern over the length of coat on long-haired dogs such as setters. Truth is, if a field bred dog summers over in the desert, his coat is going to get very thin.

Watch your dogs closely while hunting. A dog arriving from out of state won't be acclimated to the heat. You may only want to run them an hour at a time and keep them very well watered. A dog can die quickly from overheating. If your dog is staggering and incoherent, you have an emergency on your hands. Don't let it get that far.

I have seen people go to extremes in an attempt to get their dogs conditioned for the beginning of the season. Despite my best efforts, my dogs still come up short. My dogs are kenneled on gravel and run daily, yet they still go through their pads in the first month of heavy hunting. I think the most productive method a person can use is

Fritzel and Tab with a nice morning's take of Gambel's quail.

to run his dogs as often as possible. Gradually extend the dog's runs up to two hours and use rocky ground if available. Check their feet daily and give them a few days off if you observe any damage. My dogs wear holes through their pads early on and then are OK for the rest of the season. Dogs arriving from out of state need to be in excellent condition. The most that can be expected from a soft dog is one or two days in the field.

Most bird dogs have not gone through a formal training program, yet they still handle desert quail quite well. Gambel's and scaled quail, unlike Mearns', don't follow any rules. Their survival tactics can defy a dog with a formal education. Like the bird dog without a college degree, a person's education doesn't have much bearing on how they do in an alley fight. To be effective, a desert bird dog does need to be under control, but not by much.

A desert bird hunter with a fully broke dog, however, might want to look at doing some touch-up training while conditioning. When hunting Gambel's and scaled quail, stay right on top of the dog to keep it steady to wing and shot. Don't shoot birds that aren't pointed unless a dog has been trained to stop to flush. Dogs that are worked on Gambel's or scaled quail will be sorely tested. Most of the potential shots will be wild flushes. As a refresher, a hunter will do well to run his dogs through "whoa" training again because while hunting, the dog will likely be hearing that command a lot. I

The author watering Musette and Emma in the field. (Sandy McClure)

introduce a trill whistle blast as the "whoa" signal. It carries further and betrays no emotion.

While hunting desert birds, it is useful to be able to release a dog from point at a distance. I use a single whistle peep and a verbal "go on." Gambel's quail, when pointed, will work a brush or cactus patch like a grey squirrel works the top of a tree. They move to the opposite side, away from the shooter. At the flush, a bird will keep as much vegetation between it and the gun as possible. Early season trees are fully leafed and hard to see through. Therefore, the best chance of connecting is to back off to as advantageous a shooting position as possible within range and release the dog to flush.

While it's true that a steady dog marks birds more effectively, asking a dog to hold steady at the shot will limit its ability to recover cripples. One pellet in a Mearns' quail and he is down and anchored, but Gambel's and scalies are extremely tenacious of life. A shot bird can explode in a ball of feathers, do a triple somersault, pancake into the ground stone dead, and get up and run away. The desert is littered with rodent mounds and pack rat middens that a running cripple will take full advantage of in a matter of seconds. A lot of these cripples are not recovered. A dog that breaks shot will be on top of the bird when it hits the ground; therefore cutting way down on the lost rate. A word of caution regarding rodent mounds and middens: a dog will smell

Jasper and Rose cooling off during a scaled quail hunt.

a cripple in them and start digging to get at the bird. He could just as well come up with a rattlesnake. It is safer to call the dog off and then probe with a stick. Some of these structures are deep and extensive. They tend to collapse on themselves when stirred up. I have fallen through to my knees while standing on top of one of them. In my experience, unless a bird crawls in and dies right at the surface, it will not be recovered. The dog that breaks at shot can beat a running bird to the hole.

An especially important command for a dog in the desert is, "Leave it." A hunter needs to be certain that when he tells the dog to leave an area, it will respond immediately. Snake breaking a dog greatly reinforces this (refer to the section in this book on snake breaking).

Equipment Needs Afield for the Arizona Gun Dog

In the desert, water keeps dogs running. Some hunters rely on available water from tanks and running washes, but that can be a dangerous game unless a person is certain that the water is going to be there. Standing water is a mercurial thing in the desert, and a stock tank that is completely full at the beginning of the season is often bone dry at the end.

Depending on the temperature, one of my 50- to 65-pound setters will go through a quart canteen of water in an hour and a half. Hunting three dogs on a four-hour loop

Dogs that "break" will be closer to the bird when it falls and cut down on the rate of lost cripples.

requires more water than I can carry comfortably. Good hunting partners show up with their own containers and volunteer to carry their share of the dog water.

The way a person carries water is as varied as their personalities. I use two military surplus web canteen belts. My two-dog setup has two one-quart plastic canteens that I augment with an additional two-quart drinking water bottle that lies flat lengthwise in the bottom of my game bag. The four quarts it holds will keep two dogs going for three hours. For more dogs or longer time on the ground, I use a four canteen belt equipped with military "Alice style" suspenders augmented with additional water containers in the game bag. The suspenders transfer the weight to the shoulders and make walking much more comfortable.

I have seen other hunters use the larger half-gallon military water bladders. Plastic soda bottles come in a variety of sizes and work very well. A Tucson hunter, who shall go nameless, has been rumored to use Perrier bottles.

Some hunters water their dogs by pouring or squirting a water stream into the dog's mouth. This method can waste some, if not most, of the water poured. I water out of a small white plastic margarine container. There is no lost water and, in addition, the white cup held above your head has a strong association for the dog and can be seen by a dog at a distance. The time to water a dog is when you first find birds. Even hot and dead tired, a dog with a nose full of scent won't want to come in when whistled. That white cup in the air means water and brings them every time.

Snakes are a constant threat during the early dove season.

Before leaving my vehicle at the start of a hunt, I fill a bucket with water and leave it on the ground. Then, if a dog and I are separated in the field and the dog returns before I do, there will be water available. Before leaving, I encourage a dog to drink from the bucket. Once out in the field, they are watered heavily after the first 10 minutes and then again 10 minutes later. After that, I get pretty frugal with dog water. After a water stop, I pour any surplus water left in the bottom of the cup on the dog's belly to help cool him down. A word of caution regarding heat prostration: dogs can quickly die from it. Don't let a dog get overheated. When a dog is incoherent and wobbly, it is too late. Find water (such as a stock tank) and cool down his core body temperature immediately.

Harold Snyder waters his setter, Casey, during a morning lull.

Another piece of equipment as important as water is a short, quick snap lead hung from the belt. You should have one for each dog being run. When you need one, you often need it immediately. The delay caused while searching pockets could mean injury or worse for a dog.

A hunter would be well advised to carry a few first aid items in the field. After water and shells, there is not much space left in a game vest. Fortunately, just a few things will cover most contingencies. My list includes a leather sheath with a pair of needlenose pliers and suture forceps for dealing with cactus and cholla. This is covered in more detail in the section on cactus and cholla. I wear a Swiss army knife that has tweezers and a pair of scissors. I also include a bit of cord for use as a tourniquet. In the back of my game bag I carry a roll of "Vetrap" in a ziplock bag (an elastic self sticking tape used by horse fanciers and available in most feed stores) for use on tears in the skin and as a pressure wrap to control bleeding on the extremities.

Back at the truck, I have a large first aid kit housed in a watertight, steel, army surplus ammo can. It is fairly complete (see list) and includes a copy of "A Field Guide: Dog First Aid" by Randy Acker, D. V. M. and Jim Fergus.

Dog First Aid Kit List

- Vetrap bandaging tape in assorted widths
- Gauze
- Johnson and Johnson waterproof tape
- 12 fl oz aerosol can of saline (for contact lens) to clean debris from wounds
- Panolog ointment
- Benadryl (for insect and snake bite)
- Aspirin
- Nolvasan Otic Cleansing Solution (for cleaning ears)
- Opticlear (eyewash)
- Wound-kote spray wound dressing
- Cut-heal medication
- Hydrocortisone cream
- Wound powder
- Styptic pencils
- Ear, nose, throat Med-Check light
- Thermometer
- 3-inch and 6-inch tweezers
- Canine nail cutter
- Disposable razors
- Assorted scissors
- Rubber tubing (for tourniquet)
- Several cotton socks
- Tarp or sheet plastic (for carrying a bleeding dog in a vehicle)
- Wood dowel (for holding a dog's mouth open while pulling cactus or quills)
- Wire muzzle
- Book: *A Field Guide: Dog First Aid* by Randy Acker, D.V.M., and Jim Fergus
- Booklet: "A Field Guide to Dog Care," Arizona Game and Fish Department
- Note pad and pencil

Caring for the Gun Dog Afield

When a dog is in serious trouble, what you have in the way of first aid supplies may bridge the gap, but what he needs is a vet. If the dog can walk, I snap a lead on his collar and walk him out. When a dog goes down, he has to be carried. This is really a team effort, with one person carrying gear and the other the dog. Unfortunately, disaster has struck a time or two when I have been alone. In those situations, I dumped most of my water to shed weight, broke down my shotgun into two pieces and laid the pieces crosswise in the back of my game bag, picked up the dog, and walked the straightest line out.

One of the most common misconceptions that those unfamiliar with Arizona bird hunting have is that you can't hunt dogs in the desert without boots. The belief is that the cactus and cholla are unmanageable for an unshod dog. Dogs actually learn

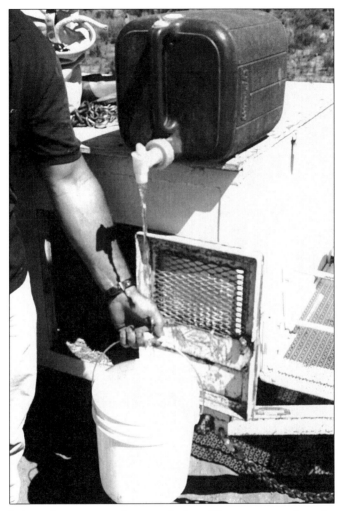

Spigoted water containers make handling water much easier.

about stickers very quickly. Within a day or two, they figure it out. This is not to deny that the break-in period can get a little grim, but the problem area is not with the dog's feet but rather his mouth when he bites the cactus to pull it out.

Dog boots come in rubber, canvas, and leather and are available through mail order catalogs. They have a very limited application as a stopgap measure for use on dogs with worn-through pads that need to be hunted another day or two. Dog boots are not necessary for hunting in the desert.

Arizona bird country has some wide open spaces, and gun dogs working there really benefit from being whistle trained. I like metal whistles: the weather doesn't

Deats, an English pointer, gets his belly spritzed to cool him down after a morning run.

get cold enough to stick to skin and be a problem, they carry further than plastic whistles, and last indefinitely. Mail order companies carry them, and referee whistles are available through most large sporting goods stores.

Over the last decade, the sound of beeper collars has become very common in bird country. While there is no denying their effectiveness, some people dislike the electronic invasion of their quiet hunting time. I confess to sharing similar sentiments. The sound reminds me of a garbage truck backing up. Bells track dogs well and are easy to listen to, but they won't help you locate a dog on point.

I have a large collection of bells. Anything I see hanging in a feed store that I don't already have, I buy. Each bell has a unique tone, and I can exercise run a dozen dogs at one time and tell who everyone is by the tone. I rig the bells with trigger snaps, so they clip on and off easily.

When hunting Gambel's and scaled quail, I prefer not to let the birds know we are coming, since they often will run from both bells and beepers. If a dog works to the gun well, they are not needed. If they don't, you don't have a choice. Beepers are a near necessity on Mearns' quail because of the oaks. We once lost an English pointer in Mearns' country and found it an hour and a half later still on point, a hundred yards from where we had last seen it. It would have been nice if that dog had been wearing a beeper. The collar I use has an optional, hawk scream mode that I tried and the birds

Harold Snyder puts boots on Casey.

still ran. The regular beep carries better and isn't quite as annoying. I set it on point beep mode only. If I need to track running dogs, I hang bells on them.

Dogs that are hunted hard can get to looking pretty tattered. A hunter from out of state, with two or three dogs, who plans on hunting for a week needs to be careful with them. Here are some ways to help extend their time in the field.

Watch their feet: when the feet are done, the dog is done, also. At the end of each hunt, spread their toes and pull any cactus you find. Large cactus spines left in the toes and webs will fester, causing the dog to go lame. Squeeze the webs with your fingers and feel for pus pockets. Open up and drain any you find. If one is particularly hot, treat it with a squirt of Panolog.

If a dog's pads wear through, the pads weren't in shape to begin with and there is not much that can be done about it. A dog with soft pads will last one day in the desert. If the pads haven't gone too far, dog boots can give the dog another day or two. At the first sign of wear-through on the backs of the main pads, use the boots.

Birds love catclaw thickets and cactus. Unfortunately, cactus and catclaw don't love dogs. This subject is covered in detail in the hazards section, but let me offer a few tips here. First, with long-tailed breeds, the tip of the dog's tail takes a real beating. It is shredded by catclaw and impaled by large cactus spines as the dog whips through cover. By the nature of their running style, some dogs have more of a problem than

A line-up of different bells used for running dogs.

others. I wrap the last 5 inches of the dog's tail with black electrician's tape. It protects it from catclaw and makes the cactus spines much more visible and easy to pull out. When a dog running in the field shows red chevrons on the rib cage (blood splashes left as the tail wags back and forth), check the dog's tail and see what is causing it. At the end of each hunt, lay the dog down and check his entire body for cactus spines. Use your finger tips to locate the problem areas. A water spritz-bottle is useful to wet the hair and flatten it out so you can see fine cactus needles. Back lighting with a small Mag-Lite helps define them, also. Don't neglect the testicles on a male dog. They are hanging out in harm's way, and a dog with a swollen, infected testicle won't run.

While hunting, I carry energy snacks for the dog. I make honey and bread sandwiches and cut them into small cubes. The snacks are carried easily in a ziplock pouch in my game bag. At the inevitable crash after three to four hours in the field, I rest the dogs and give them a snack. Also, after each retrieve I offer one. I notice that when my dogs get tired and hungry, they are much more prone to hard-mouth a retrieved bird. I also carry small, 5.5-ounce cans of gourmet cat food with pull-tab lids for dog lunches in the field.

Equipment Needs Afield for the Arizona Bird Hunter

Recommending which shotgun to use is almost as dangerous as saying which breed of dog is the "best," and you notice how neatly I dodged that bullet in the earlier section. The truth is, if it will fire shot, it will kill a bird, and the range of shotguns used in Arizona bird hunting is about that wide.

As a general guideline, if you are hunting uplands use a weapon that you don't mind getting dinged and scratched, because it will. The ground is mostly rock, and a hunter is constantly laying a gun down to pull cactus or to water dogs. For pumps and autos, synthetic stocks are a good choice. There are about two or three shell choices. Arizona has a three-shell magazine restriction. I shoot a double.

In Arizona, stuck can really mean stuck. This driver attempted to cross a flooded wash, and the truck didn't make it.

Slings are not a bad idea either. Not many people use them on shotguns simply because there is no history of it in this country. I personally don't like the feel of a shotgun with a permanent sling attached, so I use one with loops on both ends that slip on and off easily. I leave it in my game bag until needed.

I see a lot of double guns in the field. A 28-gauge will kill as well as a 12 if the bird is in the middle of the pattern. With the exception of dove shooting, a 410 is not quite enough for wild birds under field conditions. I use a 410 almost daily when dog training and kill a lot of planted birds with it. I have used it on desert quail, but I don't anymore.

On the subject of clothing, a hunter should be prepared for anything. I have frozen in October and sweated in February. Layer your clothing with a T-shirt at the bottom in case it turns hot. Even on very cool mornings, dress with the assumption that it will warm up as soon as the sun shows. A friend from Kansas gave me a nylon shell pullover with the trade name of "Gates Overshirt." It is cut like a large pullover blouse and very light in weight. The nylon stops the wind and keeps me warm. The garment fits loosely over my normal bird hunting shirts and rolls up to the size of a soda pop can to stow easily in my game bag. It is the perfect stopgap for the first two hours of the morning.

Canvas- or nylon-faced brush pants can spare a hunter some tenuous moments. They won't stop cactus or cholla but they will turn catclaw. Blue jeans that have spent the morning being pushed through catclaw thickets end up looking like a cheap pair of blue dungaree, imitation sheepskin chaps. Snakeproof cordura nylon chaps will protect against catclaw and semi-stop cactus and cholla spines, and there are snakeproof pants available that work equally well (read the hazards section on rattlesnakes). Heavy shotgun chaps stop most everything.

Boots also need to turn cactus. Modern cordura nylon composite boots are very comfortable to wear in the field until a prickly pear ear sticks to the side of one. The desert is very hard on boots. Use a good sturdy pair of leather, hightop upland boots. From March through November, I wear 17-inch-high leather snakeproof boots. They are heavy and hot to wear, but I can walk through knee-high grass all day long training dogs and never look at my feet.

A light pair of shooting gloves will protect a hunter's hands. Catclaw grabs anything that brushes by it and cuts both ways before it lets go. The best gloves I've found are goatskin gardener's models. Steerhide protects but feels too heavy to shoot with, while tennis/golfing/driving/shooting gloves shoot well but won't stop catclaw.

On the subject of shooting vests and shell bags, it's best to pay the money and buy quality gear. The cheap stuff won't last. Most desert bird hunters avoid the conventional style button/zipper front vest and prefer the open at the top shoulder strap designs. The straps carry more weight comfortably. The design is cooler to wear, carries more volume, and has a waist belt that can be adjusted to accommodate water containers worn around the waist. If one is being custom ordered, select the largest sized game bag, but pass on the zippered top, easy-clean feature. It is just one more thing to fail at the worst possible time. Also pass on the leather shell holders. They look neat, but they add more weight on the vest, and when you are in birds, it is faster to grab loose shells from a front pocket.

The best choice for dove fields is a large volume shell bag. I use a military surplus, collapsible O.D. canvas water bucket for carrying birds and empty hulls from the field and leave the shell bag for shells.

There's not much to say about hats other than to be sure to wear one. Wide-brimmed and well-ventilated in the summer, and one that is well-ventilated for the rest of the year. Remember that southern Arizona is the skin cancer capitol of the nation. Use appropriate UVA and UVB protection.

On the subject of vehicles, it is nice to have the option of 4WD, but 2WD will get you almost everywhere you want to go. If something looks dicey, don't try it. Arizona is cattle country, and if you get stuck in the middle of nowhere, there won't be any farmer's tractor along to pull you out. It will be just you and the shovel, a high-lift jack and the pair of heavy leather gloves you threw in the back of the vehicle before leaving on the trip. I travel with tools, tow cable and a few spare parts, fuel filters, electric ignition modules, etc. If you have the room, a second spare tire isn't a bad idea. Most of the flat tires I 've had have been caused by a sharp rock going through the sidewall. Have a flashlight, jumper cables, and other emergency gear. Again, if you have room, a sleeping bag and a few cans of food can be a godsend if you end up doing some unexpected overnight camping. Don't forget plenty of drinking water.

Remember to budget some of the dog's water (that you carry while hunting) for

Jim Morehouse of Arizona Quail Hunts with his dog-hauling rig set up for four dogs.

drinking yourself. The same goes for first aid. The same kit that is used for dogs will work to patch up a hunter. At the end of a hunt, despite intentions to the contrary, I often return to the vehicle after dark. I carry a small Mag-Lite (2 AA batteries size) in my game vest. After dark I wear the Mag-Lite like a miner's headlamp, in a velcro fastened nylon belt harness. The harness frees up both hands for dog leads and shotgun.

A final word about Arizona's weather. Arizona has such varied topography that an accurate forecast in one area means nothing 50 miles away. A snowed-on Mearns' hunter at 5,000 feet in southeastern Arizona may hear the Tucson weather warning golfers to reconsider shorts for the day. Trust what the sky tells you, not the radio, and plan accordingly. Arizona is contested ground between the jet stream to the north and the Gulf of California's tropical moisture to the south. There are no accurate, long-range forecasts.

Traveling with Dog and Gun

Hauling one or two dogs is not a difficult proposition, but with more than that, the logistics can get complicated. Two kennel crates will fit in the back of a truck bed and still leave room for gear. On short trips, dogs that get along together can double up in one crate or ride loose in the back of a camper shell. More than four dogs probably means a special kennel setup on the back of a pickup or a dog trailer. Organization goes a long way toward simplifying travel with dogs.

Use a water container with a spigot on the top. They are readily available in 5-gallon size through most stores selling camping supplies. Keep the jug at the back of the vehicle where it is easily tilted over to fill a water bucket. The best traveling water buckets I've found are the black rubber type sold through feed stores and used for horses. They are indestructible. Plastic 2-, 3-, and 5-gallon buckets work well in the kennel at home, but crammed in the back of a vehicle they end up cracked. I keep all the dog gear in one container so any equipment that is needed is readily at hand. Along with leads, I include tie-out cables for each dog, or a chain gang if I am traveling with many dogs. While traveling, dogs should be aired out and watered every 4 to 6 hours.

Be mindful of the temperature when hauling dogs during Arizona's summer. Travel during the night or early morning and find a cool place during the heat of the day.

For dogs being flown in, airlines have a prohibition against loading any dog if the destination's temperature is forecast to exceed 80 degrees. This means that dogs arriving during the early bird season will be routed for flights arriving in the late evening or very early morning. Be sure to talk this over with your carrier before the fact and book your flight accordingly. This is the sort of surprise information that is sprung on a traveling hunter at the last minute.

There are also other federal guidelines for shipping dogs: types of kennel container, water, feed times, etc. Each carrier has a slightly different twist on the interpretation, so be sure to coordinate with the specific carrier. Get a contact name and phone number where your dog is to land, even when you are booked on the same flight, because pup could end up at an air freight terminal on the other side of the airport. If there's any confusion, your contact person can sort it out. Dogs travel well by air, so don't be overly concerned.

Preparing Birds in the Field for Mounting

The art of taxidermy has made considerable advances in recent years. This is especially true in the realm of bird taxidermy. How you take care of your birds in the field determines the finished quality of your mounts. This crucial step is out of the control of the taxidermist. However, with a modicum of preparation, you can proceed confidently when you are holding a freshly taken bird destined for the book shelf.

Start by putting together a small kit to be carried with you in the field. Use a small plastic container, such as a plastic traveler's soap box. Throw in some cotton balls, a few wooden tooth picks, a dozen or so folded sheets of toilet paper, and a pair of panty hose.

After shooting a bird, examine it closely. First, look for pin feathers. If there are any present, you will notice them on the head directly behind the beak or bill and on the main side coverts below the bird's wing. If there are even a few pinfeathers, the specimen may not be worth mounting. By all means, save it and let your taxidermist make the decision. However, it wouldn't hurt to examine additional birds to find one with better plumage. The taxidermist can always use extra birds for spare parts.

The next step is to check for any bleeding wounds in order to prevent the taxidermist from having to wash the bird before mounting. Plug any visible wounds with cotton. Use a tooth pick as a probe to push the cotton into the holes. Now, pack the mouth and nostrils, remembering that the body is a reservoir of fluids that can drain down the neck. Make a note or take a photo of any brightly colored soft tissue parts (unfeathered areas) for the taxidermist's reference later. Fold several sheets of toilet paper and lay them between the wings and the body. Should the body bleed, this will protect the undersides of the wing from being soiled. Slide the bird head-first into the nylon stocking. Remember that feathers lay like shingles: they slide forward in the stocking smoothly, but will ruffle if you pull the bird back out the same end. The taxidermist will remove it by cutting a hole in the material at the toe and sliding the bird forward. When the specimen is all the way down, knot the nylon behind its tail. Now you are ready to slide the next one in behind it.

Place the wrapped bird in an empty game vest pocket, allow it to cool and protect it from getting wet. When you return to your vehicle, place the bird in a cool spot. At home, put it in a plastic bag to prevent freezer burn, and freeze it solid. You can safely wait several months before dropping it off at the taxidermist.

For the traveling hunter, there is the option of next-day air shipping. Provided that you can find a place to freeze the birds overnight, even a hunter on the other side of the nation can get birds to his taxidermist in good shape. Wrap the frozen birds, nylons and all, in disposable diapers. Line a shipping box with wadded newspapers. Place the birds in the middle with dry ice. Dry ice is available in some major supermarkets. Call your taxidermist to be sure someone will be there, and then ship the parcel next-day air. Be sure to contact them the next day so that a search can be instituted in the event that the parcel did not arrive.

Mounted birds are a beautiful memory of your days in the field. With just a little bit of advance preparation, you can be assured of a top-quality mount.

Hazards

In correspondence from Darrell Kincaid, a friend from Kansas, he wrote that, "Bird hunting in your area (southern Arizona) is not just a stroll to observe the dogs...no place for a hunter that walks looking at the ground, unalert, not observant of what is going on ahead of him, a constant challenge to be aware and prepared for any situation. The only situation comparable was combat as an infantryman in Korea."

By spending time in the desert, a hunter can learn how to manage it. Everybody gets "chollaed." Everybody eventually walks up on a rattlesnake. An observant, prepared hunter/dog team deals with what comes along and enjoys the hunt. The dog crosses in front of you, through a screen of brush, drops into a sand wash, and you hear a "yip!" The purpose of this section is not to scare people but to help them avoid the yip, or deal with it after the fact.

Cactus, Cholla and Catclaw

There are some formidable looking stickers in the Arizona deserts. Both hunter and dog are going to get stuck and both will survive. Dogs new to cactus have two or three bad run-ins the first day of hunting and then learn, for the most part, to avoid it. When the dog does pick some up, he quickly learns not to bite at it and to calmly wait for you to show up to remove it. Some canine cactus veterans refuse to slow down the hunt and learn to flick cholla off their legs while running, or stop and "front tooth pinch" it

Prickly pear cactus in the Verde Valley, north of Phoenix.

out with their upper lip curled back. At the end of a day, dogs will be carrying some spines, but it shouldn't slow them down.

There are five types of plant groups that are of concern to bird hunters. Prickly pear (Mickey Mouse ear) cactus, barrel/hedgehog type cactus, cholla cactus, yuccas, and catclaw. The spines or points of the different plant groups come in myriad configurations and pose different potential problems. I'll go through each and give you some idea of what to expect.

Prickly pear type cactus is found over most of Arizona. Plant concentrations are found up to 6,000 feet. This is the most common type of cactus the bird hunter will encounter in the field. When quail coveys flush into prickly pear, they generally hold. Dogs working birds in prickly pear can get pretty loaded up with spines on the front of their feet and legs while moving through cactus, and also on the face while reaching into plants to retrieve. The last third of the tail on long-tailed dogs also picks up spines. There are two types of spines: a long "guard" spine (up to 2.5 inches long) similar to the long guard hair on a wild canine's back; and very short, densely clustered "woolly" needles (no more then a quarter-inch long), packed tightly at the base of the guard spines. The ratio would be around a hundred short needles to one long guard spine.

The long guard needles are easy to see and pull out. When the dog comes in for water, give them a once over and remove any needles present. A problem area is the muscle group above the elbow on the front of the dog's foreleg. Needles are driven deep into the muscle when the dog runs into cactus pads. An infection pocket can form around the buried spine. The pocket feels similar to a caterpillar's cocoon when palpated beneath the skin. The pocket takes three or four days to develop and will require veterinary care. Avoid problems by removing the needles, if possible, before the fact.

Barrel cactus can grow to 5 or 6 feet in height.

The short spines are a translucent, golden color and much more difficult to see. Locate them by pressing lightly with your fingertips. The dog's body will absorb random needles without any complications. While skinning javelina, coyotes, and grey fox, I have seen some individuals with thousands of spines lying under the skin. The animals had been healthy and showed no sign of infection. The problem comes when a dog picks up dense patches of these fine needles. The body encapsulates them and they develop into a psoriasis-type scab with some degree of infection present. The infection doesn't warrant a veterinarian visit, but it will require cleaning and removal of as many spines as possible. Open the area up so that it can heal.

Barrel cactus and hedgehog cactus are cylindrical in shape. They range from the size of a potato to a 50-gallon drum. These plants are found in one form or another statewide.

Hedgehogs are small and carry long spines (up to 2.5 inches). Some species grow in clumps of several barrels. Dogs may step on them and carry some short-term

Hedgehog cactus are very common throughout the deserts of Arizona.

residual pain, but because the spines remain attached to the plant they don't generally offer any complications.

Barrel cactus, on the other hand, can cause serious tear wounds similar to barbed wire. However, while barbed wire tends to catch a dog high on the back in noncrucial areas while crossing under fences, barrel cactus tears a dog's lower legs, feet, and toes where there is much skin movement and agitation. Foot-skin tears can sideline a dog for a week or more.

Barrel cactus have large, curved, fishhook shaped guard spines (hence the name "fish hook cactus"). The spines are thick and have a resilient quality similar to fiberglass. Even very young plants 3 inches high sport fully developed curved guard spines. Experienced dogs avoid barrels and seldom have any problems. The only time experienced dogs abandon caution is while chasing running cripples. Youngsters or dogs new to the desert are destined for a collision or two. When you see a dog smack a barrel and cartwheel off the side, expect the worst. Check for skin tears. These tears usually don't bleed much, so don't rely on blood to locate them. On hard hits, the spines can break off in the dog and cause infections. Feel for the buried spines underneath the skin and if you can't get at them to remove them, get the dog to a vet.

Cholla cactus are the most formidable looking and the most diverse in shape and size. While some small species are found statewide, their primary range is along the Colorado River from the northwest corner of the state, south along a southeast

Chainfruit cholla with pack rat midden underneath.

diagonal line following the Mogollon rim to the New Mexico border. Areas of dense concentrations are found across southern Arizona below 4,000 feet. When a dog freezes up on a hunt, pin-cushioned, a type of cholla is usually responsible.

Cholla grows in segments that can separate and fall to the ground. Some species, like chainfruit cholla, constantly shed fully "spined" short segments that litter the ground like a mine field. In the area around dead plants, the formidable skin breaks down and spreads dry, brittle, unattached spine clusters everywhere. Rain runoff floats dried out segments and spine clusters and concentrates them in low lying areas scattered across the desert floor. Pack rats also gather cholla and weave the short segments into their middens to deter any unwelcome visitors. Cholla spines can show up anywhere.

The good news is that while cholla will stop a dog in its tracks, the spines pull easily and cleanly and seldom offer any complications. Fresh spines are very resilient and don't break off in the dog. Dry, brittle spines can snap, but a cautious removal will usually get them out. While it looks awful and hurts like hell, if I had the option of choosing what one of my dogs got stuck with, it would be cholla.

Yuccas are green, sword-leafed plants that come in a variety of shapes and sizes. The leaves generally come to some kind of hard, sharp point. They carry names like shindagger and Spanish bayonet and are represented statewide. While collisions with yucca are very unusual, they can result in severe stab wounds. I cringe when I see a dog hit sharp yucca, and then I call them in and look for holes.

Teddybear cholla.

Catclaw grows statewide from 3,500 to 6,000 feet. In some areas, concentrations are so dense that they are almost impenetrable. Catclaw is frequently encountered while hunting Mearns' and high-elevation Gambel's quail. I think it's harder on the hunters than the dogs because the dogs can move freely underneath a lot of it. Some of the largest populations of late season quail that I've found are in heavy catclaw cover. It's a good news, bad news story. The good news is that the dog has pinned a 60-bird covey in plain sight. The bad news is that there ain't no way through the catclaw to get close enough for a shot.

For dogs, catclaw is hardest on the face and the tip of the tail. Thorns load up on the eye ridges of a dog's skull as he pushes through cover and catch the tip of the tail on the other end. Other than some facial puffiness and minor tail bleeding, dogs don't seem too bothered. The puffiness recedes in about 12 hours. Combing a dog out after the hunt with a slicker brush will dislodge most of the thorns.

People, unfortunately, don't have a coat of hair to fend off the thorns. The catclaw's curved thorns bite any way you pull. A couple of days after getting scratched, small blisters (similar to very tiny poison oak) appear that itch like the devil for another day or so. I wear gloves and brush pants or chaps in catclaw and avoid the postponed discomfort.

For pulling cactus and cholla spines, hunters need three tools: needlenose pliers, forceps with a flat contact surface, and tweezers from a Swiss army knife. I carry the pliers and forceps in a leather holster secured with velcro. The holster is important because the point of the pliers will poke a hole through game vest fabric in short order. The tweezers ride with the Swiss army knife.

Somewhere lost in the annals of time, someone said that a pocket comb or pick was the ticket for removing cactus and cholla and a person who hadn't tested the procedure put it in print. Leave your combs at home. I've got pretty good dexterity in my hands, but when I used a comb or pick I ended up wearing every third cholla segment like a piece of jewelry across the top of my hand. Spines flicked on the ground will either end up in the dog's feet or the hunter's legs before the clearing job is done. It would be a pretty good trick to pull a cholla ball buried up between the pads on the bottom of a squirming dog's foot with a pick.

Needlenose pliers grasp the spines firmly, hold on, and allow the hunter to drop them safely out of the way, in the middle of an adjacent bush. The forceps work well on fine prickly pear and cholla needles in tight places, like a dog's feet, and the tweezers get the really fine "woolly" stuff.

Now, having said that, let me give you another opinion. After reading a manuscript of this book, Burt Miller of Tucson, an accomplished, long time southern Arizona bird hunter, gently reminded me that youngsters such as myself have the eyesight and reflexes to use needlenose pliers. Burt likes combs for removing cholla. He carries several and gives one to all the hunters in the party with instructions to please flick off any cholla they see on a dog. He prefers the steel combs used in dog grooming. As he explained to me about a comb's effectiveness, "It may not be pretty, but it is off the dog."

Like dogs, people who spend any time in cholla country learn to avoid it. Cholla acts like velcro: the more you try to rid yourself of it, the worse it sticks. One real problem area is a hunter's feet. As one moves through the desert, cholla sticks to the back heels of the boots. Stickers tag along unnoticed until the hunter squats down to tend to dogs and then, surprise! It can be embarrassing to ask a hunting partner to pull spines from some areas. Periodically look yourself over and remove any stickers you are carrying and always check the back of your boot heels before you stoop down.

Cactus and cholla hurt when they stick. The pain has a paralyzing quality. After the spines are pulled, they feel for some time like they are still there. Use your dog cactus kit. Yank the needles. Shake it off and get on with the hunt.

Always check your heels before stooping down.

When you see spines or cholla on a dog, pull them off. At the end of a hunt, lay a dog down and go over his entire body. Give close attention to feet, forelegs, the muscle at the top of the front elbow, and the tip of the tail. Check pads to see how they are holding up. Spines that are carried on the contact surface of a dog's pad break down into fiber strands and no longer look like spines. The 1/32 of an inch long fibrous flag that shows on the outside may be half an inch long on the inside. Feel with your finger tips to find any concentrations of fine needles. Backlighting with a small flashlight will highlight any needles or spines that are difficult to see, and spraying with a water spritzer bottle will flatten the hair so they are easier to pull. Follow up the next day with another quick onceover. Watch the dog for any sign of limping or unusual licking.

Rattlesnakes

Arizona is blessed with 11 species of rattlesnakes with overlapping ranges that extend from the tops of the mountains to the bottom of the desert floor. There are no safe areas. I have seen snakes above ground and active every month of the year. From mid-December through the middle of March (depending on the weather), most stay underground, but there are no guarantees. When the mercury hits the mid-70s, I assume the worst and get careful around rock piles.

Western diamondback rattlesnake.

Rattlesnakes can sense ground movement through their belly plates. They feel you approaching and freeze until the danger passes. Their camouflage patterns match their home ranges and are extremely effective. I don't know what the ratio is, but you unknowingly walk by dozens for every one you actually see. I use live rattlesnakes for snakebreaking dogs, so when I find one while training in the field, I catch them with a snake stick. Someone has to stay with the snake and keep an eye on its position. If I am alone in the field and leave a snake unattended for even a couple of minutes to get the stick, it won't be there when I return. I've spent 10 minutes tiptoeing around a brush patch with an intermittently buzzing snake, to no avail.

Snakes have activity periods according to the temperature. They like the 70- to 80-degree range. During the heat of summer, they are only out after dark. As the season progresses and nights cool down, they adjust their activity periods to daylight hours to take advantage of the sun's warmth. Early September dove season is very snaky the first couple of hours of the day. When the temperature breaks 85, they head for their holes. Mid-November through early December is the most dangerous time for hunter/dog teams because the snakes are active during daylight hunting hours. If I see one snake while hunting, I get cautious for the remainder of the day. If I see a second snake, we call it a day because the odds are real good that there will be a third. Some hunters can go a whole season and not see a snake. In a bad year, a hunter may come across a dozen. It depends on the year and how much time is spent in the field.

Snakes generally won't rattle a person unless they are agitated. Sometimes you can come across one that has a bad attitude, but for the most part they just want to be left alone. The presence of a dog will get them going, however. Maybe they see them as coyotes and, as such, a threat. I've had snakes not react to me until a dog shows up, and then the snake rises up off the ground like a cobra.

When you come across an unidentified snake, look at the way it carries its tail. Rattlesnakes take extra care with their rattles because they are delicate. Rattlers are careful not to drag them on the ground and travel with the tip of their tails held in a slight arch. The unique posture is visible at a distance. You can identify a rattlesnake crossing a road 50 yards out.

If a hunter wears adequate safety gear and is reasonably observant, there is very little chance of getting snakebit. Most of the bites that show up for treatment at southern Arizona hospitals are on the fingers and hands. The moral of the story is: if you don't want to be bitten, don't handle snakes. Respect them for the potentially dangerous creatures they are and give them a wide berth.

Boots and leg protection will fend off any strikes, although hunters should know that strikes on people who are not deliberately antagonizing snakes are extremely rare. I would guess that in my lifetime, there have been maybe 30 times that a snake should have struck me and didn't. Mind you, once I knew they were there I got out of the way. Asking around in preparation for this book, it was hard to find a bird hunter who, in the course of hunting, had been struck. That is certainly not reason enough to avoid preventive measures, but it does put any potential worry in proper perspective.

Currently on the market you can find snakeproof chaps, gaiters, pants, hard plastic leggings, and boots. All offer protection from the knee down. The common complaint is that snake gear is hot or heavy or both. I loaned a hunter from Atlanta, Georgia, a pair of snake chaps at the start of an early season hunt. As he was putting them on, he asked two others in our party if they used any protection. They commented that it was too hot to wear. Later in the morning, he walked up on a big, silent diamondback rattler two dogs had gone by and that I had passed within 3 feet. Our two hunting companions came over to look at the snake and made comments like "Look at the girth on that thing!" and "The head on that snake is huge!" Our Southern boy waited until there was a break in the narrative and, when he had their attention, he stuck a thumb in the front of each chap and jiggled them up and down. He told them how cool those chaps felt right about then. Comfort is relative.

Five forms of snake protection: (1) a snake-broke dog to let you know there's a snake there; (2) hard plastic leggings; (3) high-top snake boots; (4) snake-proof gaiters; and (5) full-length snake proof chaps.

Sadly, dogs don't come out as well against snakes as people. Some hunters choose not to run their dogs during the early season. Unfortunately, snakes can be present at any time, so losing the early hunts doesn't offer a guarantee of safe passage for the season. It does make sense to stay out of the rocks during warm weather. Some areas are "snakier" than others, so avoid them. If I see one snake while hunting I get very cautious, if I come upon a second we are done for the day. It is imperative that you have your dog snakebroke. A snakebroke dog will tell you by his reaction if there is a snake ahead of you.

Snakebreaking a dog is done with a live rattlesnake and an electric collar. The first step is to defang the snake so the dog is in no danger. Holding the snake securely by the neck with a snake stick, I drop the snake's body into a 6-foot-long piece of plastic 4-inch pipe. This renders the snake immobile and therefore much safer to work with. Next, using 12-inch tweezers and 8-inch forceps, bend the snake's fangs forward and pop them out. Snake fangs are multilayered, like shark's teeth. You should be able to find several fangs in descending size on each side. Pull them all.

Next, plant the snake in plain sight in the middle of an open area. Have an assistant standing by to prod the snake, keep it in place, and keep it rattling. While being controlled with a check cord, the dog needs to experience three points of association. He must first hear the snake buzzing, then locate the snake visually, and finally move into the snake's scent stream and smell the snake. When the dog's attention is fixed on the snake, his nose drinking in the scent, shock him with the highest setting the collar offers. Reinforce it with the "leave it" command. While on most dogs it "takes" the first time, the rare dog may need a second or even third exposure before he stops going for the snake. If a second or third retest is needed, relocate the snake each time.

Once the dog avoids the snake, time him out for 15 or 20 minutes. Move the snake to a new area where it is hidden in low brush. Use scotch tape to silence the snake by compressing its rattles. Retest the dog. Bring the dog through, down wind on a check cord, and allow him only the association of scent. When the dog freezes at the scent stream and moonwalks backwards to avoid it, the job is done. Retest two to three weeks later in a new area on a silent, hidden snake just to be certain.

This sort of training is best left to an experienced person who is prepared to house and handle rattlesnakes. It's a good way to get snakebit if you are not extremely careful. Please refer to the list of dog trainers who offer snake breaking. Some dog clubs will get together and offer a weekend snakebreaking clinic. They defang the snake once and run a dozen dogs through.

Going through the training is not a guarantee against future snakebites, but it's as close as you can get. If the dog is in a position to smell the snake, he should avoid it. One of our dogs got bit after the training. The fangs hit just behind her nostril, so she obviously had her nose where it didn't belong. If you knew this particular dog, you would understand. Dogs running with the wind over a snake are still at risk of getting hit, but once a dog has been snakebroke you have done all you can do.

After snakebreaking, individual dogs react differently upon encountering a snake in the field. One of my setters, Bandita, would make a curious, slight curved detour in her straight line of travel around the snake. If you didn't know her, you would miss it altogether. Belle, her daughter, yips and jumps sideways when she hits snake scents. You have to learn what your dog's reactions are.

Some hunters make it a point to kill every snake they come across. When I see a snake while hunting, I get the dogs under control and leave the area. I don't shoot snakes because I don't want to confuse the dog into thinking that I have any interest in a snake. I don't want a dog endangered by running in toward me while I'm standing around trying to shoot a snake. Sometimes the snake you are trying to kill is not the only snake there. The only snakes that I mess with are those that need to be removed because they are around the house or in a training area.

If you are going to shoot a snake, be aware that the only safe way to kill it is to vaporize its head with a load of bird shot and push it 6 inches into the ground. This can be hard to do standing in knee high brush with a snake that you can hear but not see. Blowing them in half with a shotgun could annoy them. Get the snake in sight and back off far enough so that the shot pattern covers the snake's whole body. A severed snake's head can still bite and inject poison one and a half hours later. The only safe dead snake is one that has had its head removed and buried.

If a dog does come up snakebit, remember that no two snake bites are alike. Some bites are "dry bites" where the snake injects no venom. The severity of the bite depends on the age, size, and agitation level of the snake; the size of the dog; when the snake last struck; and where the bite is located on the dog. It is now believed that a snake can control the toxicity of the venom it injects. The dog will be in a lot of pain and will usually swell severely at the site of the bite. Remove the dog's collar to avoid strangulation. Snake venom destroys the blood's ability to clot, so the fang punctures will weep a steady stream of watery blood.

The best hits are in the face because there is no muscular blood flow to disperse the venom rapidly throughout the body. The worst hits are in the vascular-filled belly, chest, and legs because the venom's effects are massive and immediate. Venom kills tissue at the bite site and can cause damage to the heart, kidneys, and liver. Anemia and blindness can occur due to retinal hemorrhage. Treatment can require blood transfusions in order to reestablish blood clotting. The primary cause of death in dogs from snakebite is cardiovascular collapse. The only treatment that will stop venom damage is antivenin.

There is a popular misconception that antivenin can easily be carried in the field by a hunter in order to be administered to a snakebit dog. This is not true. Antivenin is administered slowly by saline drip. It is a horse serum. A straight injection would cause a massive reaction and kill the dog. Antivenin is not user friendly. It comes in a two-part mix, dissolves poorly, is slow to go into solution, must be kept cold, has a short shelf life, and is very expensive.

When a dog is bit in the field, the first thing to do is to get past the panic. Get the dog away from the snake. Make a visual identification of the snake and make sure it is a rattler. Check the dog to be sure it was in fact bitten. While hunting a few years back, Belle yipped and cartwheeled as a diamondback lifted up. I was sure she had been nailed, but after a long examination and no evidence of holes or swelling, I confirmed a lucky near miss. Current wisdom discourages tourniquets or ice. Electric shock, which got so much press a few years back, has been shown to have no positive therapeutic effect. Some hunters carry injectable benadryl (antihistamine). Benadryl acts as a sedative to calm the dog, thus retarding the spread of the venom, and helps with the swelling. Also, benadryl is indicated before antivenin to prevent anaphylactic shock.

Time works against you with a snake bite. A hunter can be a long way from the middle of anywhere when bird hunting. For best results, antivenin should be administered within an hour. Three to four hours is really stretching it. The vet may tell you that too much time has passed for the antivenin to be worthwhile.

There are two schools of thought among working dog owners about whether or not to take a snakebite in for antivenin. Most dogs that are snakebit in Arizona aren't treated, ranch dogs in particular. Currently, antivenin is priced at $188 per vial. A dog may require two or three vials for treatment. The cost is prohibitive for most people. Most untreated dogs recover with no obvious ill effects, although systemic damage can appear later. One group feels that you should doctor the dog the best you can without spending a lot of money, thinking that the expense is unnecessary. A friend who runs German versatile dogs has had six dogs hit over three decades of desert hunting. All but one recovered fully without treatment. The one fatality had been bitten twice previously and recovered, but was found dead one morning in his run after being bitten during the night by a snake that had entered the kennel. Maybe the cumulative effect of all three caused the fatality.

Others, like myself, are en route to the vet's when a dog's head reaches the circumference of a three gallon pail. I have heard some sad stories from those who have treated their dog and spent a lot of money to no avail. I don't think their regret was over the lost money, but rather the lost hunting partner. They wanted to know they had done everything they could do. As Dr. Carol Rowe of Desert Small Animal Hospital in Tucson told me, "A dog can die if you don't treat them, and the only proven treatment is antivenin." Dr. Rowe, who lives with her quail hunting husband, two German shorthairs, and an English pointer, knows how valuable these dogs are to their owners. She states, "The reality is that you don't know how severe the reaction will be until it is too late to give the antivenin. You don't want to gamble with your bird dog."

I talked with ranchers about how they handle snake bites. Bob Miller of Oracle, Arizona, remembers that as a child, a snakebit dog was doctored by dipping the animal in kerosene. Suzellen Holt, of the Hundred Mile Ranch, was instructed by an old cowboy years ago to give the dog as much cold milk as it would drink. The colder the milk the better. This is how she has treated half a dozen snake bites without losing a patient. She also adds benadryl to the milk. I asked Dr. Gerry Ault of Plaza Pet Clinic in Tucson about these and other folk treatments. He said that with the exception of the benadryl, none had any known therapeutic value. He added, though, that excluding smoking around the kerosene dipped dog, none would necessarily hurt the animal, either. Dr. Ault has heard of folk remedies such as painting the bit area with tar and wrapping the site with Saran wrap. One elderly gentleman brought in a dog that he had treated with a poultice of orange juice and fresh horse manure.

In rural Arizona, dog/snake contacts are common. A non-snakebroke ranch dog who has survived one bite often develops an animosity toward snakes. They go to battle with any snake they come across and end up bitten several times over a period of several years. Because the dog goes right at the snake, they are hit in the face (the best place for a bite) and skulk back up to the house, feeling sick and swelling up like a balloon. If someone is at home to witness it, they will doctor the dog and hope for the best. Either way, the dog then crawls up underneath a trailer to sleep it off. If the dog comes out a couple of days later, he made it. If not, a person waits for a warm day, fashions a grappling hook on the end of a long piece of stout steel cable, and goes fishing where it smells the worst.

Other Reptiles

There are other poisonous reptiles in Arizona, but most are seldom encountered and don't offer any risk. Coral snakes carry a very potent venom but don't have the inclination or bite radius to deliver it.

Gila monsters, although uncommon, are occasionally seen in the field during spring and summer. One could be encountered in the early dove season, but by the

Gila monster. (Randall D. Babb, Arizona Game & Fish Department)

opening of quail in October, they have pretty much gone underground. Gila monsters are very defensive and will bite a dog. Once they bite, they hang on like a pair of vise grip pliers. They do not inject venom like a viper, but rather chew the poison in through hollow rear teeth. The longer they hang on, the greater the potential for serious envenomation.

Ranchers occasionally have dogs come in wearing Gila monsters. I asked my vet about the frequency of Gila bites presented for treatment and, in a three decade career, he has only seen a handful. In the dogs he has treated, envenomation was not the problem. The dogs carried laceration wounds with broken teeth left embedded from prying the Gila off the dog. The dogs had to be treated for removal of broken teeth and infection. If you have to remove a Gila from a dog, be careful to avoid getting bit yourself. They move very quickly.

Animals

Arizona is still very wild in some places, complete with a large host of critters. We (the dogs and myself) have come across most of the locals while bird hunting. I give the "leave it" command and retreat one way, and the local takes the opening and goes the other. To get in trouble, your dog will generally have to start it. If your dog likes to chase and bite things, snakebreak him so he learns that some things hurt more than the battle is worth.

There are fluke situations you could encounter, such as a rabid coyote or a surprised bobcat. Range cows drop their calves in January in Arizona's quail country. Dogs commonly will work in and point a newborn like it was a bird. Mama often takes exception with this, lowers her head, and comes running from out of nowhere. Take mama's advice and move over a couple of hundred yards.

Coatimundis live in southern Arizona quail country also, mostly in Mearns' areas, in riparian zones along water. They look like a smooth-tailed, long-nosed version of a brown raccoon, to which they are related. They travel in groups of 20 or 30, working both the ground and the trees like a troop of baboons. They have the temperament of a boar coon and travel in a gang. Leave them alone.

Most animal contacts are random, nonthreatening occurrences. There is one animal, though, which is very common and found over the lower two-thirds of Arizona. Basically, this animal is found anywhere Gambel's quail are found. Javelina are very dangerous. They aren't a threat to people, but they can kill a dog in short order.

When we first moved to Arizona, we lived in Sedona. The Cottonwood paper ran weekly articles about a local javelina that would stroll through town, kill a dog or two, and then head back home like a lumberjack who had come into town to visit the ladies, drunk up the rest of his paycheck, and needed a fight before going back out. If my memory serves me, the local constable curtailed his string of victims at 7 or 8 dogs. Here in Oracle, my neighbor down the hill was leaving food scraps for wildlife in the draw behind his house. A herd of pigs were regular diners. The javelina, discovering that he fed his shorthair on the back step of the house, took to coming up after dark and emptying the dog's food bowl. One afternoon the javelina arrived early, while the dog was still there, and chewed him up. The shorthair died three days later. I could relate a dozen similar stories.

A javelina's appearance is that of a shy, retiring creature who runs away from trouble, and mostly they do. I have spent some time lying in herds, waiting for a shot while bow hunting. Herd members constantly keep in contact with each other by "woofing." It is a very soft sound that you feel more than hear. Once a herd member makes you, it woofs a warning. If they smell scent and know it's human, they leave en masse. If some sound or movement gave you away, it could mean anything to the pigs. A piglet is a tasty morsel to a hungry coyote. If the pigs think a baby is in danger, the sows and young retreat while the boars bristle up and charge forward to protect the herd. An experienced bow hunter woofs to let them know where the intruder is, then does his best to deflate the largest pig that comes forward.

If you and your dogs blunder into a herd of pigs while hunting, get your dogs in and observe their reaction. Most of the time, they take off and keep going. Sometimes their defensive responses get triggered, especially if a dog bites or chases one of the them. If you hear woofing, watch out.

Javelina don't exhibit any fear around dogs. They come in during the summer to eat the peaches that fall to the ground below our trees. The herd forages with complete indifference to dogs barking at them behind chain link 3 feet away. If anything, I would interpret their attitude as contempt.

Javelina.

Mike Merry, formerly of Oracle, Arizona, and now living in Ely, Nevada, had a run-in with a herd of javelina that illustrates how aggressive pigs can get. I chose this story because it has a happy ending. Most of the stories I hear don't.

Mike took Gizzy, his two-year-old female Brittany, for a run north of Oracle. The quail season was open, and he hoped to move a covey or two. They parked the truck at the top of a series of shallow sandwich canyons. He put a check cord on Giz and headed out, side-hilling along toward the bottom of a canyon.

With Mike watching from the hillside above, Giz dropped through the mesquite trees that lined the edge of the wash and took off running and yipping. He could see a group of pigs running in front of her. He whistled and yelled, but she ignored him and disappeared up the wash. Mike came down off the sidehill and ran after her. He had gone 50 yards up the wash when Giz appeared running toward him with a dozen pigs in hot pursuit. Mike grabbed Giz's check cord and ran for the sidehill so they could clear the heavy vegetation lining the wash. The javelina followed them through the trees and hung at the edge of the brush while Giz and Mike made their way uphill.

The pigs milled around, bristled up and woofed for a minute, and then charged directly at them. Mike said that he was certain the pigs saw him, but it didn't deter them. They wanted the dog. Mike waved his arms and screamed. He stomped his feet and ran at them like a madman. The pigs stopped short on their charge and returned to the brush line 40 yards away.

Mike made for the top of the hill, dragging Giz in tow on the end of the check cord. The pigs gave them a 30-second head start and then charged uphill after them. He turned the second charge by firing a shot into the dirt in front of them and held them in place with more yelling and arm waving. The javelina momentarily hung back, bristling up and teeth clattering, then lined out and came again.

He turned them with a second shot and ran for a mesquite tree above him on the hill. He had just enough time to back into the tree when the pigs closed around them. As a pig ran by at 3 feet, Gizzy broke free and ran after it and nipped it in the ass. The pigs closed in to kill the dog, so Mike waded in and kicked one pig in the side, grabbed Giz's check cord and lifted her out.

The pigs backed off and Mike used the opportunity to run for the top of the hill. The reprieve was shortlived. Thirty seconds later the herd came again. As Mike tells it, "This time they were serious to get something or somebody." The pigs closed around them. He kicked several to no avail. As a pig came at him, he clubbed it across the snout with his shotgun barrel and that turned the pigs. The javelina retreated.

The pigs regrouped for 30 seconds and came at them again. As Mike turned to run, he stumbled and fell to the ground. A pig charged over the top of him to get to Gizzy behind him, and Mike swung his shotgun like a golf club, cracking the pig alongside the head and accidentally discharging the gun. The javelina withdrew uninjured from the shot, and the herd dispersed momentarily. Mike decided he was going to have to start shooting for effect when they came at him again.

He tried to open the action to reload and discovered that while gripping his shotgun in the melee of clubbing, he had bent the trigger back and jammed the action. The weapon was inoperable.

The pigs charged again, stopped short and fell back. Mike knew he was in trouble and had to lose the herd. He ran, circling downwind to break the scent trail. He made 40 yards before they caught him. The pigs circled and then charged, running at him downhill. Mike got a good hold on Giz's rope and ran for all he was worth. He stopped at 100 yards, out of breath and looked back to see the pigs searching around on the hillside trying to find his trail. Mike didn't slow down until he got back to the truck.

Mike estimated that the encounter lasted 15 to 20 minutes. Miraculously, neither he nor Giz were bitten. His shotgun had three dents in the barrel that had to be removed by a gunsmith. There were several, deep rope gouges where the check cord had lain between his hand and the pistol grip on the stock while flying Gizzy on their escape runs. I asked Mike what he would have done differently, and I recommended a full auto with a bayonet lug up front. Mike answered that he would have shot a whole bunch of warning shots in the beginning, made a whole bunch of noise and run like hell. Sounds like a good plan to me.

In Arizona, javelina are legal game only to valid tag holders during prescribed seasons with legal weapons, birdshot not being one of them. What happened to Mike was an unusual occurrence and told only as an example of extreme behavior.

If a hunter is unfortunate enough to get a dog torn up, he will have to act quickly. Javelina have long, triangular-shaped canine teeth. Their canines inflict a deep, wicked wound. Use a shirt or jacket to wrap the dog up and hold the wound together. The blood loss can be massive. Secondary infection is a certainty. Get to a vet as soon as possible.

Insects and Others

In Arizona we have a host of bugs to match our diversity of thorns. While some of crawlers look pretty wicked, dog owners shouldn't be overly concerned. I've had dogs stung by scorpions, and one of our setters picked up a young tarantula and got stung in the mouth while carrying it around the yard. With insect bites and stings, I treat the dog with benadryl. They swell up and then sleep it off. They will be fine in the morning. With scorpions and spiders they can lose hair at the site of the bite or sting. There is a magazine article account of an adult German shorthair pointer dying after a scorpion sting to the mouth, but that is the only account of serious injury I could find. My dogs kill scorpions they come across in the dog room and yard by flattening them with a quick slap of their front paw, without receiving any stings.

An insect that Arizona dog owners should be aware of is a one-inch-long, pumpkin-seed-shaped bug called a conenose beetle or kissing bug. They are active during the summer, before the monsoons, and common in undeveloped areas of the Sonoran desert. Conenose beetles are parasitic and feed on blood from unsuspecting hosts, both animal and human. They live and breed in pack rat middens.

After dark, these insects fly in search of a blood meal. They are adept at secreting themselves in bedding and clothing and then emerging after their intended target goes to sleep. Once bitten, a person learns to roll back every blanket on a bed and check for conenose before getting in it. The initial bite is painless because the conenose injects a poison that deadens the area. After the insect has fed and left, the numbing effect wears off, and a person awakes to severe burning and itching at the bite. A red welt will be visible at the bite 1 to 3 inches in circumference, and the surrounding 4 to 8 inches of skin will be raised and white. The sensation is similar to nettles and burns like fire.

Conenose target dogs and like to feed between the toes and at the cuticle where the toenail grows from the toe. I have had dogs bitten repeatedly, and the effects are fairly consistent. Between the toes, a white welt is visible at the site of the bite. A secondary infection is present on the surface of the skin the following day. For bites at the toenail, a hard knot develops behind the cuticle that runs from ¼ to ½ inch in diameter. The knot itches and the dog licks and worries the bite for a couple of days. In some bites, the toe bone bends and starts to deform. In any case, I give the dog benadryl for the first couple of days to help alleviate the itching and then let it heal on its own. The secondary skin infection I treat with an aerosol spray wound dressing used for horses called Wound-Kote Blue Lotion. It usually knocks it out with one application. It can take up to three months before the toe returns to normal.

When we first moved to the desert and started having these strange dog foot problems, I didn't have a clue about what was happening. There were a lot of these harmless looking brown bugs flying around after dark, but I didn't know what they were. On one dog with a severe toe deformation, we ran up a $220 bill with a local vet. He prescribed several types of antibiotics and ran tests for valley fever. When nothing worked, he said we might have to consider amputation. About that time, my wife and I were at a store thumbing through a book called *Poisonous Dwellers of the Desert* by Natt N. Dodge. We turned a page to see a picture of our innocent looking brown beetles that came out after dark, and the mystery was solved. We stopped treatment and started looking for a new vet. The toe was back to normal in a few months.

Africanized bees are a recent import to the Southwest. Dogs and several people have been killed in southern Arizona as far north as the Phoenix metro area. Africanized bees are reported to respond to any perceived threat within a 150-yard radius of their hive. A loud noise (such as a gun report or a barking dog) has precipitated some attacks. It was thought that the shift from native bees to Africanized bees would take many years and possibly dilute the final inhabitant's aggressiveness, but a recent mite infestation is wiping out native hives and leaving their territories open for colonization by the aggressive newcomers. Texas has had Africanized bees present for several years, and it hasn't chased hunters from the field. However, it is wise to give any swarms or hives seen in the field a wide berth.

Since Africanized bees are new to Arizona, there has been little time to gain a history of bee/people/dog interactions. Let me relay the particulars of one attack that took place in mid-May of 1996. Bill Kuvlesky, one of the quail biologists on the Buenos Aires Refuge, was leaving his home one morning to start his work day. Bill's two bird dogs, an English setter and an English pointer, spent their days in the fenced yard attached to the house.

On the way out to his vehicle, he was stung by a bee. His home is on the refuge surrounded by large mesquite trees, and it is common to have large numbers of bees in the area gathering mesquite pollen. When he arrived at his office a few minutes later, his neighbor called and told him that one of his dogs had jumped the fence and had just run by. The thought of the earlier bee sting came back to him, and he returned home to find his pointer running the yard, frantically trying to escape a swarm of attacking bees. By Bill's account, the swarm was concentrating on the dog's head. After Bill ran into the yard to bring the dog into the house, the bees shifted their focus and started stinging him. The pointer's head was literally covered with bees. With the pointer safe, he then collected the runaway setter who had also been stung repeatedly. He gave both dogs 50 mg. of benadryl before starting the one-hour drive to the nearest vet.

The pointer, stung over a thousand times on the head, went into convulsions and died during the drive. The setter, having escaped the yard and thus avoiding the brunt of the attack, still sustained over 100 bee stings to the head. She died at the vets later that evening.

The hive was 15 yards away from the dog area and had not been there the night before. The bees had set up housekeeping within just hours of the attack. Unlike the literature, which says that bees will respond out to 150 yards from the hive, this group's attack zone was only 50 yards. In light of this experience, Bill feels that a hunter and dog attacked in the field could easily outrun a swarm and avoid serious injury. He felt that the fact that his dogs were confined in an enclosed area was the reason they were so severely stung.

Colorado River toads (*Bufo alvarius*) are very common in some areas during the summer monsoon season, July through September. They are primarily nocturnal.

Their range approximates that of Gambel's quail. The 7-inch-long Colorado River toad is the largest native toad in the United States. During monsoon rains, toads appear seemingly out of nowhere. They often take up stations under outdoor lighting and bug zappers and eat insects that are attracted by the light. They have no qualms about entering dog yards and kennels.

Colorado River toads have an elongated, 2-inch parotoid gland that runs from the rear corner of the eye back toward the shoulder. This gland produces a potent, poison slime that coats the mucus membranes in a dog's mouth when it picks up a toad. The poison takes effect immediately—the dog becomes incoherent and the pupils dilate. In matter of minutes, this is followed by a complete loss of muscle control, including the bladder, and convulsions. Depending on the severity of reaction, convulsions are followed by death.

I have had three toad poisonings with my dogs. Thankfully, I saw the toad prior to the first incident, so I knew what had caused the collapse. Toad poisoning symptoms can look like a lot of different things.

The treatment for toad poisoning is to remove the poison slime from the dog's mouth. A garden hose works best. If not available, use whatever stream of water is available. A spray bottle could work in an emergency. Use a low pressure stream of water and irrigate the dog's mouth while you rub the slime off the dog's gums. Use plenty of water. It could take half an hour before the dog regains full muscle control.

Valley fever (*Coccidioidomycosis*) is a disease that is found in the Southwest. It can affect both animals and people. It is caused by inhalation of fungus spores that are present in the soil. With surface disruptions caused by large scale construction developments, the spores become airborne. While most people and animals don't exhibit any reaction, some suffer from chronic coughing, elevated temperature, skin abscesses, swelling of the joints, and weight loss among other symptoms. If you or your dog experience these symptoms, a simple blood test can screen for valley fever. Left untreated, this condition can result in death. Valley fever is a two-stage infection, primary and disseminated. Prognosis is best for primary form valley fever when treated within the first one to four weeks. Once a disseminated form infection spreads past the lungs and lymph nodes and enters the bone, brain or other organs, it can be very difficult and expensive to treat successfully. Because of the high cost of Ketoconazol, the drug used to treat valley fever, many people cross the border and buy their prescriptions in Mexico, where its cost is a fraction of U.S. prices.

Manmade Dangers

Arizona was built on mining and ranching. In remote areas, traces of these enterprises can turn up anywhere. This is especially the case with mining. Most of Arizona is public land and many old mining sites have returned to public ownership, complete with messes that weren't cleaned up. The desert reverts back to its original state quickly. In a few decades, most of the above-ground, visual indications of a previous habitation disappear into the landscape. As Arizona is peppered with thousands of abandoned, unmarked mine shafts and hand-dug wells, this poses a hazard to hunters and gun dogs. Keep your eyes open!

An illustration of how difficult it can be to see a mine shaft before it is too late. The top photo shows the ground level view. The photo below shows the shaft that is not visible in the center of the first photograph until a person is right on top of it.

Another concern is the border separating Arizona and Mexico. In actuality, the international border along nondeveloped areas is a nondescript barbed wire fence. The only indication to be found of national sovereignty in these areas is labels on litter: to the south they are written in Spanish; to the north in English. Be sure to study a map before hunting so you know where the line is.

Contrary to the immigration laws, there are a lot of people heading north. A few of these folks are engaged in criminal endeavors. Much of the best Mearns' quail habitat is right on the border. If you see men wearing pack frames or leading a pack string of mules loaded with bales, don't ask them for directions.

Gambel's Quail Distribution

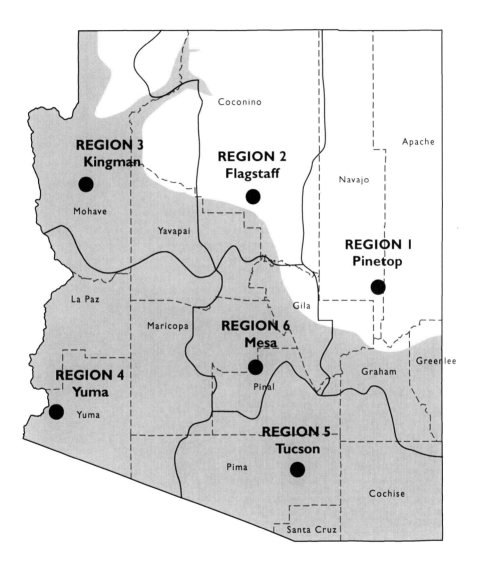

Scaled Quail Distribution

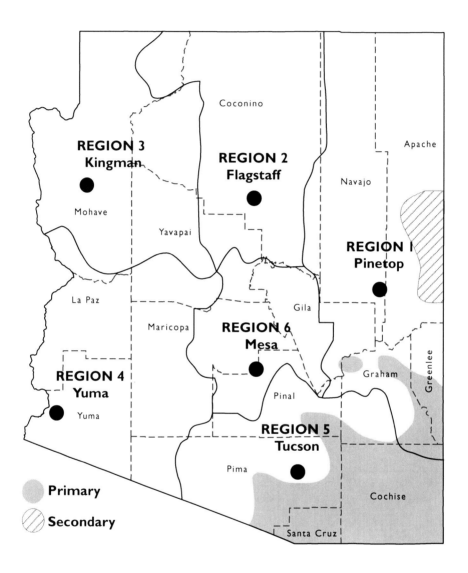

REGION 3
Kingman

Coconino

Apache

REGION 2
Flagstaff

Navajo

Mohave

Yavapai

REGION 1
Pinetop

La Paz

Gila

REGION 6
Mesa

Maricopa

Graham

Greenlee

REGION 4
Yuma

Yuma

Pinal

REGION 5
Tucson

Pima

Cochise

Santa Cruz

Primary

Secondary

MEARNS' QUAIL DISTRIBUTION

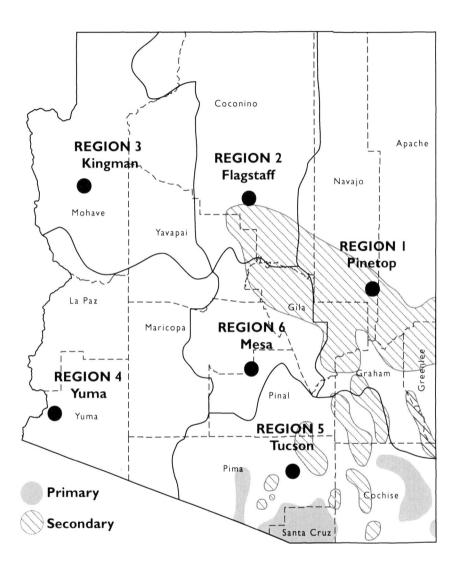

MOURNING DOVE DISTRIBUTION

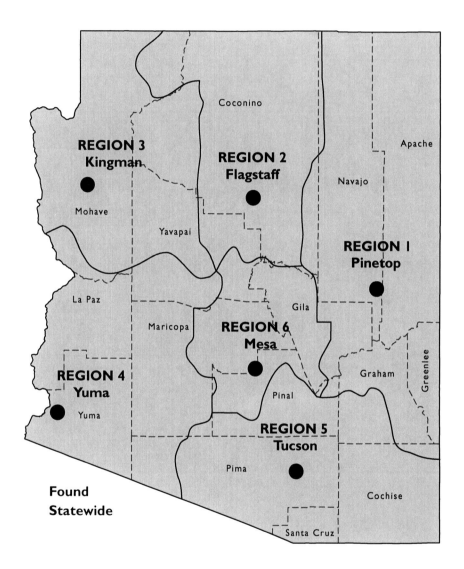

Found
Statewide

WHITE-WINGED DOVE DISTRIBUTION

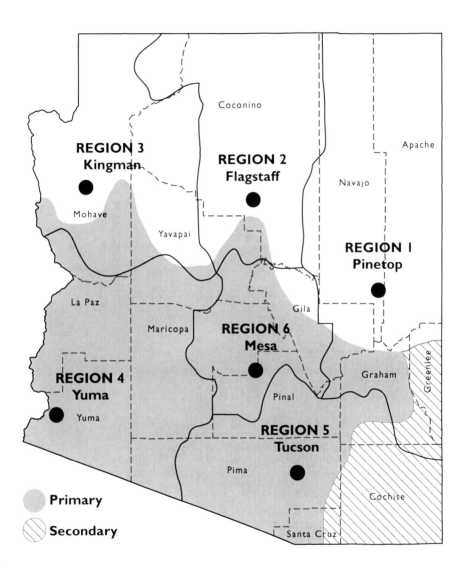

Coconino

Apache

REGION 3
Kingman

REGION 2
Flagstaff

Navajo

Mohave

Yavapai

REGION 1
Pinetop

La Paz

Gila

Maricopa

REGION 6
Mesa

Greenlee

REGION 4
Yuma

Graham

Yuma

Pinal

REGION 5
Tucson

Pima

Cochise

Primary

Secondary

Santa Cruz

Band-tailed Pigeon Distribution

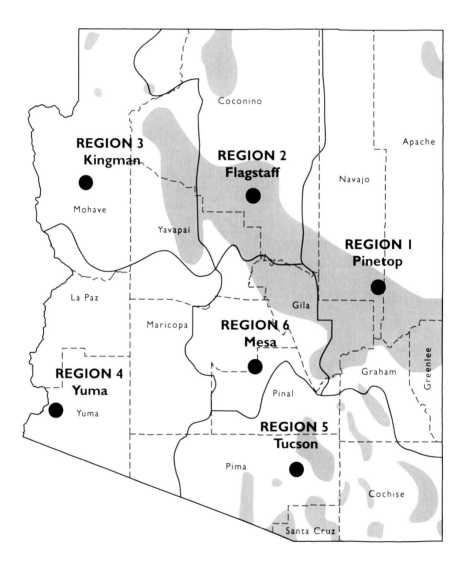

BLUE GROUSE DISTRIBUTION

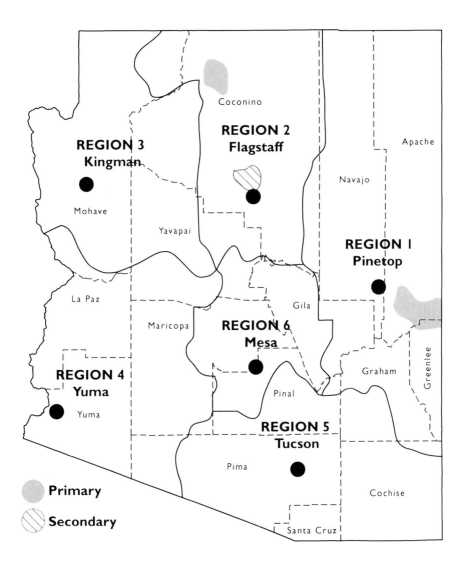

REGION 3
Kingman

Mohave

Coconino

REGION 2
Flagstaff

Apache

Navajo

REGION 1
Pinetop

Yavapai

La Paz

Gila

Maricopa

REGION 6
Mesa

REGION 4
Yuma

Yuma

Pinal

Graham

Greenlee

REGION 5
Tucson

Pima

Cochise

Primary

Secondary

Santa Cruz

MERRIAM'S WILD TURKEY DISTRIBUTION

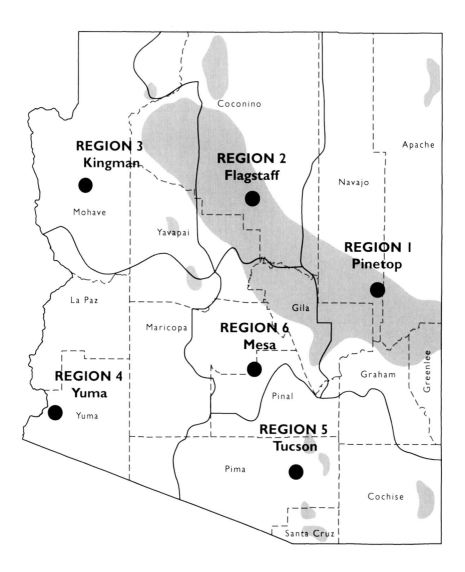

SANDHILL CRANE DISTRIBUTION

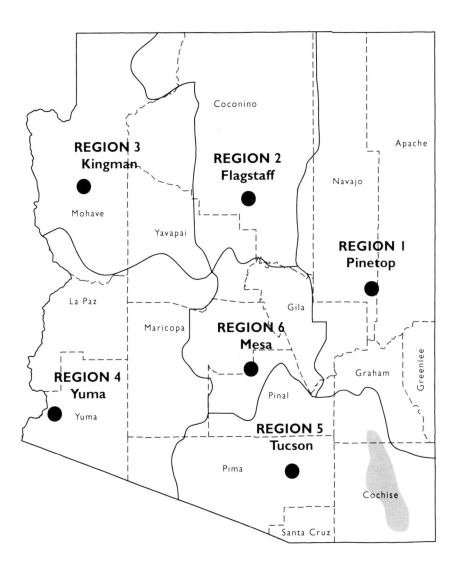

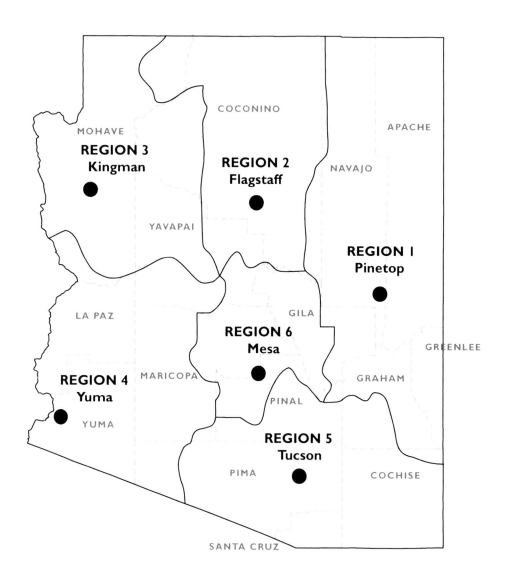

A Place to Hunt

ARIZONA GAME AND FISH DEPARTMENT REGIONAL OFFICES

Main Office

5000 West Carefree Highway
Phoenix, AZ 85086
602-942-3000
www.gf.state.az.us/

Region 1

2878 East White Mountain Drive
Pinetop, AZ 85935
928-367-4281
www.gf.state.az.us/

Region 2

3500 South Lake Mary Road
Flagstaff, AZ 86001
928-774-5045
www.gf.state.az.us/

Region 3

5325 North Stockton Hill Road
Kingman, AZ 86401
928-692-7700
www.gf.state.az.us/

Region 4

9140 East 28th Street
Yuma, AZ 85365
928-342-0091
www.gf.state.az.us/

Region 5

555 North Greasewood
Tucson, AZ 85745
928-628-5376
www.gf.state.az.us/

Region 6

7200 East University
Mesa, AZ 85207
480-981-9400
www.gf.state.az.us/

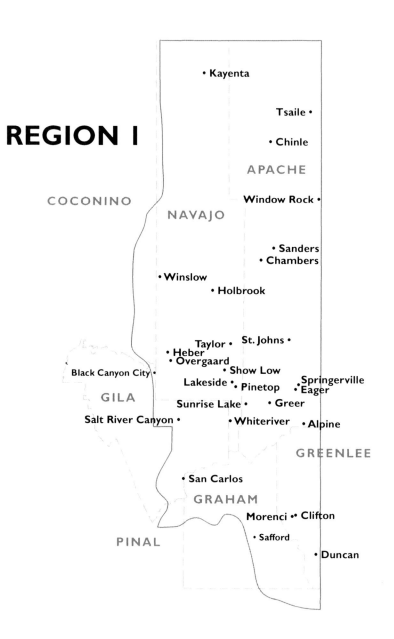

REGION I

COCONINO

NAVAJO

APACHE

• Kayenta

Tsaile •

• Chinle

Window Rock •

• Sanders
• Chambers

• Winslow

• Holbrook

Taylor •   St. Johns •
• Heber
• Overgaard
Black Canyon City •   • Show Low
Lakeside •   Springerville
• Pinetop   • Eager
GILA   Sunrise Lake •   • Greer
Salt River Canyon •   • Whiteriver   • Alpine

GREENLEE

• San Carlos

GRAHAM

Morenci • • Clifton

PINAL   • Safford

• Duncan

REGION 1:
Eastern Arizona

Region 1 spans nearly the entire length of Arizona's eastern boundary. Elevation begins at 3,000 ft. in the southern area and extends above 11,000 ft. in the White Mountains. The Navajo, White Mountain Apache, and San Carlos Apache Reservations are found in this section of the state. Major cities are Safford in the south, Show Low and Pinetop/Lakeside in the center of the region, and Holbrook along I-40 north of the White Mountains. Eager/Springerville is close to the New Mexico border at the north/south center point of the state line.

Gambel's and scaled quail are found at the extreme southern end of Region 1. Depending on rainfall, the lower elevation desert quail country around Safford can be very productive. Isolated coveys of Mearns' quail are seen on rare occasions in the mountainous areas. A widely scattered, seldom seen population of prairie subspecies, scaled quail live in the high desert grasslands north of Springerville and east of the Little Colorado River.

Blue grouse are found above 8,000 ft. in the White Mountains. Band-tailed pigeons migrate through the region's higher elevations.

Waterfowl are found on available water throughout the region. Duck hunters might best focus their efforts on the Gila River and Little Colorado River drainages and adjacent water.

UPLAND BIRDS
Gambel's Quail, Scaled Quail, Mearns' Quail, Mourning Dove, White-winged Dove, Band-tailed Pigeon, Blue Grouse, Merriam's Turkey

WATERFOWL
Ducks & Geese

COUNTY STATISTICS FOR REGION 1

County	Population	Area (sq.mi.)	Max. Jan. Temp.	Annual Precip.	Percent Public Land	Percent Reservation
Apache County	63,275	11,171	51.7°	13.46"	20%	65%
Gila County	43,350	4,748	61.5°	20.77"	59%	38%
Graham County	30,625	4,618	64.3°	9.53"	56%	36%
Greenlee County	8,425	1,878	64.3°	14.55"	94%	—
Navajo County	81,750	9,910	57.5°	8.82"	16%	54%

Region 1: Eastern Arizona Hub Cities

ALPINE
Elevation – 8,000 ft. • Population 256

Alpine is a small, picturesque community nestled in the conifers due south of Escudilla Mountain in the White Mountains. Accommodations are few and rustic in nature. Blue grouse and turkey are found in appropriate habitat surrounding the area. Waterfowl hunting can be good on the many lakes scattered throughout the White Mountains.

ACCOMMODATIONS

Tal WiWi Lodge, (has restaurant) / 928-339-4319 / No dogs allowed / $$-$$$ /
   www.talwiwilodge.com
Hannagan's Meadow Lodge, Hannagan's Meadow (has restaurant) /
   928-339-4370 / No dogs allowed / $$-$$$
Coronado Trail Cabins, & RV Park / 928-339-4772 / dogs allowed with fee / $$

RESTAURANTS

Bear Wallow Cafe, 42650 US Hwy 180 /928-339-4310
Millard & Millard, County Road 2054 / 928-339-4378

FOR MORE INFORMATION

Alpine Chamber of Commerce
   PO Box 410
   Alpine, AZ 85920
   928-339-4330
   www.alpinearizona.com

BLACK CANYON CITY
Elevation – 2,600 ft. • Population – 2,697

Found on Interstate 17, north of Phoenix, Black Canyon City is a small town that rambles over some beautiful Sonoran desert hill country. The town offers moderate services. The surrounding country is predominantly Gambel's quail cover with some mourning doves present.

ACCOMMODATIONS

Mountain Breeze Motel, 34500 S Old Black Canyon Hwy / No dogs allowed /
   623-374-5361 / www.mountainbreezemotel.com

Campgrounds & RV Parks

Bradshaw Mountain RV Resort, 33900 S. Old Black Canyon Hwy / 623-374-9800 / bradshawmtnrvresort.com
Black Canyon KOA, 19600 E St Josephs Rd / 623-374-5318 / www.koa.com
River's Edge RV Park/Campground, HC01, PO Box 964 / 623-374-9448 / riversedgebccaz.com

Restaurants

Four Bees Cafe, Old Black Canyon Hwy, / 623-374-5736
Byler's Amish Kitchen, 34351 N Old Black Canyon Hwy / 623-374-9330 / www.arizonaamish.com
Rock Springs Cafe, 37569 Old Black Canyon Hwy, / 623-374-5794/ rockspringscafe.com
Kid Chilleens Bad Ass Barbeque and Steak House, 33125 S Coldwater Rd / 623-374-5552 / www.badassbbq.net

Veterinarians

Foothills Veterinary Service, 48410 N. Black Canyon Hwy, New River / 623-465-9488 / www.foothillsvet.com

Auto Repair

Doug's Car Care, 19135 E K Field Rd / 602-374-5248
Canyon Service Center, 34400 S Old Black Canyon Hwy / 602-374-5236 Service / 602-374-9443 Parts

Medical

Community Association Medical Center, 4601 S. Phyllis St., PO Box 1008, / 602-374-9777

For More Information

Black Canyon City Chamber of Commerce
PO Box 1919
Black Canyon City, AZ 85324
602-374-9797
www.blackcanyoncity.org

CLIFTON/MORENCI
Elevation – 4,000 ft. • Combined Population – 4,144

These two small communities support a large copper mining operation. Clifton/ Morenci is surrounded by large tracts of public lands at approximately 4,000 ft. elevation. The area contains mostly Gambel's quail, with some scaled quail also available. Waterfowling is productive along the Gila River. Turkeys and Bandtails are present in the mountains to the north.

RESTAURANTS

Marla's Pizzeria, 352 N. Coronado Blvd., Clifton / 928-865-5291
Dairy Queen Brazier, Morenci / 928-865-3456 / www.dairyqueen.com
Golden City Chinese Restaurant, Hwy 191#1, Morenci / 928-865-5941

AUTO REPAIR

B & D Auto Supply, 200 N. Coronado Blvd., Clifton / 928-865-2950

MEDICAL

Morenci Health Care Center, Coronado Blvd., Clifton / 928-865-4511

EAGER
Elevation – 7,090 ft. • Population – 4,265

Eager/Springerville sits in the picturesque Round Valley. These old ranching communities developed to the south of the Little Colorado River. The two cities have many services and accomodations for the traveling bird hunter. National Forest lands to the south are the principal stronghold of blue grouse in Arizona. Turkey is also common on National Forest lands. Waterfowl are found along the Little Colorado River and on adjacent waters.

ACCOMMODATIONS

Best Western Sunrise Inn, 128 N. Main St. / Dogs allowed / 800-528-1234 / $$ / www. bestwesternarizona.com

FOR MORE INFORMATION

Round Valley Chamber of Commerce
PO Box 31 / 418 E. Main Street
Springerville, AZ 85938
928-333-2123 / Fax 928-333-5690
www.roundvalley.org

PINETOP/LAKESIDE
Elevation – 7,200 ft. • Population – 4,442

Pinetop/Lakeside is a sprawling community thath stretches among the pine trees on the northern border of the White Mountain Apache Indian Reservation. Show Low is a few miles to the west, and the two communities are connected along Highway 260 by an unbroken string of shops and businesses. The three cities of Pinetop, Lakeside, and Show Low are the center of commerce for the region and provide a full array of services for the traveling sportsman. Blue grouse are found on the higher elevations to the east. Turkeys are present in fair to good numbers. Waterfowl hunting can be excellent on the many lakes dotting the region.

ACCOMMODATIONS

Mountain Hacienda Lodge, PO Box 713, Pinetop-Lakeside / Dogs allowed / 928-367-4146 / $-$$ / www.mountainhacienda.com

Econo Lodge, 458 White Mountain Rd., Pinetop / Dogs allowed / 800-553-2666 / $-$$$ / www.econolodge.com

Best Western Inn of Pinetop, PO Box 1005, Pinetop / Dogs allowed / 800-528-1234 / $$-$$$ / www.bestwesternarizona.com

RESTAURANTS

Red Devil Restaurant & Bar, 1774 E. White Mountain Blvd, Pinetop / 928-367-5570 / www.reddevilrestaurant.com

Pasta House, 2188 W. White Mtn Blvd, Pinetop / 928-367-2782 / www.pastahouse.com

Charlie Clark's Steak House, Hwy 260, Pinetop / 888-333-0259 / www.charlieclarks.com

Brickman's Grill, 1450 E. White Mountain Blvd., Pinetop / 928-367-7400 / www.brickmansgrill.com

VETERINARIANS

White Mountain Animal Hospital, 1939 W. White Mountain Blvd., Pinetop / 928-368-8425

SPORTING GOODS

Pinetop Sporting Goods, 747 E. White Mountain Blvd. #4, Pinetop / 928-367-5050 / White Mountain Apache Tribe Hunting License Vendor

Hon Dah Service Station, Pinetop / 928-369-4311 / White Mountain Apache Tribe Hunting License Vendor

MEDICAL

Navapache Regional Medical Center, 2200 E Show Low Lake Rd, Show Low / 928-367-2506 / www.nrmc.org

FOR MORE INFORMATION

White Mountain Apache Tribe
The Office of Tourism
928-338-1230
www.wmat.nsn.us

SAN CARLOS

Elevation – 3,800 ft. • Population – 3,716

San Carlos is located on the San Carlos Apache Reservation just north of Highway 70. It is best to be fully provisioned while traveling on a reservation because most offer little in the way of amenities. Quail and waterfowl are the primary birds hunted on the reservation.

RESTAURANTS

Apache Gold Casino, 5 miles east of Globe on Hwy 70 / 928-475-7800 / www.apachegoldcasinoresort.com
San Carlos Cafe / 928-475-2722

SPORTING GOODS

Noline's Country Store, US Hwy 70, Peridot / 928-475-2334 / San Carlos Reservation license vendor
San Carlos Lake Store, US Hwy 70, Peridot / 928-475-2756 / San Carlos Reservation license vendor

FOR MORE INFORMATION

Graham County Chamber of Commerce
1111 Thatcher Blvd.
Safford, AZ 85546
928-428-2511 / Fax 928-428-0744
www.graham-chamber.com

SHOW LOW

Elevation – 6,331 ft. • Population – 9,885

Show Low, due west of Pinetop/Lakeside on Highway 260, is the center of commerce for that portion of the White Mountains. As such, there are ample services for visiting bird shooters. Blue grouse are found in the mountains to the east, along with turkey that utilize similar habitat. Good waterfowl hunting is found throughout the region.

ACCOMMODATIONS

K C Motel, 60 W. Deuce of Clubs / Dogs allowed / 928-537-4433 / $$ / www.kcmotelinshowlow.com
Kiva Motel, 261 E. Deuce of Clubs / Dogs allowed / 928-537-4542 / $-$$

Mearns' quail take is monitored by the Arizona Game and Fish Department with "wing barrel" surveys. Hunters are asked to leave one wing per bird in the barrel.

RESTAURANTS

Branding Iron Steak House, 1261 E. Deuce / 928-537-5151
Fiesta Mexicana restaurant 350 E. Duce of Clubs/ 928-532-3424
Asia Garden Restaurant, 59 W. Deuce of Clubs, 928-537-9333

VETERINARIANS

Aspen Ridge Animal Hospital 5624 White MT Top Ave, Lakeside, AZ/
    928-537-4000
Alta Sierra Veterinary Clinic, 100 S Clark Rd / 928-537-2880

Sporting Goods

Big Five Sporting Goods 4441 S.White Mountain Rd./928-537-555
A to Z Gunsmithing, 8470 Antelope Dr / 928-537-2121

Air Service

Show Low Airport, 3200 E. Deuce / 928-537-5629

Auto Rental

Enterprise Rent-a-Car, 980 E. Deuce / 928-537-5144 / www.enterprise.com

For More Information

Show Low Chamber of Commerce
PO Box 1083
Show Low, AZ 85901
Phone / Fax 928-537-2326
www.showlowchamberofcommerce.com

SAFFORD
Elevation – 2,900 ft. • Population – 8,981

Safford, found due east of the San Carlos Indian Reservation on Highway 70, runs along the southern edge of the Gila River. Safford is a growing commercial center built on agriculture. Much of the area is still in agricultural fields. The city offers a full range of services for the traveling bird hunter. The predominant game bird species is Gambel's quail with scaled quail also present. Mourning and white-wing dove and migrating waterfowl are found on available water and along the agricultural fields that line the Gila River.

Accommodations

Best Western-Desert Inn of Safford, 1391 Thatcher Blvd. / Dogs allowed /
928-428-0521 / $$-$$$ / www.bestwesternarizona.com
Comfort Inn, 1578 W. Thatcher Blvd. / Dogs allowed / 800-221-2222 / $$ /
www.comfortinn.com

Restaurants

Brick's Steaks Seafood 4367 S. US Hwy 191/928-348-8111
El Charro Restaurant, 601 W. Main St. / 928-428-4134 / www.elcharrocafe.com
Casa Manana, 502 S 1st Ave / 928-428-3170

Veterinarians

All About Pets Animal Hospital,114 W 5th St / 928-428-4900
Companion Animal Clinic, 1765 S 20th Ave / 928-348-8432

Don Prentice reaches out to accept a bird from Fritzel.

SPORTING GOODS

Kmart, 1987 W. Thatcher Blvd. / 928-428-4985 / www.kmart.com
Gila Outdoor, 408 W Main St / 928-348-0710 / www.gilaoutdoor.com
Q's Gun and Supply 7648 S. Chuckwagon/928-965-1556

AUTO RENTALS

Enterprise Rent A Car, 715 5th / 928-428-0955
Hatch Brothers Auto Center, 1623 W. Thatcher / 928-428-6000

AIR SERVICE

Safford Aviation, 4550 E. Aviation Way / 928-428-7670

FOR MORE INFORMATION

Graham County Chamber of Commerce
1111 Thatcher Blvd.
Safford, AZ 85546
928-428-2511 / Fax 928-428-0744
www.graham-chamber.com

REGION 2

REGION 2
North Central Arizona

Region 2 encompasses much of Arizona's beautiful higher elevation, forested areas. The Verde River is found in the southern section of the region, and the Colorado River runs out of Lake Powell and south along the state's northern boundary. Vast tracts within the region are uninhabited, and hunting can be excellent. The area contains many of Arizona's turkeys. Bandtail pigeons and Mourning doves migrate through and are found in available habitat. While Gambel's quail hunting can be very good, available habitat is limited and they are found only in the extreme southern portion of the region, in the Verde valley area. There are rare sightings of Mearns' quail on National Forest lands. Blue grouse are found only on the Kaibab Plateau and the San Francisco Peaks, north of Flagstaff. The state's only huntable population of Chukars are found in the Kanab Creek Wilderness/Snake Gulch area on the western edge of the Kaibab Plateau.

Waterfowl migrate through and are found on available water throughout the region.

UPLAND BIRDS
Gambel's Quail, Mearns' Quail, Mourning Dove,
White-winged Dove, Band-tailed Pigeon, Blue Grouse,
Merriam's Turkey, Chukar

WATERFOWL
Ducks and Geese

COUNTY STATISTICS FOR REGION 2

County	Population	Area (sq.mi.)	Max. Jan. Temp.	Annual Precip.	Percent Public Land	Percent Reservation
Coconino County	96,591	18,540	47.5°	22.10"	49%	45%
Yavapai County	107,714	8,091	55.9°	3.21"	91%	—

North Central Arizona Hub Cities

CAMP VERDE

Elevation – 3,160 ft. • Population – 9,451

Camp Verde is found along the main travel corridor, Interstate 17, between Flagstaff and Phoenix. The Verde River runs through Verde Valley and contains the northernmost finger of Gambel's quail habitat in the central part of the state. Turkeys are found on adjoining national forest lands. Some duck hunting is found along the Verde River and on the many stock tanks throughout the area. Huntable concentrations of mourning doves are sometimes found. Band-tailed pigeons are seen in the higher elevation national forest lands.

CAMPGROUNDS AND RV PARKS

Zane Grey RV Park (Dick Reynolds), 4500 East Highway 260 / 80 Sites / 928-567-4320 / www.zanegreyrvpark.com
Verde River Resort, HC 75-1526 Horseshoe Bend / 150 Sites / 928-567-5262

ACCOMMODATIONS

Comfort Inn of Camp Verde, 340 North Goswick Way / 928-567-9000 / .www.comfortinn.com
Super 8 1550 State Rt.250 / 866-539-0036

RESTAURANTS

Las Margaritas. 77 General Cook Trl / 928-567-2435
Babe's Roundup, 90 S Montezuma Castle Hwy / 928-567-6969

VETERINARIANS

Anasazi Animal Clinic, 407 W Highway 260 / 928-567-3807
Camp Verde Veterinary Clinic, 100 S. Montezuma Castle Rd. / 928-567-9400

SPORTING GOODS

Canyon Outfitters, Inc., 2701 W Highway 89A, 928-282-5293

AUTO REPAIR

Beaver Creek Service Center, 3718 E. Beaver Creek Rd., Rim Rock / 928-567-5652

MEDICAL

Marcus J. Lawrence Medical Center / 928-567-3884 / www.nahealth.com

FOR MORE INFORMATION

Camp Verde Chamber of Commerce
PO Box 1665 / 435 S. Main Street
Camp Verde, AZ 86322
928-567-9294 / 567-6715
www.visitcampverde.com

Cottonwood
Elevation – 3,320 ft. • Population 9,179

Found in the western extreme of the Verde Valley, Cottonwood has ample accommodations and services. Gambel's quail are found in the surrounding desert grasslands. Ducks frequent the upper stretches of the Verde River. Turkey and band-tailed pigeon populations are found in the higher elevation national forest land. Huntable populations of migrating mourning doves may be present.

CAMPGROUNDS AND RV PARKS

Thousand Trails/Verde Valley (Sharon Glover), PO Box 1779 / 333 Sites / 928-567-9562/ www.thousandtrails.com
Turquoise Triangle RV Resort (Eli Planedin), 2501 Highway 89A East / 60 Sites / 928-634-5294

ACCOMMODATIONS

Best Western Cottonwood Inn, 993 S. Main / Dogs allowed / 800-528-1234 / $$-$$$ / www.bestwesternarizona.com
Quality Inn, 301 W. SR 89A / Dogs allowed / 800-221-2222 / $$-$$$ / www.qualityinn.com
The View Motel, 818 S. Main / Dogs allowed / 928-634-7581 / $-$$ / www.theviewmotel.com

RESTAURANTS

Sizzler Steak Seafood & Salad, 1041 S Highway 260 / 928-634-3605 / www.sizzler.com
Murphy's Grill, 747 S. Main St. / 928-634-7272 / www.murphysgrill.us
Stromboli's Restaurant and Pizzeria, 321 S. Main / 928-634-3838 / www.strombolis.com

VETERINARIANS

Airpark Animal Hospital, 515 S Airpark Rd # 103 / 928-649-8387 / www.airparkanimalhospital.com
Verde Veterinary Hospital, 1201 E. Cherry / 928-399-7519/ www.verdevethospital.com

SPORTING GOODS

Wal-Mart, 1100 State Route 2 / 928-634-0378 / www.walmart.com

Auto Repair

A & B Motors, 335 S. Main St. / 928-634-3297
Phillips Auto Repair, 395 Airpark Rd / 928-634-7395 / www.phillipsautorepair.com

Auto Rental

Enterprise Rent A Car, 1423 E. US Hwy 89A / 928-634-0049 / www.enterprise.com

Medical

Marcus J. Lawrence Memorial Hospital / 928-634-5708
Marcus J. Lawrence Medical Center, 202 S. Willard St. / 928-634-2251

For More Information

Cottonwood/Verde Valley Chamber of Commerce
1010 S. Main Street
Cottonwood, AZ 86326
928-634-7593 / Fax 928-634-7594
www.cottonwood.verdevalley.com

Flagstaff

Elevation – 6,905 ft. • Population – 52,894

Flagstaff is northern Arizona's major city. At 6,900 feet in elevation, it bears no resemblance to the cactus studded mountains found throughout much of Arizona. Ponderosa pine and aspen light up the mountain slopes. Home of Northern Arizona University, Flagstaff is a hub where Interstates 40 and 17 and Highways 89 and 180 meet. A wide range of services and amenities are available.

Turkey numbers can be good in the surrounding national forest lands. Band-tailed pigeons and mourning doves migrate through the area and sometimes congregate in huntable numbers. Blue grouse were transplanted on the San Francisco Peaks, and while I have not been successful in finding them there, other hunters have. Elevations here are too high to sustain quail, and as a result, none are present, with the exception of rare Mearns' quail sightings.

Waterfowl hunting can be outstanding on the many lakes surrounding Flagstaff.

Campgrounds and RV Parks

J & H RV Park (Harvey Mickelson), 7901 North Highway 89 / 55 Sites / 928-526-1829 / www.flagstaffrvparks.com
Flagstaff KOA (Jerry Sanders), 5803 Highway 89 / 195 Sites / 928-526-9926 / www.koa.com
Meteor Crater RV Park (George Shoemaker), 603 North Beaver / 72 Sites / 928-289-4002
Woody Mountain Campground (Larry Skrobut), 2727 West Highway 66 / 146 Sites / 928-774-7727 / www.woodymountaincampground.com

A large flock of Canada and snow geese along the Colorado River. (Randall D. Babb, Arizona Game and Fish Department)

ACCOMMODATIONS

Motel 6, 2440 E Lucky Ln / Dogs allowed / 928-774-8756 / $ / www.motel6.com
Super 8 Motel, 3825 Kasper Ave. / Dogs allowed / 800-800-8000 / $-$$ / www.super8.com
Travelodge Suites, 2755 Woodlands Village Rd. / Dogs allowed / 928-773-1111 / $$-$$$ / www.travelodge.com

RESTAURANTS

Outback Steakhouse 2600 E Lucky Ln. /928-774-7630
Historic Saginaw House, 717 Riordan Rd. / 928-774-3929
Hunan Restaurant East, 1926 N 4th St # 8 / 928-526-1009
Josephine's, 503 N. Humphreys / 928-779-3400 / www.josephinesrestaurant.com
Monte Vista Coffee Shop, 104 N. San Francisco St. / 928-774-8211
The Cottage Place Restaurant, 126 W Cottage Ave / 928-774-8431 / www.cottageplace.com

VETERINARIANS

Kaibab Veterinary Clinic, 1000 E. Butler Ave. / 928-774-8731
Alpine Animal Hospital, 1066 W. Highway 66 / 928-774-9441
Aspen Veterinary Clinic, 7861 N. Hwy 89 / 928-526-242

SPORTING GOODS

Big 5 Sporting Goods, 2775 Woodlands Village Blvd / 928-214-0590 / www.big5sportinggoods.com

MOTELS

Babbitt's Backcountry, 12 E Aspen Ave / 928-774-4775

AUTO REPAIR

Bill's Welding & Repair Service, 11850 N. US Hwy 89 / 928-526-2816
Coconino Motors, 1141 W. Kaibab Ln. / 928-774-4408
Economy Auto Repair, 204 Mike's Pike / 928-774-1931

AUTO RENTAL

AAA Discount Car Rental, 602 W. Route 66 / 928-774-7394
Budget Rent A Car, 201 N. Switzer Canyon Dr. / 928-779-3534 / www.budget.com
Enterprise Rent A Car, 3470 E. Route 66 / 928-526-1377 / www.enterprise.com

AIR SERVICE

Flagstaff Pulliam Airport Terminal / 928-556-1234
Flagstaff Pulliam Airport Operations / 928-774-1422

MEDICAL

Aspen Hill Hospital, 305 W. Forest Ave. / 928-773-1060
FMC Walk In Medical, Care, 1355 N. Beaver St., #100 / 928-556-9564

FOR MORE INFORMATION

Flagstaff Chamber of Commerce
101 W. Route 66
Flagstaff, AZ 86001
928-774-4505 / Fax 928-779-1209
www.flagstaffchamber.com

SEDONA
Elevation – 4,240 ft. • Population – 11,220

Sedona is a rapidly growing community set in the picturesque red rock formations along the Mogollon Rim. Connected by Highway 89 through Oak Creek Canyon, Flagstaff is 40 minutes away. Sedona is an upscale resort community, and this is reflected in the price of accommodations. The surrounding grasslands can provide productive Gambel's quail hunting during good years. Higher elevation national forest lands to the north hold turkey and band-tailed pigeons. Migrating dove and waterfowl are found on available water.

ACCOMMODATIONS

Desert Quail Inn, 6626 Hwy 179 / Dogs allowed / 928-284-1437 / $$-$$$ / www.desertquailinn.com
Sedona Super 8 2545 W. State Rt. 89A/ 928-282-1533

RESTAURANTS

Coffee Pot Restaurant, 2050 W. State Route 89A / 928-282-6626
Heartline Cafe, 1600 W Hwy 89A / 928-282-0785 / www.heartlinecafe.com
Cowboy Club 241 N. State Rt. 89A /928-282-4200
Shugrue's Hillside Grill, 671 State Route 179 / 928-282-5300 / www.shugrues.com
L'Auberge Restaurant, 301 Lauberge Ln / 928-282-1667 / www.lauberge.com

VETERINARIANS

Oak Creek Small Animal Clinic, 3130 W. Highway 89A / 928-282-1195 /
    www.acsacdvms.com
Sedona Animal Hospital, 100 Posse Ground Rd. / 928-282-4133

AUTO REPAIR

Canyon Automotive Repair & Service, 2025 Yavapai Dr. / 928-282-4424
Sedona Tire and Auto Repair, 3035 W Highway 89A / 928-282-2500

AUTO RENTAL

Sedona Jeep Rentals, 235 Air Terminal Dr. / 928-282-2227

AIR SERVICE

Sedona Airport, 1225 Airport Rd. / 928-282-4409 / sedonaairport.org
Sedona Airport Terminal, 235 Air Terminal Dr. / 928-282-4487

MEDICAL

Marcus J. Lawrence Medical Center / 928-282-1831
Sedona Medical Center, 35 Dry Creek Rd. / 928-282-1285 / www.nahealth.com

FOR MORE INFORMATION

Sedona Chamber of Commerce
    45 Sunset Dr.
    Sedona, AZ 86336
    (928) 204-1123
    www.sedonachamber.com

REGION 3

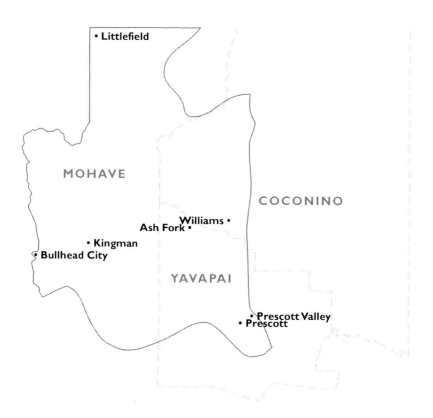

REGION 3
Northwest Arizona

Sparsely populated, Region 3's major cities are Kingman and Bullhead City. The Colorado River runs along the region's western border and is one of Arizona's principal water recreation zones. Interstate 40 is the main travel artery running east to west. Gambel's quail are found throughout the desert regions and in the lower elevations along the Colorado River. Mourning and white-winged dove frequent the agricultural fields that line the Colorado River, and early-season dove populations can be very impressive. Some turkeys are found north of the Grand Canyon and in the region's higher elevations. Waterfowl, both ducks and geese, use the federal refuges along the Colorado River drainage.

UPLAND BIRDS

Gambel's Quail, Mourning Dove, White-winged Dove,
Band-tailed Pigeon, Merriam's Turkey,
Sandhill Crane (currently not legal game in this area)

WATERFOWL

Ducks & Geese

COUNTY STATISTICS FOR REGION 3

County	Population	Area (sq.mi.)	Max. Jan. Temp.	Annual Precip.	Percent Public Land	Percent Reservation
Coconino County	96,591	18,540	47.5°	22.10"	49%	45%
Mohave County	93,497	13,217	70.5°	2.58"	84%	6%
Yavapai County	107,714	8,091	55.9°	3.21"	91%	—

Northwest Arizona Hub Cities

Bullhead City
Elevation – 504 ft. • Population – 40,225

Bullhead City is a popular resort area and offers the traveler many amenities. Located due north of the Fort Mojave Indian Reservation and the Havasu National Wildlife Refuge, it is a convenient home base for early season mourning and white-wing dove hunters. Gambel's quail and waterfowl hunting is available on Fort Mojave Indian Reservation and Topock Marsh on Havasu National Wildlife Refuge.

Campgrounds and RV Parks

Blackstone RV Park (Jerry Rowland), 3299 Boundry Cove Road / 136 Sites / 928-768-3303

Accommodations

Silver Creek Inn, 1670 Hwy 95, / Dogs allowed / 928-763-8400 / $$
Best Western, 1126 Highway 95 / 800-827-8298 / www.bestwesternarizona.com

Restaurants

China Szechuan, 1890 S. Hwy 95 / 928-763-2610
Iguana's Mexican River Cantina, 2247 Clearwater Dr. / 928-763-9109
Perkins Family Restaurant, 2250 S. Hwy 952 / 928-763-1960 / www.perkinsrestaurants.com
Black Bear Diner, 1751 Hwy 95, Ste. 25 / 928-763-2477 / www.blackbeardiner.com

Veterinarians

Spirit Mountain Animal Hospital, 1670 Lakeside Dr. / 928-758-3979

Sporting Goods

K Mart, 2250 S. Hwy 95 / 928-763-7878 / www.kmart.com
Wal-mart, 2350 S. Miracle Mile / 928-758-7222 / www.walmart.com
Big 5 Sporting Goods, 1835 Hwy 95 / 928-763-0608 / www.big5sportinggoods.com
Longhorn Trading Co., 1091 US Hwy 95 / 928-754-3434 / www.longhornguns.com

Auto Repair

Lance's Auto Repair, 1305 Baseline Rd / 928-754-2314
Bullhead Auto Repair, 165 Lee Ave. / 928-754-2405

Auto Rental

Avis Rent A Car, 2750 Locust Blvd. / 928-754-4686 / www.avis.com
Budget Rent A Car, 600 Hwy 95 / 928-754-3361 / www.budget.com

Gundogs quickly learn to scan the horizon for incoming birds.

AIR SERVICE

Laughlin Bullhead International, 2550 Laughlin View / 928-754-2134 / www.bullheadcity.com

MEDICAL

Bullhead Community Hospital, 2735 Silver Creek Rd. / 928-763-2273

Mohave Valley Hospital & Medical Center, 1225 Hancock Rd. / 928-758-3931 or 758-4531

Silver Ridge Village, 2812 Silver Creek Rd. / 928-763-1404

FOR MORE INFORMATION

Bullhead Area Chamber of Commerce
1251 Hwy 95
Bullhead City, AZ 86429
928-754-4121 / Fax 928-754-5514
www.bullheadchamber.com

Kingman
Elevation – 3,345 ft. • Population – 27,271

Kingman is a rapidly growing city that has many amenities for the traveling bird hunter. Interstate 40 transects the city, and many motels and eating establishments are found just off of the freeway. Gambel's quail as well as mourning and white-wing dove hunting is found in the area. Good waterfowl hunting and dove shooting is to be found further west along the Colorado River.

CAMPGROUNDS AND RV PARKS

Blake Ranch RV Park (Bob Beck),9315 East Blake Ranch Road / 55 Sites / 928-757-3336 / www.blakeranchrv.com
Kingman KOA Kampground, 3820 N. Roosevelt / 928-757-4397 / www.koa.com

ACCOMMODATIONS

Motel 6, 3270 E. Andy Devine / Dogs allowed / 928-757-7121 / $ / www.motel6.com
Super 8 3401 Andy Devine/dogs allowed/1-800-276-7415
Best Western King's Inn, 2930 E. Andy Devine / Dogs allowed / 800-528-1234 / $$ / www.bestwesternarizona.com

RESTAURANTS

Carl's Jr., 789 W. Beale St. / 928-753-1989 / www.carlsjr.com
Golden Corral Steakhouse, 3157 Stockton Hill Rd. / 928-681-3900 / www.goldencorral.com
Chili's Bar & Grill 3840 Stockton Hill road/928-681-3444
Redneck's Southern Pit Barbecue 420 E. Beale St/928-757-8227
Mattina's Ristorante italiano 318 E. Oak St/928-753-7504

VETERINARIANS

Kingman Animal Hospital, 1650 Northern /928-757-7979 / www.kingmananimalhospital.com
Manzanita Animal Hospital, 2323 E. Detroit Ave. / 928-753-6138
Stockton Hill Animal Hospital, 4335 Stockton Hill Rd. / 928-757-7979 / www.stocktonhillah.com

SPORTING GOODS

Big 5 Sporting Goods, 3320 N Stockton Hill Rd # F /928- 692-4944 / www.big5sportinggoods.com
Wal-Mart, 3320 Stockton Hill Rd. / 928-692-0555 / www.walmart.com
K-Mart, 3340 E. Andy Devine / 928-757-3202 / www.kmart.com

AUTO REPAIR

Steve's Route 66 Auto Repair, 731 E. Andy Devine Ave. / 928-753-8020
D & S Auto Repair, 941 E. Andy Devine Ave. / (928) 753-6939

AUTO RENTAL

Budget Rent A Car, 3730 Stockton Hill Rd. / 928-692-6555 / www.budget.com
Enterprise Rent A Car, 3505 Stockton Hill Rd / 520-692-9229 / www.enterprise.com

AIR SERVICE

Kingman Airport Authority, Inc., 7000 Flightline Dr. / 928-757-2134 /
www.kingmanairportauthority.com

MEDICAL

Kingman Regional Medical Center, 3269 Stockton Hill Rd. / 928-757-2101 /
www.azkrmc.com

FOR MORE INFORMATION

Kingman Area Chamber of Commerce
PO Box 1150 / 333 W. Andy Devine
Kingman, AZ 86402
928-753-6106 / Fax 928-753-6867
www.kingmanchamber.org

PRESCOTT
Elevation – 5,410 ft. • Population – 33,938

Prescott is one of Arizona's more rapidly growing cities. It is a popular retirement and recreational area. Prescott is a fair-sized city that offers traveling bird hunters a wide range of amenities. Located in the Prescott National Forest, the area is predominantly public land and open to hunting. Gambel's quail are plentiful during good years. Mourning dove and migrating waterfowl are present on available water. Turkeys and band-tailed pigeons are available at higher elevations.

CAMPGROUNDS AND RV PARKS

Willow Lake RV & Camping Park (Burt Kruglick),1617 Heritage Park Road, / 199 Sites / 928-445-6311
Point of Rocks Campground (Charles Horsley),3025 North Highway 89 / 92 Sites / 928-445-9018 / www.pointofrockscampground.com

ACCOMMODATIONS

Motel 6, 1111 E. Sheldon St. / Dogs allowed / 928-776-1666 / $-$$ / www.motel6.com
Super 8 Motel, 1105 E. Sheldon St. / Dogs allowed / 800-800-8000 / $$ / www.super8.com

Best Western Prescottonian Motel, 1317 E. Gurley St. / Dogs allowed / 800-367-2966 / $$-$$$ / www.bestwesternarizona.com

RESTAURANTS

Schlotzsky's Deli, 1385 Iron Springs Rd., #B1 / 928-771-8008
Dog House Restaurant, 126 S. Montezuma St. / 928-445-7962
Dry Gulch Steakhouse, 1630 Adams St. / 928-778-9693 / www.drygulchsteakhouse.com
El Charro Restaurant, 120 N. Montezuma St. / 928-445-7130 / www.elcharro-restaurant.com
Peacock Room Hassayampa Inn, 122 E. Gurley St. / 928-778-9434 / www.hassayampainn.com

VETERINARIANS

Animal Care Clinic of Prescott, 803 E. Sheldon / 928-445-5442
Mile Hi Animal Hospital, 1205 White Spar Rd. / 928-445-4581 / www.milehianimal.com
Prescott Animal Hospital, 1318 Iron Springs Rd. / 928-445-2190 / www.prescottvets.com
Thumb Butte Animal Hospital, 1441 W. Gurley St. / 928-445-2331 / www.vcathumbbutte.com

SPORTING GOODS

High Country Guns & Knives, 555 White Spar Rd. / 928-445-7704
American Gun Shop, 122 Grove Ave. / 928-776-1873
Davidson's Gallery of Guns, 6100 Wilkinson Drive / 928-776-8055
Classic Barrel and Gunworks, 339 Grove Avenue / 928-772-4060 /
  www.cutrifle.com

AUTO REPAIR

A & W Automotive, 4749 N Verde Vista Dr, Prescott Valley / 928-775-0582
Auto Max, 221 W. Willis St. / 928-445-4740
Napa Auto Parts, 533 Madison Ave. / 928-445-2240 / www.napaonline.com

AUTO RENTAL

Budget Rent A Car, 1031 Commerce Dr. / 928-778-3806 / www.budget.com
Enterprise Rent A Car, 1500 E State Route 69 / 928-778-6506 / www.enterprise.com

AIR SERVICE

Airport Manager, 6500 MacCurdy Dr. / 928-776-6338
Airport Operations, 928-445-7860

MEDICAL

Yavapai Regional Medical Center, 1003 Willow Creek Road / 928-445-2700 /
  www.yrmc.com
Brookhaven Medical Center, 864 Dougherty Street / 928-445-2744

FOR MORE INFORMATION

Prescott Chamber of Commerce
  117 W. Goodwin Street
  Prescott, AZ 86303
  928-445-2000
  www.prescott.org

WILLIAMS
Elevation – 6,750 ft. • Population – 10,745

Williams, located west of Flagstaff on Interstate 40, is a tourist-oriented community with ample accommodations for traveling bird hunters. Turkey and band-tailed pigeons are found in the surrounding national forest lands. Migrating mourning doves and waterfowl occasionally frequent the area's small lakes and many stock tanks.

CAMPGROUNDS AND RV PARKS

Grand Canyon KOA (Alan Spicer), North Arizona Highway 64 / 10 sites / 520-635-2307 / www.koa.com

Circle Pines KOA (Al Barany), 1000 Circle Pines / 120 Sites / 520-635-4545 / www.koa.com

ACCOMMODATIONS

Highlander Motel, 533 W. Bill Williams Ave. / Dogs allowed / 520-635-2541 / $-$$ / www.highlander-motel.com

Ramada Limited, 710 W. Bill Williams Ave / Dogs allowed / 800-272-6232 / $-$$$ / www.ramada.com

Budget Host Inn, 620 Bill Williams Ave. / Dogs allowed / 520-635-4415 / $-$$$ / www.budgethost.com

RESTAURANTS

Denny's Restaurant, 2550 W. Bill Williams Ave. / 520-635-2052 / www.dennys.com

Miss Kitty's Steak House, 642 E. Bill Williams Ave. / 520-635-9161

Pancho McGillicuddy's Mexican, 140 Railroad Ave. / 520-635-4150

Pronto Pizza, 106 S. 3rd St. / 520-635-4157

SPORTING GOODS

Sportway Supplies, 400 W. Route 66/ 928-635-4571

Tom Quinn Firearms Dealer, 103 N. Grand Canyon Blvd. / 928-635-0763

AUTO REPAIR

Canyon Gateway Mobil, 711 N. Grand Canyon Blvd. / 520-635-2623

Sandoval's Auto Repair, 999 N Grand Canyon Blvd / 928-635-1934

Malone's Automotive, 808 E Route 66 / 928-635-2934

AIR SERVICE

Williams Airport, 5100 N. Airport Rd. / 520-635-4937 / www.valleaiport.com

MEDICAL

Williams Health Care Center, 301 S. 7th St. / 520-635-4441

*Randy Babb and Ken Crawford with a morning's worth of band-tailed pigeons.
(Randall D. Babb, Arizona Game and Fish Department.)*

FOR MORE INFORMATION

Williams Chamber of Commerce
200 W. Railroad Avenue
Williams, AZ 86046
520-635-1418 / Fax 520-635-1417
www.williamschamber.com

REGION 4

REGION 4
Southwest Arizona

Located in Arizona's southwest quarter, much of Region 4's land lies along the southern stretches of the Colorado River near sea level. The desert itself is predominantly creosote bush with grasslands beginning in the region's eastern areas. Heavy cover is found along the river and irrigation channels, where Gambel's quail populations will be found. Major cities are Yuma and Lake Havasu City.

The Colorado River's lower elevations are a destination spot for traveling nonresident early season dove hunters, and both mourning and white-winged doves can be present in truly impressive numbers. Gambel's quail are also present, but typically coveys are jumped at the edge of inpenetrable riparian cover and provide marginal shooting. In the creosote flats away from water, Gambel's quail run from an approaching gun. A major flyway exists for waterfowl migrating south into the Colorado River delta in Mexico.

UPLAND BIRDS
Gambel's Quail, Mourning Dove, White-winged Dove,
Sandhill Crane (not legal game in this area)

WATERFOWL
Ducks & Geese

COUNTY STATISTICS FOR REGION 4

County	Population	Area (sq.mi.)	Max. Jan. Temp.	Annual Precip.	Percent Public Land	Percent Reservation
La Paz County	13,844	4,430	69.9°	4.50"	87%	9%
Maricopa County	2,122,101	9,155	70.8°	4.95"	64%	5%
Pima County	666,880	9,240	69.5°	11.63"	45%	42%
Yavapai County	107,714	8,091	55.9°	3.21"	91%	—
Yuma County	106,895	5,561	72.6°	3.21"	91%	—

Region 4: Southwest

Arizona Hub Cities

BUCKEYE

Elevation – 888 ft. • Population – 29,615

Buckeye is found near the confluence of the Hassayampa and Gila Rivers. It is located off of Interstate 10, west of the Phoenix metropolitan area. The town offers a moderate level of services. According to Forbes Magazine in 2007, Buckeye is the second-fastest growing town in America.

The agricultural fields and river channel attract good numbers of both mourning and white-winged dove, and waterfowl in season. The surrounding desert hills can hold good numbers of Gambel's quail.

ACCOMMODATIONS

Comfort Inn, Goodyear / No dogs allowed / 602-932-9191 / Dogs allowed / $-$$ / www.comfortinn.com

The Ranch House Motel & Apartments, 1009 E. Monroe Ave. / No dogs allowed / 623-386-4207 / $

Days Inn, 25205 W. Yuma Road, dogs allowed,fee / 623-386-5400

RESTAURANTS

Flat Tortilla Restaurant, 301 E. Monroe Ave. / 623-386-6227

La Placita Cafe, 424 E. Monroe Ave. / 623-386-4632

Wild West Cowboy Steakhouse, 104 E. Monroe Ave. / 623-386-1400

VETERINARIANS

Animal Health Services/Buckeye Animal Clinic, 24090 W US Highway 85 / 623-386-2532/ www.buckeyevetservices.com

SPORTING GOODS

Wal-mart, 23701 W. Southern / 623-386-3319 / www.walmart.com

Modern Call Products, 22511 W Hilton Ave / 623-386-3187 / www.moderncallproducts.com

AIR SERVICE

Buckeye Municipal Airport, 3000 S. Palo Verde Rd., #7 / 623-386-3353

MEDICAL

Buckeye Medical Center, 213 E. Monroe / 623-386-9111

FOR MORE INFORMATION

Buckeye Valley Chamber of Commerce
PO Box 717 / 508 E. Monroe Street
Buckeye, AZ 85326
623-386-2727 / Fax 623-386-7527
www.buckeyevalleychamber.org

EHRENBERG
Elevation – 250 ft. • Population – 1,357

Located along the Colorado River, Ehrenberg/Blythe is sandwiched between the Colorado River Indian Reservation to the north, and Cibola National Wildlife Refuge to the south. Ehrenberg/Blythe are popular traveler's stops along the much-traveled Interstate 10, and as such, have a full range of services.

Principal shooting is for mourning and white-winged dove during the early season. Gambel's quail are present. Waterfowl hunting is available along the Colorado River and other available water.

ACCOMMODATIONS

Best Western Desert Oasis, S Frontage roadcampgrounds / Dogs allowed / 928-923-9711 / $$ / www.bestwesternarizona.com

RESTAURANTS

Cookery Restaurant and Buffett, 14380 S Frontage Rd / 928-923-9600
Charlies's Chuckhouse, 49424 Post & Parker Rd / 928-923-7730
Wendy's, 14320 Flying J Rd / 928-923-8911

GILA BEND
Elevation – 737 ft. • Population – 1,980

Gila Bend is so named because it was founded on a bend in the Gila River. Painted Rocks Dam was built and can back up a huge section of water during rainy years. Much of the Gila's drainage water flows from agricultural fields, and as a result, Painted Rocks Reservoir is contaminated with high levels of pesticides. Fish from its waters are not considered safe table fare. The shallow reservoir basin is a magnet for waterfowl, and hunting there can be excellent. Gila Bend is geared to service traveler's on Highway 8. The town offers a full range of services.

Gambel's quail and both mourning and white-winged dove hunting is excellent during good years.

CAMPGROUNDS AND RV PARKS

Wheel Inn RV Park (Roger Simon), 606 West Williams / 44 Sites / 928-683-2951

ACCOMMODATIONS

Best Western Space Age Lodge, 401 E. Pima / Dogs allowed / 800- 528-1234 or 928-683-2273 / $$-$$$ / www.bestwesternarizona.com
Yucca Motel, 836 E. Pima / Dogs allowed / 928-683-2211
Super 8 Motel, 2888 Butterfield Trail, PO Box 943 / No dogs allowed / 928-683-6311 / $$ / www.super8.com

RESTAURANTS

Little Italy Pizza, 502 E. Pima St. / 928-683-2221 / littleitaliapizza.com
Sofia's Mexican Food, 616 W. Pima / 928-683-6382
Space Age Restaurant, 401 E. Pima St. / 928-683-2761

AIR SERVICE

Gila Bend Municipal Airport, Hwy 85 / 928-683-2733

FOR MORE INFORMATION

Gila Bend Chamber of Commerce
PO Box CC
Gila Bend, AZ 85337
928-683-2002
www.gilabendaz.org

LAKE HAVASU CITY
Elevation – 500 ft. • Population – 56,355

Lake Havasu City is a resort oasis on the Colorado River, a popular retirement community that flourishes in one of the places with the highest recorded temperatures in the United States. A full range of services and amenities are available. The city is founded on the shores of Lake Havasu, which is, in fact, a wide lake on the Colorado River channel. The Fort Mojave Indian Reservation and the Topock Marsh unit of the Havasu National Wildlife Refuge are found to the north, and the Colorado River Indian Reservation is found to the south. All three sites provide superior hunting opportunities for mourning and white-winged dove and waterfowl. Gambel's quail are also present.

ACCOMMODATIONS

Super 8 Motel, 305 London Bridge Rd. / Dogs allowed / 800-800-8000 / $-$$ / www.super8motel.com
Days Inn 1700 McCulloch Bld N/dogs allowed/928-855-7841 $-$$
Island Inn Hotel, 1300 W. McCulloch Blvd. / Dogs allowed / 928-680-0606 / $$$

RESTAURANTS

BarleyBrothers Brewery, 1425 N. McMulloch Blvd / 928-505-7837
BBQ Bill's Big Easy, 3557 Maricopa Ave/928-680-1100 / www.bbqbillsbigeasybistro.com

Troy Hawks cools down his GSP, Pepper, after a morning hunt.

Char-Bones Steakhouse & Tapas Bar, 112 London Bridge Rd./928-854-5554 /
www.charbones.com
Angelina's Italian Kitchen, 1530 El Camino Way / 928-680-3868
Casa Serrano, 150 Swanson Ave. / 928-854-5500 / www.serranoent.com

VETERINARIANS

Animal Hospital of Havasu, 1990 Mesquite Ave. / 928-855-8122 /
www.animalhospitalofhavasu.com
Animal Medical Center, 2761 Paseo Dorado / 928-855-4540

SPORTING GOODS

Big 5 Sporting Goods 251 S. Lake Havasu Ave/928-854-2770
Wal-mart, 1795 Kiowa Ave. / 928-453-8515 / www.walmart.com
Southwest Firearms, 2148 McCulloch Blvd. N. #101 / 928-453-4867
Sam's Shooters Emporium, 2183 Mcculloch Blvd N. # 101 / 928-680-7000 /
www.samsguns.com
Pima Gun Works, 4063 Little Finger Rd. / 928-855-4213

AUTO REPAIR

Joe's Service Center, 561 N. Lake Havasu Ave. / 928-855-5823 /
www.joesautorvtruck.com
Lakeside Tire and Auto Service, 1891 Industrial Blvd. / 928-855-4969

Auto Rental

Avis Rent A Car, 5600 N. State Route 95 / 928-764-3001 / www.avis.com
Budget Rent A Car, 1690 Industrial Blvd. / 928-453-3361 / www.budget.com

Air Service

Lake Havasu City Municipal Airport, 5600 N. State Route 95 / 928-764-3330

Medical

Havasu Regional Medical Center, 101 Civic Center Ln. / 928-855-8185

For More Information

Lake Havasu City Chamber of Commerce
1930 Mesquite Ave., Ste 3
Lake Havasu City, AZ 86403
928-855-4115 / Fax 928-680-0010
www.havasuchamber.com

PARKER

Elevation – 420 ft. • Population – 3,140

Parker is found at the extreme northern edge of the Colorado River Indian Reservation. A full range of services and amenities are available. It makes a popular home base for those wishing to hunt the Colorado River Indian Reservation. Gamebirds available include mourning and white-winged dove, Gambel's quail, and waterfowl.

Accommodations

Best Western Parker Inn, 1012 Geronimo Avenue / 928-669-6060 /
   www.bestwesternarizona.com
Stardust Motel, 700 California Ave. / Dogs allowed / 928-669-2278 / $$

Restaurants

Blimpie's Subs & Salads, 212 W. Riverside Dr. / 928-669-5595 / www.blimpies.com
Road Runner Dock Bar & Grill, 7000 Riverside Dr. 928-667-4252
El Sarape Restaurant, 621 W. Riverside Dr. / 928-669-0110
Blue Water Resort and Casino, 11300 Resort Drive / 888-243-3360 /
   www.bluewaterfun.com

Veterinarians

Colorado River Animal Hospital, 8972 Riverside Dr. / 928-667-3341

Auto Repair

Crit Auto Shop, 2nd Avenue and Mohave / 928-669-1376
Above All Automotive Repair, 1500 S Geronimo Ave / (928) 669-8900

AUTO RENTAL

Parker Motor, 920 Arizona Ave. / 928-669-2291 / www.parkermotor.net

AIR SERVICE

Crit Air Avi Suquilla, 26600 Mohave Rd. / 928-669-2168

MEDICAL

Parker Community Hospital, 1200 W. Mohave Rd./ 928-669-9201

FOR MORE INFORMATION

Parker Area Chamber of Commerce
1217 California Avenue
Parker, AZ 85344
520-669-2174 / Fax 520-669-6304
www.parkerareachamberofcommerce.com

QUARTZSITE
Elevation – 870 ft. • Population – 3,397

Quartzsite is located on Interstate 10, to the east of Ehrenberg, AZ. The town has few permanent residents but swells into a small city with the influx of retirees in motor homes and travel trailers during the winter. There are open air, swap meet style vendors of rockhounding paraphernalia, minerals, fossils, and the like. Quartzsite is surrounded by BLM land. Game birds available would be Gambel's quail, white-winged dove and mourning dove. Concentrations of birds would be located to the west, along the Colorado River.

CAMPGROUNDS AND RV PARKS

Rose RV Park, 600 E. Kuehn St./405-306-2309 / full hook ups, pet friendly

ACCOMMODATIONS

Super 8 Motel, 2050 Dome Rock Road / No dogs allowed / 928-927-9233 / www.super8.com
Stagecoach Motel, 904 W Main St / 928-927-8161
Quartzite Yacht Club Motel, 1090 W Main, / 928-927-5628

RESTAURANTS

Sweet Darlene's, 776 E. Main / 928-927-9338
Silly Al's Pizza, 175 W. Main / 928-927-5585
Palo Verde Cafe, 305 N. Central Blvd. / 928-927-7676

VETERINARIANS

Quartzite Animal Clinic, 745 W. Main / 928-927-6404

AUTO REPAIR AND RENTAL

Kar Kare, 928-927-5273
Best Auto RV and Truck Repair, 585 N Central / 928-927-8787
Everett's Towing and Repair, 77 Plymouth Ave / 928-927-6101

MEDICAL

La Paz Medical Services, 150 E Tyson St / 928-927-8747 / www.lapazhospital.org
Palo Verde Hospital, 928-927-4115 / www.paloverdehospital.org

FOR MORE INFORMATION

Quartzsite Chamber of Commerce
PO Box 85, Hwy 95
Palm Plaza, Quartzsite, AZ 85346
928-927-5600
www.quartzsitetourism.us

WICKENBURG

Elevation – 2,070 ft. • Population – 5,082

Wickenburg is located northwest of Phoenix. It's a medium-sized town with a Western flair and provides ample services and amenities. The land surrounding Wickenburg is a mix of BLM and state trust lands. The cover is true Sonoran desert with a mix of cholla, saguaro, and ocotillo. Gambel's quail are present in good numbers during good years. Mourning dove, white-winged dove, and waterfowl are present on available water.

ACCOMMODATIONS

Best Western Rancho Grande Motor Hotel, 293 E. Wickenburg Way / Dogs
allowed / 800- 528-1234 / $$-$$$ / www.bestwesternarizona.com
Westerner Motel, 680 West Wickenburg Way / Dogs allowed / 928-684-2493 / $$

RESTAURANTS

Rancho 7 Restaurant and Lounge, 111 E Wickenburg Way / 928-684-2492
House Berlin, 169 E. Wickeburg Way, 928-684-5044
Golden Nugget Restaurant, 222 E. Wickenburg Way / 928-684-0648

VETERINARIANS

Bar S Animal Clinic, 3920 Industrial / 928-684-7846
Wickenburg Veterinary Clinic, 1127 W. Wickenburg Way / 928-684-7866

SPORTING GOODS

Gun Trader, 36 E. Yavapai St. / 928-684-2149

A pair of English setter Gambel's specialists, Rose and Emma, trap a running Gambel's covey by pointing from two sides.

AUTO REPAIR
Jones Auto Center, 781 W. Wickenburg Way / (928) 684-5481 /
www.jonesautocenters.net
Agnew Automotive, 885 W. Wickenburg Way / (928) 684-5042

FOR MORE INFORMATION
Wickenburg Chamber of Commerce
PO Drawer CC, 216 N. Frontier Street
Wickenburg, AZ 85358
928-684-5479 / Fax 928-684-5470
www.wickenburgchamber.com

YUMA
Elevation – 138 ft. • Population – 77,515

Yuma, a large city in Arizona's extreme southwest corner, is an agricultural center. The city itself provides ample services and amenities for traveling bird hunters. The Cocopah Indian Reservation is located to the south, and the Fort Yuma Indian Reservation to the north. This area is the location of one of the last good, early season white-winged dove shoots in Arizona. Nonresident hunters traveling from California and Nevada headquarter in Yuma and travel north and south to hunt on the Indian reservations. Gambel's quail are also present. Waterfowl migrate through the area on their way into Mexico.

ACCOMMODATIONS

Motel 6, 1640 Arizona Ave. / Dogs allowed / 928-782-6561 / $ / www.motel6.com
Best Western Coronado, 233 4th Ave. / Dogs allowed / 800- 528-1234 / $-$$$ / www.bestwesternarizona.com
Holiday Inn Express, 3181 S. 4th Ave. at 32nd St. / Dogs allowed / 928-344-1420 / $$-$$$ / www.hiexpress.com

CAMPGROUNDS AND RV PARKS

Rollie's Lynda Vista RV Park (Robert Rolle), 2900 West Fifth Street / 65 sites / 928-782-9009
Arizona Sands RV Park, 5510 E. 32nd St. / 928-726-0160 / www.arizonasandsrvpark.com

RESTAURANTS

Julianna's Patio Cafe, 1951 W 25th St / 928-317-1961 / www.juliannaspatiocafe.com
Crossing Restaurant, 2690 S. 4th Ave. / 928-726-5551
Hungry Hunter Steakhouse, 2355 S. 4th Ave. / 928-782-3637
Rocky's NY Style Pizza & Restaurant, 2601 S. 4th Ave. / 928-344-4260

VETERINARIANS

Chaparral Veterinary Clinic, 1963 Arizona Ave. / 928-782-9219
Desert Veterinary Clinic, 1195 S. 5th Ave. / 928-783-5010 / www.desertvet.com
Foothills Animal Hospital, 11769 S. Frontage Rd. / 928-342-0448 / www.foothillsanimalhospital.com
Yuma Veterinary Clinic, 13340 Avenue No. 4-E / 928-344-1956

SPORTING GOODS

Yuma Coin & Gun Shop, 905 S. Orange Ave. / 928-783-9268
Sprague's Sports, 345 W 32nd St. / 928-726-0022 / www.spragues.com

AUTO REPAIR

McCloud Russell Auto Repair, 1495 S 3rd Ave / 928-783-7307 /
www.yumacarcare.com
Campbell's Auto Service, 350 E. 24th St. / 928-782-4424
Purcell's Western States Tire, 1150 S 4th Ave / 928-783-8815
Napa Auto Parts, 3080 S Pacific Ave / 928-341-4688 / www.napaonline.com

AUTO RENTAL

Avis Rent A Car, 3040 S. Pacific Ave. / 928-344-5772 / www.avis.com
Enterprise Rent A Car, 661 E. 32nd St., #A / 928-344-5444 / www.enterprise.com

AIR SERVICE

Yuma International Airport, 928-726-5882 Ext. 160

MEDICAL

Yuma Regional Medical Center, 2400 S. Aven, #A / 928-344-2000 /
www.yumaregional.org

FOR MORE INFORMATION

Yuma County Chamber of Commerce
PO Box 10230 / 377 S. Main Street
Yuma, AZ 85366
928-782-2567 / Fax 928-343-0038
www.yumachamber.org

REGION 5

MARICOPA

GRAHAM

PINAL

Florence • Kearny •
Winkelman •

•Picacho   • Mammoth
    • Oracle • San Manual

• Ajo   • Marana

PIMA   • Tucson   Bowie •
                              • Willcox

                                    COCHISE
                        • Benson
        • Green Valley

                    • Sonoita • Tombstone
        • Tubac   Sierra Vista
              • Patagonia
SANTA CRUZ   • Nogales   • Bisbee Douglas

REGION 5
Southeast Arizona

Region 5, southeastern Arizona, is the center of Arizona's three-season quail hunting. Vast expanses of mesquite-studded grasslands support scaled and Gambel's quail. Mearns' quail are found on the higher elevation, oak-dotted mountain ranges. Both mourning and white-winged dove provide shooting for early season gunners, and mourning doves remain on through the second season. Turkeys are found in some of the larger, higher elevation, sky island mountain ranges, although few are harvested. The Willcox Playa area of the Sulphur Springs Valley, has a limited draw sandhill crane hunt. Migrating waterfowl frequent the many tanks that are spread throughout the region.

UPLAND BIRDS
Gambel's Quail, Scaled Quail, Mearns' Quail, Mourning Dove, White-winged Dove, Band-tailed Pigeon, Merriam's Turkey, Sandhill Crane

WATERFOWL
Ducks & Geese

COUNTY STATISTICS FOR REGION 5

County	Population	Area (sq.mi.)	Max. Jan. Temp.	Annual Precip.	Percent Public Land	Percent Reservation
Cochise County	108,225	6,256	64.5°	16.21″	59%	—
Graham County	26,554	4,618	64.3°	9.53″	56%	36%
Pima County	728,425	9,240	69.5°	11.63″	45%	42%
Pinal County	132,225	5,388	69.1°	5.22″	51%	23%
Santa Cruz County	32,400	1,246	67.2°	20.05″	61%	—

Southeast Arizona Hub Cities

Ajo
Elevation – 1,300 ft. • Population – 3,705

Ajo is a mining community with a long history in southern Arizona. A full service of accommodations and amenities are available. Surrounded on four sides by areas closed to hunting, Ajo sits in a large chunk of BLM land. The vast Tohono O'odham reservation sits to the east, Organ Pipe Cactus National Monument sits to the south, the Cabeza Prieta National Wildlife Refuge sits to the west, and the Barry M. Goldwater Gunnery Range sits to the north. The BLM land around Ajo is classic Sonoran desert and contains Gambel's quail and mourning and white-wing dove.

CAMPGROUNDS AND RV PARKS

Shadow Ridge RV Resort (Dick Jensen), 431 North 2nd Avenue / 78 Sites / 520-387-5055 / www.shadowridge.biz

Ajo Heights RV Park, 2000 N Highway 85 / 520-387-6796 / www.ajorvparks.com

ACCOMMODATIONS

Marine Motel, 1966 2nd Ave. / Dogs allowed / 520-387-7626 / $-$$$ / www.marinemotel.com

Mine Manager's House (Bed & Breakfast), 1 Greenway Dr. / No dogs allowed / 520-387-6505

La Siesta Motel, 2561 N Ajo Gila Bend Hwy / No dogs allowed / 520-387-6569 / www.ajolasiesta.com

RESTAURANTS

Bamboo Village, 1810 N. 2nd Ave. / 520-387-7536

Ranch House Restaurant, 663 N 2nd Ave / 520-387-6226

Gringo Pass Cafe, 175 W Solana Ave / 520-387-3547

Pugsy's Place, 1135 W Hoover St / 520-387-6797

FOR MORE INFORMATION

Ajo District Chamber of Commerce
400 E Taladro Ave
Ajo, AZ 85321
520-387-7742
www.ajochamber.com

BENSON

Elevation – 3,685 ft. • Population – 4,934

Benson, found due east of Tucson on Highway 10, is a thriving community built up aong the banks of the San Pedro River. A full range of services and amenities are provided. Both Gambel's and scaled quail are found in the grass lowlands. Mearns' quail are found in the higher elevation national forest to the south. Both mourning and white-winged dove are available during the September season. Late season mourning dove tend to frequent agricultural fields and available water. Waterfowl migrate through the area and are found on both stock tanks and rivers.

CAMPGROUNDS AND RV PARKS

Chief Four Feathers KOA (William Nutt), 180 West Four Feathers Lane / 94 sites / 520-586-3977

Red Barn Campground, 711 N. Madison / 520-586-2035

ACCOMMODATIONS

River's Edge Sporting Retreat (Norman & Barbara Crawford), HC 1, PO Box 742 / Dogs allowed / 520-212-4868 / $-$$

Best Western Quail Hollow Inn, 699 N Ocotillo Road / Dogs allowed / 520-586-3646 / $-$$ / www.bestwesternarizona.com

RESTAURANTS

Galleano's Restaurant, 601 W. 4th St. / 520-586-3523

Horse Shoe Restaurant, 154 E. 4th St. / 520-586-3303

Ruiz's Family Restaurant, 687 W. 4th St. / 520-586-2707

VETERINARIANS

All Creatures Veterinary Clinic, 655 E. 4th Street / 520-586-3777 / benson-arizona.com/allcreatures/

AUTO REPAIR

Big Dave's Towing and Roadside Service, 688 E. 4th Street / 520-586-4620 / www.bigdavestowing.com

Oakley's Garage, 203 W. 4th St. / 520-586-2251

MEDICAL

Benson Hospital, 450 S. Ocotillo Ave. / 520-586-2261

For More Information

Benson-San Pedro Valley Chamber of Commerce
249 E 4th St
Benson, AZ 85602
520-586-2842 / Fax 520-586-7477
www.bensonchamberaz.com

Bisbee

Elevation – 5,350 ft. • Population – 6,177

Bisbee is an historical visit into Arizona's Victorian past. Once the seat of Arizona's government, Bisbee's pre-eminence has eclipsed, but the former trappings of the state's mineral wealth are still present. Bisbee is a popular tourist destination and offers a full range of services, amenities and antique shopping.

All three species of quail (Gambel's, scaled, and Mearns') are found in close proximity. Dove species found include both mourning and white-winged dove.

Waterfowl hunting can be productive on the ample stock tanks that dot the area.

Accommodations

Jonquil Motel, P.O. Box 1658 / 317 Tombstone Canyon / Dogs allowed / 520-432-7371 / $ / www.thejonquil.com
The Bisbee Grand Hotel, 61 Main St. / 520-432-5900/ www.brisbeegrandhotel.net

Restaurants

Cafe Roka, 35 Main St. / 520-432-5153 / www.caferoka.com
Old Tymers Restaurant, 202 Tombstone Cyn / 520-432-7304

Veterinarians

Cochise Animal Hospital, 1993 S Barnett Rd / 520-432-3296

Auto Repair

Gila Auto Parts, 200 Bisbee Rd. / 520-432-5363
Warren Service Center, 215 Arizona St. / 520-432-5107

Air Service

Bisbee Airport / 520-432-6030

Medical

Chiricahua Community Health Center, 108 Arizona St, Bisbee / 520-432-3309 / www.cchci.org
Copper Queen Community Hospital, 101 Cole Ave / 520-432-5383 / www.cqch.org

Don Prentice holds a lesser sandhill crane.

FOR MORE INFORMATION

Bisbee Chamber of Commerce
  1 Main St.
  Bisbee, Arizona 85603
  520-432-7684, Fax 520-432-2597
  www.cqch.org

BOWIE
Elevation – 3,750 ft. • Population – 660

While not necessarily a hub of commerce, Bowie is a hub of southern Arizona's quail hunting. Principal quail species are Gambel's and scaled. Mearns' quail are found in the mountain ranges to the south. Mourning dove and some whitewing provide shooting for area dove hunters. Migrating waterfowl use the area's many stock tanks.

STORES
Store-n-More, 1275 Business Loop Ext 366 / 520-847-2288

FOR MORE INFORMATION
Bowie Chamber of Commerce
PO Box 286
Bowie, AZ 85605

DOUGLAS
Elevation – 4,020 ft. • Population – 14,312

Douglas is a border city in the extreme southeast corner of Arizona. The city reflects the influences of its intimate contact with Old Mexico. The city had a ringside seat during the Mexican Revolution, and the old buildings are still ripe with history. The beautiful old Victorian homes that line the broad boulevards reflect the time's affluence. The Gadsden Hotel has played host to every governor in Arizona's history.

Surrounding areas can support good numbers of both scaled and Gambel's quail in good years. Mearns' quail are found at higher elevations in the surrounding mountain ranges. Dove species include both mourning and white-winged dove. Waterfowl are found throughout the area on available water.

ACCOMMODATIONS
Motel 6, 111 16th St. / Dogs allowed / 520-364-2457 / $
Travelers Motel, 1030 E 19th St / 520-364-8434

RESTAURANTS
Church's Chicken, 94 W 5th St / (520) 364-1449
Chatita's Mexican Restaurant, 301 E 10th St / 520-364-1144
La Fogata, 1008 Cochise Ave. / 520-364-7355

SPORTING GOODS
Kmart, 50 W. 16th St. / 520-364-7596 / www.kmart.com
Wal-mart, 204 W. 5th St. / 520-364-1279 / www.walmart.com
Ortega's Sportsworld, 1017 N G Ave / 520-364-5721

VETERINARIANS
High Desert Veterinary Services, 2555 E. 9th St. / 520-364-3268

AUTO REPAIR
Fuentes Auto Repair, 559 E 9th St / 520-364-2682

AIR SERVICE
Douglas Bisbee International Airport, 6940 N Air Terminal Blvd / 520-364-2771

MEDICAL
Southeast Arizona Medical Center, 2174 W Oak Ave / 520-364-7931 /
www.samcdouglas.org

FOR MORE INFORMATION
Douglas Chamber of Commerce
345 E 16th St
Douglas, AZ 85607
520-364-2477 / Fax 520-364-6403
www.douglasaz.gov

FLORENCE
Elevation – 1,500 ft. • Population – 17,054

Florence has figured prominently in Arizona state history. Once a center of government and currently the seat of Pinal County government, the town's main strip has a host of historical buildings. The area economy is built on agriculture and the Arizona State Prison at Florence. The city hosts a good number of services and amenities for the traveling bird hunter. Due to the area's popularity as an early season dove hunting area, interested hunters should book accommodations well in advance.

Mourning and white-winged dove are found in good numbers. The desert areas south and east of Florence are very productive Gambel's quail habitat. Jump-shooting waterfowl is a popular pastime on the area's many stock tanks.

ACCOMMODATIONS
Inn at Rancho Sonora, 9198 North Hwy 79 / No dogs allowed / 520-868-8000 /
$$ / www.ranchosonora.com
Blue Mist Motel, 40 S Pinal Pkwy / No dogs allowed / 520-868-5875 / $-$$ /
www.bluemistmotel.com

RESTAURANTS
A & M Pizza, 445 W. Hwy 287 / 520-868-0170
Old Pueblo Restaurant, 505 Main St. / 520-868-4784
A Taste of Italy, Highway 287 / 520-868-3440

VETERINARIANS
Coolidge Veterinary Hospital 435 W.Coolidge/520-723-5500

Auto Repair

Florence Automotive, 625 S. Main / 520-868-3911
Big O Tires, 801 N Highway 79 / (520) 868-0800 / www.bigotires.com

Medical

Florence Clinic, 150 S Main St / 520-868-5811

For More Information

Greater Florence Chamber of Commerce
PO Box 929 / 291 N. Bailey Street
Florence, AZ
520-868-9433
www.florenceaz.org

Kearny

Elevation – 2,020 ft. • Population – 2,765

Kearny is located on Highway 77 between Superior and Winkelman. Kearny is a mining community built on the north bank of the Gila River. Services and amenities are at a minimum. The predominant game bird in the area is Gambel's quail. Dove species include both mourning and whitewing. Waterfowl hunting can be productive along the Gila River and area stock tanks.

Accommodations

General Kearny Inn, 301 Alden Rd / Dogs allowed / 520-363-5505 /
www.generalkearneyinn.com

Restaurants

Buzzy's Drive In, 111 Tilbury Dr. / 520-363-7371
General Kearny Inn, 301 Alden Rd / 520-363-5505
Old Time Pizza, 370 Alden Rd / 520-363-5523

Veterinarians

Kearny Veterinary Clinic, 396 Alden Rd /520-363-9630

Medical

Community Medical Complex, 300 Alden Rd. / 520-363-5573

For More Information

Copper Basin Chamber of Commerce
PO Box 206 / 355 Alden Road
Kearny, AZ 85237
520-363-7607 / Fax 520-363-7527
www.copperbasinaz.com

Dr. John Sherman moves in to flush a Mearns' quail pointed by Musette.

NOGALES
Elevation – 3,865 ft. • Population – 20,878

Nogales is closely tied to its twin city, Nogales, Sonora, directly across the border. It is a commercial center for international trade and import/export concerns. There are ample services and accommodations. The country around Nogales is typical Mearns' quail habitat—rolling hills sprinkled with oak trees. Some pockets of Gambel's quail are found along the Santa Cruz Valley. Both mourning and white-winged dove are present on available water. The national forest land around Nogales can be very productive for jump-shooting waterfowl on stock tanks.

ACCOMMODATIONS

Motel 6, 141 W. Mariposa Rd. / Dogs allowed / 520-281-2951 / $
Super 8 Motel, 547 Mariposa Rd / Dogs allowed / 800-800-8000 / $-$$
Time Motel, 921 N. Grand Ave. / Dogs allowed / 800-528-1234

RESTAURANTS

El Zarape, 694 N. Grand Ave. / 520-287-3920
Las Vigas Steak Ranch, 180 W. Loma St. / 520-287-6641

Peter Piper Pizza, 466 N Grand Court Plz / 520-287-6511
La Cabana, 840 N Grand Ave / 520-287-8208

VETERINARIANS

Nogales Veterinary Clinic, 1660 Tucson/Nogales Hwy / 520-287-2888
Companion Veterinary Clinic, 762 N Morley Ave / 520-281-0900

SPORTING GOODS

Kmart, 300 W. Mariposa Rd. / 520-761-4844 / www.kmart.com
Wal-mart, 351 W. Mariposa Rd. / 520-281-2594 / www.walmart.com
Nogales Ammunition, 1152 N Hohokam Dr # 1 / 520-287-5635

AUTO REPAIR

Pep Boys, 470 N Grand Court Plz / 520-287-3626 / www.pepboys.com
Cropper's Auto Center, 1831 N Grand Ave / 520-281-2438 / www.croppercars.com

AUTO RENTALS

Enterprise Rent A Car, 1831 N. Grand Ave. / 520-281-0425 / www.enterprise.com
Hertz Rent A Car, 1012 N. Grand Ave. / 520-287-2012 / www.hertz.com

MEDICAL

Holy Cross Hospital, 1171 W Target Range Rd / 520-285-3000 / www.carondelet.org

FOR MORE INFORMATION

Nogales/Santa Cruz County Chamber of Commerce
123 W. Kino Park Place
Nogales, AZ 85621
520-287-3685 / Fax 520-287-3688
www.thenogaleschamber.com

ORACLE
Elevation – 4,350 ft. • Population – 3,043

Oracle is a small, eclectic mining community with a unique mix of cowboys, miners, writers, artists, and others. Services and accommodations are minimal. Oracle sits on the northern edge of the Catalina Mountain range and overlooks a vast expanse of Sonoran desert grasslands that spread to the north. The predominant game bird species in the area are Gambel's quail, interspersed with small populations of scaled quail. Both mourning and white-winged doves frequent the area. Migrating waterfowl use the many water tanks as loafing areas on their migration south.

Accommodations

Cherry Valley Ranch B & B, 2505 E Mount Lemmon Hwy / 520-896-9639
Triangle L Ranch B & B Retreat, 2805 N. Triangle L Ranch Rd. / No dogs allowed /
    520-896-2804 / $$$
Chalet Village Motel, 1245 W. American Ave. / No dogs allowed / 520-896-9171 /
    $-$$

Restaurants

De Marco's Pizzeria and Italian, 1885 W American Ave / 520-896-9627
Casa Rivera's Taco Express, 1975 W American Ave / 520-896-3747
Oracle Inn and Steakhouse, 305 E American Ave / 520-896-3333

Auto Repair

Precision Tune-up Car and Truck, 300 E. American Ave. / 520-896-2721
Oracle Auto Repair, 1535 W. American Ave. / 520-896-9110

Medical

University Medical Center, 265 W Ina E / 520-694-8170 / umcmedical.org

For More Information

SMOR Tri-Community Chamber of Commerce
    PO Box 1886
    Oracle, AZ 85623
    520-896-9322 / Fax 520-385-4846
    www.smorchamber.org

Patagonia
Elevation – 4,044 ft. • Population – 940

Patagonia, long considered the center of Mearns' quail hunting in Arizona, is a picturesque town nestled in the surrounding rolling hills and oak trees. Accommodations are at a minimum but have historically served Mearns' hunters well. Breakfast at the Stage Stop Inn Hotel is a Mearns' hunter's rite of passage. The predominant game bird species in the area is the Mearns' quail. Both Gambel's and scaled quail are seen at lower elevations. Mourning and white-winged dove are present, as well as migrating waterfowl. Both frequent the area's many stock tanks.

Accommodations

Stage Stop Inn, PO Box 777, Patagonia, AZ 85624 / Dogs allowed / 520-394-2211
    / $$-$$$

A point and back in prime scaled quail habitat.

RESTAURANTS

Velvet Elvis Pizza Company, 292 Naugle Avenue / 520-394-2102 /
www.velvetelvispizza.com

Gathering Grounds Deli, 319 McKeown Ave. / 520-394-2097 /
www.mygatheringgrounds.com

Home Plate, 303 McKeown Ave. / 520-394-2344

Wagon Wheel Saloon and Restaurant, 400 W Naugle Ave. / 520-394-2433

SIERRA VISTA
Elevation – 4,636 ft. • Population – 36,855

Sierra Vista sits on the north end of the Huachuca Mountains and provides a support community for Fort Huachuca Military Reservation. The amount of available services and accommodations for a traveling bird hunter are extensive. Both Gambel's and scaled quail can be found in the adjoining Sulphur Spring Valley's extensive bottom grasslands and brush-choked hillsides. Mearns' quail are found at higher elevations on forest service land. Both mourning and white-wing dove are present. Waterfowl hunting can be very productive on the area's many small water tanks.

Accommodations

Motel 6, 1551 E. Fry Blvd / Dogs allowed / 520-459-5035 / $ / www.motel6.com
Ramada Inn, 2047 S. Hwy 92 / Dogs allowed / 520-459-5900 / $$-$$$ /
www.ramada.com
Super 8 Motel, 100 FAB Ave / Dogs allowed / 800-800-8000 / $-$$ /
www.super8.com

Restaurants

Outback Steakhouse, 99 S. Hwy 92 /520-458-1313
Daisy Mae's Stronghold, 332 N. Garden Ave/ 520-452-8099

Veterinarians

Coronado Veterinary Clinic, 4181 E. Glenn Rd. / 520-378-0911
Apache Animal Center, 2145 S State Highway 92 / 520-458-0930 /
www.vcaapache.com
Sierra Animal Hospital, 900 S. Highway 92 / 520-458-8656 /
www.sierraanimalhospital.com

Sporting Goods

Big 5 Sporting Goods, 135 S Highway 92 # C / 520-459-1801 /
www.big5sportinggoods.com
Wal-mart, 657 S. State Highway / 520-458-9690 / www.walmart.com
Trail Boss Outfitters, 124 W Fry Blvd / 520-515-0048

Auto Repair

Midas Auto Service, 1317 E Fry Blvd / 520-459-3090 / www.midas.com
Brake Masters, 1750 E. Fry Blvd. / 520-458-4000
Monty's Motors Auto Repair, 601 E Fry Blvd / 520-458-2061

Auto Rentals

Enterprise, 743 E Fry / 520-458-2425 / www.enterprise.com
Ideal Car Rental, 645 S Highway 92 / 520-458-4441

Air Service

Sierra Vista Municipal Airport, 1224 N. North Ave. / 520-458-5775

Medical

Sierra Vista Community Hospital, 300 S. El Camino Real / 520-458-4641 /
www.svrhc.org

FOR MORE INFORMATION

Sierra Vista Chamber of Commerce
   77 Calle Portal, Suite A-140
   Sierra Vista, AZ 85635
   520-458-6940 / 1-800-288-3861 / Fax 520-452-0878
   www.sierravistachamber.org

TOMBSTONE
Elevation – 4,540 ft. • Population – 1,569

Tombstone is a popular tourist destination and the site of the OK Corral shootout. Tombstone offers a host of amenities, all steeped with a Western flair. Surrounding hillsides and valleys have also played host to both scaled and Gambel's quail shooting. Mearns' quail are found in the higher elevations. Migrating dove and waterfowl frequent the many area water tanks.

ACCOMMODATIONS

Best Western Lookout Lodge, PO Box 787 / Dogs allowed / 800-652 6772 / $$-$$$ / www.bestwesterntombstone.com

RESTAURANTS

Longhorn Restaurant, 501 E. Allen / 520-457-3405
OK Cafe, 220 W Allen St / 520-457-3980
Ranch 22 Bar and Restaurant, 781 N Highway 80 / 520-457-9122 / www.bestwesterntombstone

SPORTING GOODS

Diamond Jim's, 336 E. Allen / 520-457-3227
Lefty's Corner Store, 17 S 4th St / 520-457-3227

FOR MORE INFORMATION

Tombstone Chamber of Commerce
   PO Box 995, 4th & Allen
   Tombstone, AZ 85638
   520-457-9317
   www.tombstone.org

TUCSON
Elevation – 2,410 ft. • Population – 518.956

Tucson is Arizona's second largest metropolitan area and home to the University of Arizona. As such, there are an extensive array of services and accommodations. Surrounding areas provide good areas for Gambel's and scaled quail. Mearns' quail are found on the mountain ranges to the south. The agricultural lands to the west and northwest of Tucson have historically provided fine mourning and white-winged dove shooting. Waterfowl are found on the many stock tanks throughout the area.

CAMPGROUNDS AND RV PARKS

Mission View RV Resort (Don James), 31 West Los Reales / 152 sites / 520-741-1965

Whispering Palms Travel Trailer Park (Ray Bratton), 3445 North Romero Road / 81 sites / 520-888-2500 / www.whisperingpalmsrv.net

ACCOMMODATIONS

Best Western Ghost Ranch Lodge, 801 W. Miracle Mile / Dogs allowed / 800-528-1234 / $-$$$ / www.ghostranchlodge.com

The Lodge on the Desert, 306 North Alvernon Way / Dogs allowed / 520-325-3366 / $$-$$$ / www.lodgeonthedesert.com

Motel 6, 4630 W. Ina Rd. / Dogs allowed / 520-744-9300 / $ / www.motel6.com

Super 8-Central East, 1990 S. Craycroft Rd. / Dogs allowed / 800-800-8000 / $$ / www.super8.com

Windmill Inn at St. Phillip's Plaza, 4250 N. Campbell Ave. / Dogs allowed / 520-577-0007 / $$-$$$ / www.windmillinns.com

RESTAURANTS

Anthony's in the Catalinas, 6440 N. Campbell Ave. / 520-299-1771 / www.anthonyscatalinas.com

Bistro Zin, 1865 E. River Rd / 520-299-7799 / www.foxrc.com

El Carro Cafe, 311 N. Court Ave. / 520-622-1922 / www.elcharrocafe.com

The Grill at Hacienda del Sol, 5601 N. Hacienda del Sol Rd / 520-529-3500 / www.haciendadelsol.com

Fuego Restaurant, 6958 E Tanque Verde Rd / 520-866-1745 / www.fuegorestaurant.com

Jano's, 150 N. Main Ave. / 520-884-9426 / www.janos.com

Acacia at St. Philips, 4340 N. Campbell / 520-232-0101 / www.acaciatucson.com

Jonathan's Cork, 6320 E Tanque Verde Rd / 520-296-1631 / www.jonathanscork.com

Veterinarian

Animal Medical Clinic of Tucson, 3325 N. 1st Ave. / 520-293-5470 (Emergency clinic: nights & weekends) / www.vcaanimalmedicaltucson.com
Plaza Pet Clinic, 2840 W. Ina Rd., Suite# 100 / 520-544-2080

Sporting Goods

Sportsmans Warehouse, 3945 W. Costco Dr. / 520-877-4500 / www.sportsmanswarehouse.com
Big 5 Sporting Goods / www.big5sportinggoods.com
  4901 N. Stone Avenue, 520-292-2778 / 6441 S. Midvale Park Rd, 520-573-4135 / 5695 E. Speedway Blvd, 520-296-3326

Auto Repair

Art's Pit Stop, 5656 E. Speedway Blvd. / 520-745-0388
Desert Refrigeration & Auto Service, Inc., 3675 N. Romero Rd. / 520-887-6961
Precision Tune-up, 2580 N. Oracle Rd. / 520-882-4847

Auto Rentals

Budget Rent A Car, 3085 E. Valencia Rd. / 520-889-8800 / www.budget.com
Enterprise Rent A Car, 1401 W. Valencia Rd. / 520-295-9051 / www.enterprise.com

Air Service

Tucson International Airport / 520-573-8100

Medical

Carondelet St. Joseph's Hospital, 350 N. Wilmot Rd. / 520-296-3211 / www.carondelet.org
Kino Community Hospital, 2800 E. Ajo Way / 520-294-4471 / www.uph.org
Northwest Medical Center, 6200 N. La Cholla Blvd. / 520-742-9000 / www.northwestmedicalcenter.com
University Medical Center, 1501 N. Campbell Ave. / 520-694-0111 / www.umcarizona.org

For More Information

Tucson Metropolitan Chamber of Commerce
  PO Box 991 / 465 W. St. Mary's Rd.
  Tucson, AZ 85702
  520-792-2250 / Fax 520-882-5704
  www.tucsonchamber.org

WILLCOX

Elevation – 4,182 ft. • Population – 3,828

Willcox services a large ranching and farming community in the northern end of the Sulphur Springs Valley. Many nonresident hunters traveling to southeastern Arizona set up housekeeping in Willcox. The community provides an ample opportunity for services and accommodations. Both scaled and Gambel's quail are found throughout the Willcox area. Mearns' quail are found on the higher elevation mountain ranges that border the valley. The agricultural fields in the Sulphur Springs Valley provide opportunities for both dove and sandhill crane in season. Tank-jumping for waterfowl is a popular pursuit in the area.

ACCOMMODATIONS

Motel 6, 921 N. Bisbee / Dogs allowed / 520-384-2201 / $ / www.motel6.com
Best Western Plaza Inn, 1100 W. Rex Allen Dr. / Dogs allowed / 520-384-3556 / 800-528-1234 / $$$ / www.bestwesternarizona.com

RESTAURANTS

Big Tex BBQ, 130 E Maley St, 520-384-4423
Salsa Fiesta, 1201 W Rex Allen Dr / 520-384-4233
Carter's Drive In, 575 S Haskell Ave / 520-384-2277

VETERINARIANS

Pencin Veterinary Clinic, 1250 N Fort Grant Rd / 520-384-5322
Willcox Veterinary Clinic, 889 N Taylor Rd / 520-384-2761

AUTO REPAIR

TechNet Professional Auto Service, 220 N Haskell Ave / 520-384-6410
Big O Tires, 651 N Bisbee Ave / 520-384-0466 / www.bigotires.com
Buddy'z Auto Repair, 100 W Rex Allen Dr / (520) 384-0307

AIR SERVICE

Cochise County Airport, 780 N Vista Ave / 520-384-2908

MEDICAL

Northern Cochise Community Hospital, 901 W. Rex Allen Dr. / 520-384-3541 / www.ncch.com

FOR MORE INFORMATION

Willcox Chamber of Commerce
1500 N. Circle 1 Road
Willcox, AZ 85643
520-384-2272 / 1-800-200-2272 / Fax 520-384-0293
www.willcoxchamber.com

REGION 6

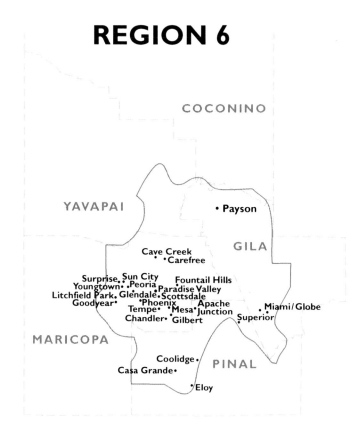

COCONINO

YAVAPAI

• Payson

GILA

Cave Creek
• •Carefree

Surprise• Sun City   Fountail Hills
Youngtown• •Peoria Paradise Valley
Litchfield Park• Glendale•Scottsdale
Goodyear•   •Phoenix   Apache
        Tempe• •Mesa•Junction   •Miami/Globe
    Chandler• Gilbert   Superior

MARICOPA

Coolidge •
Casa Grande•   PINAL

•Eloy

REGION 6
Central Arizona

Region 6 is found close to the geographic center of Arizona. It contains the state's major urban area. The Phoenix metropolitan basin is a continuous series of large cities that afford a visiting bird hunter a full range of services and accommodations.

Surprisingly, good bird hunting is close at hand for those headquartered in the Phoenix basin. Much of the developed land started as agricultural fields, and much of the land to the south and west of the municipalities is still in agriculture. The Gila River flows through the valley and supports good numbers of mourning doves and some whitewings. Waterfowl and dove frequent the Gila River drainage west of the basin in the Buckeye/Arlington area. Gambel's quail are found throughout the region in suitable habitat. National forest land in the northeast section of Region 1 rises up to the ponderosa pines. Both turkeys and band-tailed pigeons can be found in the high country.

UPLAND BIRDS

Gambel's Quail, Mourning Dove, White-winged Dove, Band-tailed Pigeon, Merriam's Turkey

WATERFOWL

Ducks & Geese

COUNTY STATISTICS FOR REGION 6

County	Population	Area (sq.mi.)	Max. Jan. Temp.	Annual Precip.	Percent Public Land	Percent Reservation
Gila County	43,350	4,748	61.5°	20.77"	59%	38%
Maricopa County	2,122,101	9,155	70.8°	4.95"	64%	5%
Pinal County	132,225	5,388	69.1°	5.22"	51%	23%
Yavapai County	107,714	8,091	55.9°	3.21"	91%	—

Central Arizona Hub Cities

APACHE JUNCTION
Elevation – 1,715 ft. • Population – 19,175

Apache Junction is a rapidly growing community on the extreme eastern edge of the Phoenix basin. Highway 60 transects the city from west to east. A full range of accommodations and services are available.

The Salt River and the lakes of the Salt River Project are found to the north and northeast. Ample national forest and state trust lands provide hunting for Gambel's quail. Farmlands to the south can host good numbers of doves. Some ducks are found on the Salt River.

CAMPGROUNDS AND RV PARKS

Mesa Apache Junction KOA, 1540 S Tomahawk Rd / 800-562-3404/ www.koa.com
La Hacienda RV Resort (Joyce Pinseth), 1797 West 28th Avenue / 280 sites / 480-982-2808 / www.lahaciendarv.com

ACCOMMODATIONS

Apache Junction Motel, 1680 W. Apache Trail / Dogs allowed / 480- 982-7702 / $-$$ / www.ajmotel.com
Super 8, 251 E. 29th Ave. / 480-288-8888 / www.super8.com

RESTAURANTS

Whataburger, 11518 E. Apache Trail / 480-986-0045 / www.whataburger.com
Feedbag Restaurant, 300 S. Phelps / 480-983-3521
Mammoth Steak House, 4650 E. Mammoth Mine Rd. / 480-983-6402 / www.mammothsteakhouse.net
Village Inn, 575 W. Apache Trail / 480-982-4579 / www.villageinnrestaurants.com

VETERINARIANS

VCA Apache Junction Animal Hospital, 17 N. Mountain Rd. / 480- 984-2114 / www.vcaapache.com

SPORTING GOODS

AJI Sporting Goods, 10444 E Apache Trl / 480-984-8616 / www.ajisports.com

AUTO REPAIR

Junction Auto Parts & Machine Shop, 2204 W.Apache Trail / 480- 982-0363 / www.napaonline.com
Big O Tires, 740 W Apache Trl / 480-982-2600 / www.bigotires.com

FOR MORE INFORMATION
Apache Junction Chamber of Commerce
PO Box 1747 / 1001 N. Idaho Rd., Bldg. H
Apache Junction, AZ 85217
480- 982-3141 / Fax: 480- 982-3234
www.apachejunctioncoc.com

CAREFREE
Elevation – 2,200 ft. • Population – 3,799

Carefree sits up against the Tonto National Forest on the northern edge of the Phoenix metropolitan area and is primarily a residential community. Carefree's surrounding country is rolling, Sonoran desert hills that can sustain good numbers of Gambel's quail in wet years. Migrating doves and waterfowl are present on available water.

ACCOMMODATIONS
The Boulders, 34631 N. Tom Darlington Rd. / Dogs allowed / 800-553-1717 / $$$ / www.theboulders.com

RESTAURANTS
Black Mountain Coffee Shop, Spanish Village / 480-488-9261
Boulder's Resort & Club, 34631 N. Tom Darlington Dr. / 480-488-9771 / www.theboulders.com
Sundial Garden Cafe, 7 Sundial Circle / 480-488-9825

VETERINARIANS
Carefree Animal Clinic, 6718 E Cave Creek Rd, Cave Creek / 480-488-3080 / www.carefreeanimalhospital.com

AIR SERVICE
Carefree Airport, 8302 E Carefree Rd / 480-488-3571 / www.skyranchcarefree.com

FOR MORE INFORMATION
Carefree/Cave Creek Chamber of Commerce
PO Box 734 / 748 Easy Street
Carefree, AZ 85377
480-488-3381
www.carefreecavecreek.org

Cave Creek
Elevation – 2,200 ft. • Population – 4,951

Cave Creek is situated next to Carefree in the beautiful Sonoran desert foothills of the Tonto National Forest. The town is predominantly a residential community. Gambel's quail, white-winged, and mourning dove are found in the surrounding area. Migrating waterfowl may be present on available water.

ACCOMMODATIONS

The Boulders Resort, 34631 N. Tom Darlington Dr., Carefree / No dogs allowed / 602-488-3128 / $$$ / www.theboulders.com

The Tumbleweed Hotel, 6333 East Cave Creek Rd. / No dogs allowed / 602-488-3668 / $$ / www.tumbleweed.com

RESTAURANTS

Buffalo Chip Saloon & Steakhouse. 6811 E. Cave Creek Rd. 480-488-9188

El Encanto Mexican Cafe, 6248 E. Cave Creek Rd. / 602-488-1752 / www.elencantorestaurant.com

Satisfied Frog Cave Creek Rd. 480-488-317

Horny Toad Restaurant, 6738 E Cave Creek Rd / 480-488-9542 / www.thehornytoad.com

VETERINARIANS

Animal Health Services, 6920 Cave Creek Rd. / 602-488-6181 / www.ahsvet.com

AUTO REPAIR

Fletcher's Tire & Auto Service, 4915 E Carefree Hwy / 480-575-1790 / www.fletcherstireandauto.net

Cave Creek European Ltd., 37608 N. Cave Creek Rd / 602-488-0501

MEDICAL

Desert Foothills Medical Center, 36889 N Tom Darlington Dr # A4, Carefree / 602-488-9220 / Emergency Services Open 24 Hours A Day, 7 Days A Week

FOR MORE INFORMATION

Carefree/Cave Creek Chamber of Commerce
PO Box 734 / 748 Easy Street
Carefree, AZ 85377
602-488-3381
www.carefreecavecreek.org

COOLIDGE
Elevation – 1,418 ft. • Population – 7,786

Historically, Coolidge is one of Arizona's top early season dove hunting areas. An older community that relies heavily on agriculture, the area surrounding Coolidge is a patchwork of cultivated fields. The town provides a good amount of accommodations and services, however, early season hunters would do well to make arrangements well in advance. Both white-winged and mourning dove are found in good numbers. Picacho Reservoir to the south, near Eloy, is a popular southern Arizona waterfowl hunting area. Gambel's quail are found in the surrounding desert.

CAMPGROUNDS & RV PARKS

Indian Skies RV Resort, 1050 S. Arizona Blvd. / 520-723-7831 / www.indianskiesrvresort.com

ACCOMMODATIONS

Grande Vista Motel, 1211 N. Arizona Blvd. / No dogs allowed / 520-723-7793 / $
Moonlight Motel, 1087 N. Arizona Blvd. / No dogs allowed / 520-723-3475 / $

RESTAURANTS

Casa Palomino, 1076 N Arizona Blvd / 520-723-4223
Tag's Restaurant, 156 N. Arizona Blvd. / 520-723-1013

VETERINARIANS

Coolidge Veterinary Hospital, 435 W. Coolidge Ave. / 602-723-5500

AUTO REPAIR

Day Auto Supply, 403 W. Central Ave. / 520-723-9551 / www.napaonline.com
The Tire Factory, 2311 S 5th St / 520-723-7840

AUTO RENTALS

Tate's East Valley Ford Mercury, 296 N. Arizona Blvd. / 520-723-5479 / tateseastvalleyfordmercury.dealerconnection.com/

AIR SERVICE

Coolidge Municipal Airport / 520-723-9169 (contact Sam Berneto) / www.coolidgeaviation.com

MEDICAL

Horizon Human Services Outpatient Clinic, 5497 W Mccartney Rd / 520-723-9800 / www.horizonhumanservices.com

For More Information

Coolidge Chamber of Commerce
PO Box 943 / 320 W. Central Avenue
Coolidge, AZ 85228
520-723-3009
www.coolidgechamber.org

Globe/Miami
Elevation – 3,450 / 3,411 ft. • Population – 7,141/ 1,936

Globe/Miami is found on Highway 60 and is a popular home base for those hunting the vast San Carlos Reservation. The community's economy is primarily based on mining. Historic period buildings line the center of the city, while more modern accommodations are available along the main traveled corridors. Ample services and accommodations are available.

The principal game bird species is Gambel's quail, and impressive numbers can be found there in wet years. Small pockets of scaled quail are occasionally seen in the eastern portion of the San Carlos Apache Reservation. The Gila River, which flows through the San Carlos Reservation into San Carlos Reservoir, is a popular waterfowl hunting area.

Campgrounds & RV Parks

Apache Trail RV Park, HCO2, Box 279, Globe / 928-425-7979
El Rey Motel/RV, 1201 E. Ash St., Globe / 928-425-4427
Gila County RV Park, 300 S. Pine St., Globe / 928-425-4653

Accommodations

Cloud Nine Motel, 1649 E. Ash St., Globe / Dogs allowed / 928-425-5741 / $$
El Rey Motel, 1201 East Ash St., Globe / Dogs allowed / 928-425-4427 / $-$$
Days Inn, 1630 East Ash St., Globe / 928-425-5500 / www.daysinn.com

Restaurants

Burger House, 812 Live Oak St., Miami / 928-473-9918
Crestline Steakhouse, 1901 E. Ash St., Globe / 928-425-6269
Irene's Real Mexican Food, 1601 E. Ash St., Globe / 928-425-7904
Jasmine Teahouse, 1097 N. Broad St., Globe / 928-425-2503
Jerry's Restaurant, 699 E. Ash St., Globe / 928-425-5282
La Luz del Dia, 304 N. Broad St., Globe / 928-425-8400

Veterinarians

Samaritan Veterinary Center, 1776 East Maple Street, Globe / 928-425-5797

Sporting Goods

Circle K Store #423, 1951 East Ash, Globe / San Carlos Reservation License Vendor / www.circlek.com
Globe Gun Shop, 1300 N. Broad, Globe / 928-425-5244
United Sporting Goods and Jewelry, 135 N Broad St, Globe / 928-425-7300

Auto Repair

Dr. J's Precision Automotive, 710 N. Willow St., Globe / 928-425-8173
Big O Tires, 1790 N Broad St, Globe / 928-425-8222 / www.bigotires.com

Air Service

San Carlos Apache Airport / 520-475-2361

Medical

Savin Medical Center, 5886 S Hospital Dr, Globe / 928-425-7108

For More Information

Greater Globe/Miami Chamber of Commerce
PO Box 2539 / 1360 N. Broad Street
Globe, AZ 85502
928-425-4495 / 1-800-804-5623 / Fax 928-425-3410
www.globemiamichamber.com

Phoenix / Scottsdale
Elevation – 1,117 ft. / 1,160 ft. • Population – 1,552,259 / 202,705

Phoenix is the largest city in Arizona and is the state capital. Found at nearly the geographical center of the state, access is provided by Interstates 10, 17, and 60. While all the surrounding lands are incorporated, good hunting is found with a minimum amount of travel. Dove hunting is good in the surrounding agricultural fields, and the Gila River provides near access to those interested in hunting waterfowl. Gambel's quail are found throughout Region 6 and, during wet years, can be available in impressive numbers. Vast tracts of national forest lands are found to the north and northeast of Phoenix and provide hunting opportunities for turkey and band-tailed pigeon.

Scottsdale is known as an upscale arts community with an established downtown shopping area. Although surrounded by incorporated land to the south, west, and north, and the Salt River Indian Reservation to the east, good hunting is available to those willing to travel a moderate distance. Agricultural areas to the south and southwest are known as good early season dove hunting areas. Waterfowl and dove populations are concentrated on the Gila River. Gambel's quail are found throughout the region.

Campgrounds and RV Parks

Covered Wagon RV Park (Aime Ricci), 6540 North Black Canyon, #53, Phoenix / 45 sites / 602-242-2500

Phoenix Metro RV Park (Marlene Adams), 22701 N. Black Canyon Hwy I-17, Phoenix / 308 sites / 602-582-0390 / www.phoenixmetrorvpark.com

Westworld of Scottsdale (Mitzi Pollack), 16601 North Pima Road, Scottsdale / 100 sites / 602-585-4392

Accommodations

Best Western Bell Motel, 17211 N. Black Canyon Hwy, Phoenix / Dogs allowed / 800-528-1234 / $-$$$ / www.bestwesternarizona.com

Comfort Inn-Turf Paradise, 1711 W. Bell RD., Phoenix / Dogs allowed / 800-221-2222 / $-$$$ / www.comfortinn.com

Red Roof Inn Camelback, 502 W. Camelback Rd., Phoenix / Dogs allowed / 602-264-9290 / $$-$$$ / www.redroof.com

Econo Lodge, 1520 N. 84th Dr., Tolleson / Dogs allowed / 800-424-4777 / $$-$$$ / www.econolodge.com

Motel 6, 2330 W. Bell Rd., Phoenix / Dogs allowed / 602-993-2353 / $ / www.motel6.com

RESTAURANTS

Christopher's Fermier Brasserie, 25884 E Camelback Rd, Phoenix / 602-522-2344 / www.fermier.com

The Farm at South Mountain, 6106 S. 32nd St, Phoenix / 602-276-8804 / www.thefarmatsouthmountain.com

Bill Johnson's Big Apple, 3757 E. Van Buren St., Phoenix / 602-275-2107 / www.billjohnsons.com

Bloom, 8877 N. Scottsdale Rd, Scottsdale / 480-922-5666 / www.foxrc.com

Mosaic Restaurant, 10600 E Jomax Rd, Scottsdale / 480-563-9600 / www.mosaic-restaurant.com

North, 15024 N. Scottsdale Rd, Scottsdale / 480-948-2055 / www.foxcr.com

Razz's Restaurant, 10315 N Scottsdale Rd, Scottsdale / 480-905-1308 / www.razzsrestaurant.com

Sassi Ristorante, 10455 E Pinnacle Pkwy, Scottsdale / 480-502-9095 / www.sassi.biz

Musette pointing a bird holed up below a chainfruit cholla. Her eyes say, "Put down that camera and kill this bird." (Sandy McClure)

Veterinarians

All Creatures Animal Clinic, 4022 E. Greenway Rd., Ste#7-8, Phoenix / 602-345-0974/ www.allcreaturesac.com

Emergency Animal Clinic, 2260 W. Glendale Ave., Phoenix / 602-995-3757 /

Aztec Animal Hospital, 8140 E. McDowell Rd. Scottsdale / 480-331-5986 / www.aztecanimalhospital.net

Sporting Goods

Big 5 Sporting Goods / www.big5sportinggoods.com
Phoenix: 3560 E. Thomas Rd., 602-955-9601 / 1717 W. Bethany Home Rd, 602-242-1806 / 10202 Metro Parkway W, 602-674-3189 / 7710 W. Thomas, 623-848-4800 / 4623 E. Cactus Rd, 602-953-0305 / 1919 W Bell Rd, 602-863-1309
Scottsdale: 3330 Hayden Rd, 480-941-4387 / 14987 N. N.sight Blvd, 480-948-9277

Sportsman's Warehouse, 19205 N. 27th Avenue, Phoenix / 623-516-1400 / www.sportsmanswarehouse.com

Sports Authority / www.sportsauthority.com
Phoenix: 9620 Metro Pkwy W, #119, 602-870-3620 / 7000 E Mayo Blvd, #15, 480-563-4009 / 12869 N. Tatum Blvd, 602-494-7715 / 1625 E. Camelback Rd, 602-277-9000 /
Scottsdale: 9009 E. Indian Bend Rd, 480-922-8811

Auto Repair

Blackwell Automotive, 15440 N. 40th St., Phoenix / 602-992-5478 / www.blackwellautomotive.com

Jack's Automotive Service, 2623 E. McDowell Rd. / 602-273-0717

Weaver's Auto Service, 2925 N. 29th St., Phoenix / 602-956-0667

Automotive Machine Scottsdale, 3011 N. 73rd St. #107, Scottsdale / 480-945-0934

Rayco Car Service, 8245 E Butherus Dr # 101, Scottsdale / 480-951-4054 / www.raycocarserviceaz.com

Auto Rentals

Avis Rent A Car, 3400 E Sky Harbor Blvd, Phoenix / 602-273-3222 / www.avis.com

Dollar Rent A Car, 3400 E Sky Harbor Blvd, Phoenix / 602-392-0695 / www.dollar.com

Hertz, 1125 N Scottsdale Rd, Scottsdale / 480-949-2420 / www.hertz.com

Air Service

Phoenix Sky Harbor International Airport, 3400 E. Sky Harbor Blvd, Phoenix / 602-273-3300 / www.phoenix.gov/aviation

Phoenix Deer Valley Municipal Airport, 702 W. Deer Valley Rd., Phoenix / 602-869-0975

Scottsdale Airport, 15000 N. Airport Dr., Scottsdale / 480-994-2321

MEDICAL

John C. Lincoln Deer Valley Hospital, 19829 N. 27th Ave., Phoenix / 623-879-6100 / www.jcl.com

Maricopa Medical Center, 2601 E Roosevelt St # 7, Phoenix / 602-344-5011

Saint Joseph's Hospital & Medical Center, 350 W. Thomas Rd., Phoenix / 602-285-3000 / www.stjosephs-phx.org

Scottsdale Healthcare, 9003 E Shea Blvd, Scottsdale / 480-323-3000 / www.shc.org

Mayo Clinic, 13400 East Shea Blvd, Scottsdale / 800-446-2279 / www.mayoclinic.org

FOR MORE INFORMATION

Phoenix Chamber of Commerce
201 N. Central Ave., Ste 2700
Phoenix, AZ 85073
602-254-5521 / Fax 602-495-8913
www.phoenixchamber.com

Scottsdale Chamber of Commerce
4725 N Scottsdale Rd # 210
Scottsdale, AZ 85251-4498
480-355-2700
www.scottsdalechamber.com

ARIZONA'S INDIAN RESERVATIONS

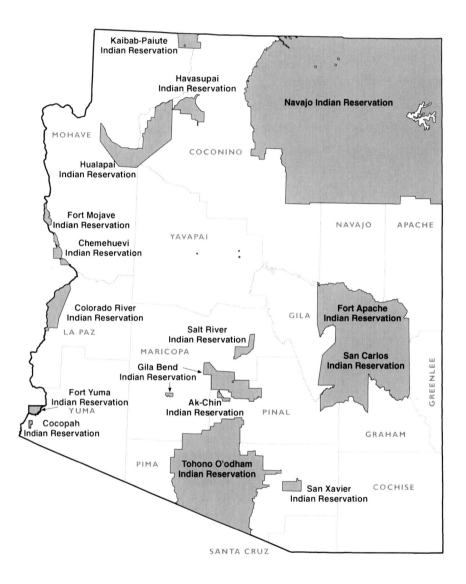

Hunting on Indian Reservations

Arizona is home to 20 Indian reservations that encompass 26,051,026 acres of land. The eight reservations that allow nontribal hunting contain 20,991,701 acres. That means that 81% of the land set aside as tribal reservations is open to hunting by nontribal members.

Tribal reservations are considered sovereign nations and those hunting there are exempted from state hunting license requirements. Arizona game and fish statute R12-4-117 states "No state license, tag or permit is required to hunt or fish on any Indian Reservation in this state. Wildlife lawfully taken on an Indian Reservation may be transported or possessed anywhere in the state when it can be identified as to species and legality as provided in A.R.S. 17-309A.20."

Hunting on Arizona's Indian reservations is a real bargain. The cost of a reservation small game license, with the exception of the more expensive San Carlos Apache, is a fraction of the cost of a $61.25 three-day small game nonresident Arizona license or the annual $151.25 nonresident Arizona general hunting license. Hunters get ample opportunity for minimal expense. Some outstanding hunting is found on tribal lands. Some of the larger reservations are the size of small states and very sparsely populated.

Reservations offer few amenities, so the visiting bird hunter should be provisioned before arriving. Accommodations are generally available in the cities nearest the reservation borders.

WHITE MOUNTAIN APACHE RESERVATION
(appears on maps as Fort Apache Indian Reservation)

1,664,872 acres
Game and Fish Department
P.O. Box 220
Whiteriver, AZ 85941
928-338-4385/ 877-338-9628
Guide list available upon request
Species available: Gambel's quail, Mearns' quail, band-tailed pigeons, Merriam's turkey, ducks, and geese

The White Mountain Apache Reservation is famous for its very high dollar big game hunting program, world record class elk in particular. The reservation also offers a very reasonable priced small game license with opportunities for Gambel's quail, limited Mearns' quail, bandtails and waterfowl. Guided spring turkey hunts are also available.

Much of the reservation is higher in elevation and covered in pines, so quail habitat is at a minimum, but for those willing to focus, good Gambel's hunting is available in the Salt River Canyon and along the western border. Rare sightings of Mearns' quail are reported along the entire rim to Williams. Mearns' are legal game on the reservation, but those wishing specifically to target Mearns' should concentrate their efforts in the southern part of the state.

Band-tailed pigeon numbers varies from year to year. In some years reservation hunting is very good. Turkey hunting is reported to be outstanding.

Both ducks and Canada geese use the many stock tanks and lakes spread throughout the reservation. On the southern boundary, the Black and Salt Rivers hold birds through the season when weather closes higher elevation water.

Blue grouse season is currently closed.

Small game hunting permits are priced at $5 for a day and $50 dollars for the season. Three-day guided spring turkey hunt permits are $750 dollars. Bag limits and seasons conform to Arizona Game and Fish guidelines.

The nearest services are on the northern border in Show Low and Pinetop/Lakeside.

White Mountain Apache Tribe Hunting License Vendors

Wildlife & Outdoor Recreation Division / Whiteriver, AZ / 928-338-4385
Pinetop Sporting Goods / Pinetop, AZ / 928-367-5050
Hon Dah Service Station / 3 Miles south of Pinetop / 928-369-4311
Salt River Canyon Inn / Salt River Canyon / No Phone
Tempe Marine / Chandler, AZ / 480-782-6813
Woody's Food Stores / Show Low, AZ / 520-537-4667
Circle B Market / Greer, AZ / 928-735-7540
Western United Drug / Springerville, AZ / 928-333-4321
Bob's Bang Room / Show Low, AZ / 928-368-5040
Texaco Rebel Quik Mart / Globe, AZ / 520-425-4275

SAN CARLOS APACHE RESERVATION

1,853,841 acres
Recreation and Wildlife Department
P.O. Box 97
San Carlos, AZ 85550
928-475-2343 or 888-475-2344
Guide list available upon request
Species available: Gambel's, scaled, and Mearns' quail, doves, band-tailed pigeon, Merriam's turkey, ducks, and geese

The San Carlos Reservation has a wide range of habitat types that run from rolling Sonoran desert grasslands in the south to ponderosa pine forests above the Nantac Rim in the north. Most of San Carlos contains Gambel's quail. Some areas are rugged, thick, and present difficulties in working birds. The reservation quail populations are also subject to the whims of rainfall and, like the rest of the state, birds get harder to find without precipitation. Taken on the whole, reservation Gambel's hunting is fair to excellent. There are small populations of both scaled and Mearns' quail on the reservation, but hunters committed to finding either species should hunt further south, closer to the Mexican border.

Dove hunting is also available during the season, with the early September hunt producing the best shooting. With very little agriculture on the San Carlos Reservation to condense dove populations, shooting is over water tanks with success running from moderate to nonexistent. Shooters looking for prime dove hunting on an Indian reservation should consider other tribal reservations on the Colorado River.

Band-tailed pigeons are a unique species not often pursued by hunters. San Carlos has an open season that runs concurrent with the Arizona state season. There is ample bandtail habitat in the northern part of the reservation and while pigeon hunting is by nature mercurial, if a hunter can locate birds he could get some shooting.

Turkey hunting on San Carlos is consistently excellent. Hunt success runs 70 to 80 percent. One nine-day, any turkey fall season is offered. Fall permits cost $100. Two bearded turkey spring seasons are offered. One runs nine days and the other six days, spread over three weekends, respectively. Spring tags cost $200.

San Carlos has the water to attract and hold good numbers of ducks and Canada Geese. The San Carlos Reservoir alone, when full, has 17,410 acres of surface area and 158 miles of shoreline. The Gila River, whose water forms the San Carlos Reservoir, is the most important waterfowl corridor in central Arizona. Waterfowl use these and additional tanks, rivers and smaller lakes on the reservation high country. San Carlos is, and should continue to be, one of the best waterfowl areas in the state.

Regulations follow Arizona Game and Fish Department guidelines. One-day permits cost $15 for units A,B,and C. Unit D one-day permits run $25. Three-day permits cost $30 and $50, respectively. Seven-day permits are priced at $60 and $100. Nearest services are in Globe to the west and Safford to the east.

San Carlos Apache Reservation Hunting License Vendors

Noline's Country Store, Peridot, AZ / 928-475-5393
San Carlos Lake Store, Peridot, AZ / 928-475-2756
Tempe Marine, Chandler, AZ / 480-782-6813
Circle K Store #423, Globe, AZ / (928) 425-4142
Pinky's Bait & Tackle, Safford, AZ / 928-428-0056
Bob Keen's Store, Ft. Thomas, AZ / 928-485-2261

THE NAVAJO NATION

16,000,000 acres
Navajo Fish and Wildlife
P.O. Box 1480
Window Rock, AZ 86515
928-871-6451 or 871-6452
Species available: Scaled quail, ring-necked pheasants, Gambel's quail, mourning doves, blue grouse, Merriam's turkey, chukar, ducks, and geese

The Navajo Reservation is a huge piece of real estate. Much of the land is sparsely vegetated sandstone buttes and vista that have no resident upland birds.

The northeast quadrant of the reservation, which spills into New Mexico, Colorado and Utah, holds most of the bird hunting.

Some scaled quail are found along the reservation's eastern border in New Mexico. The four corners area has huntable numbers of ring-necked pheasants and Gambel's quail in the San Juan River Valley. Some mourning doves can be found on the reservation.

The Chuska, Lukachukai and Carrizo Mountains near four corners rise above 9,000 feet in elevation. Turkey and blue grouse are found at higher elevations. Chukar partridge are found in the Utah section of the four corners region.

By all reports, waterfowl hunting can be very good on the reservation. The northeast corner has many small lakes that hold ducks, sometimes in large numbers. The San Juan River flowing northeast from Shiprock, New Mexico, through the four corners into Utah is used heavily by ducks and Canada geese.

Annual small game licenses are $30. There is an additional $5 pheasant stamp for each pheasant taken. Call the Wildlife Department for regulations and current charges.

Because of the sheer size of the Navajo Reservation, many cities could serve as a home base depending on which part of the reservation a hunter was visiting. Page, Arizona, sits on the northwest boundary. On the southern border are the cities of Flagstaff, Winslow, Holbrook, and Gallup, New Mexico. Farmington, New Mexico, is found to the northeast. The Navajo Reservation is a tourist destination and many of the sightseeing areas and national monuments have well developed restaurants and overnight accommodations.

Navajo Nation Hunting License Vendors

Bond & Bonds, P.O. Box 640, Shiprock, NM 87420 / 505-368-4448
City Market, Inc., US Highway 666 & Nm Hwy 64, Shiprock, NM
    87420 / 505-368-4248
Four Corners Windsurfing, P.O.Box 751, Fruitland, NM 87416 / 505-598-6688
Handy Bait & Tackle, 504 Aztec Blvd., Aztec, NM 87410 / 505-334-9114
Kirtland Pawn Shop, P.O. Box 166, Kirtland, NM 87417 / 505-598-6969
Navajo Fish and Wildlife, P.O. Box 1480, Window Rock, AZ 86515 / 928-871-6451
Red Barn Trading Post, P. O. Box 245, Sanders, AZ 86512-0245 / 520-688-2762
Copper Valley Development. Corp., Sheep Springs Trading Post, Sheep Springs,
    NM 87364 / 505-732-4211
Ross Sporting Goods, 204 West Main, Farmington, NM 87401 / 505-325-1062
Swift's Sporting Goods, 1725 South 2nd Street, Gallup, NM 87301 / 505-863-9331
Wal-Mart Store, 1308 W. Metro, Gallup, NM 87301 / 505-722-2296
Wal-Mart Store, 700 Mikes Pike Blvd., Winslow, AZ 86047 / 520-289-4641
Zia Sporting Goods, 500 East Main, Farmington, NM 87401 / 505-327-600

FORT MOJAVE INDIAN RESERVATION

33,884 acres
1601 Plantation Drive
Mohave, AZ 86440
928-346-1521, ask for Chief Ranger Rick Boyd
**Species available: Mourning & white-winged dove, Gambel's quail,
ducks, and geese**

Fort Mojave Indian Reservation is the northernmost of the four reservations on the Colorado River that allow nontribal hunting. Fort Mojave shares borders with Arizona,California, and Nevada and has land in all three states. Of the 33,000 acres enclosed in the reservation, approximately 20,000 are open to hunting, 15,000 acres of which are in agriculture. Cotton and alfalfa are the principal crops. Lesser amounts of grain are also planted.

The Colorado River Valley has historically offered excellent hunting for both mourning and white-wing dove. Large concentrations of birds build through the summer and, unless pushed into Mexico by weather, hold into the September 1st opening. Much of the hunting pressure is from shooters traveling from California and Nevada.

The region's natural vegetation is sparse, low desert creosote community. Desert washes are lined with sporadic mesquite trees. The areas adjacent to water have thick bands of nearly impenetrable salt cedars and arrowheat. Gambel's quail, the third upland species available, are concentrated in these thick salt cedar jungles. It is not what would be called traditional quail cover, but it is possible to take a few birds along the edges. Hunters wanting to experience classic Arizona quail cover will need to travel east.

The Fort Mojave Reservation adjoins the Havasu National Wildlife Refuge, and of the four Colorado River reservations, it offers the best waterfowl hunting. The 12-mile portion of the river that travels through the reservation has three backwaters totaling approximately 900 acres of flooded cattail marsh. Ducks, snow geese, and Canada geese use these areas.

Season dates and bag limits follow Arizona state guidelines. Season permits for dove and quail are priced at $ 20 per species. An inclusive season permit, allowing dove, quail, duck and geese, is priced at $50.

Nearest services are in Bullhead City and Laughlin.

Fort Mojave Hunting License Vendors

Kmart, Hwy 95, Bullhead City, AZ / (928) 763-7272
Fort Mojave Smoke Shop, Avi Hotel & Casino, Laughlin, NV
Fort Mojave Smoke Shop, 8501 Hwy 95, Mojave Valley, AZ

COLORADO RIVER INDIAN TRIBES RESERVATION

268,691 acres
Department of Fish and Game
P.O. Box 777
Parker, AZ 85344
520-669-9285
Species available: White-winged & mourning dove, Gambel's quail, ducks, and geese

The Colorado River Indian Tribes Reservation is approximately 70% agriculture and all is open to hunting. It is located in both California and Arizona, on the Colorado River between Parker and Ehrenberg, Arizona, with 225,995 acres of reservation land falling within the boundaries of Arizona.

Cottonwoods and willows shade thick growth tamarisk that is found along water. Remaining desert is typical, low density creosote plant community. Agricultural crops include wheat, oats, cotton, alfalfa,corn, and melons.

Both white-winged and mourning doves, as well as Gambel's quail are the upland bird species available. Waterfowl are sometimes found along the Colorado River and the reservation's irrigation canals. Contact the reservation for current information on season dates and hunt regulations. Annual hunting permits cost $25 and are valid from January 1 through December 31.

Nearest services are on the northern boundary of the reservation in Parker, Arizona.

QUECHAN INDIAN RESERVATION
(appears on maps as Fort Yuma Indian Reservation)

44,000 acres
P.O. Box 1899
Yuma, AZ 85366
(760) 572-0213
Species available: White-winged & mourning doves, Gambel's quail, ducks, and geese

The Quechan Indian Reservation is cut by the Colorado River between California and Arizona, with 95% on the California side. It is three miles east of Yuma. Unless posted, the whole reservation is open to hunting. Cottonwood, willow, arrowheat and tamarisk are found along the river and creosote desert on the higher ground. One third of the reservation is in agriculture. Crops include milo, sesame seed, grain, and citrus groves.

Both mourning and white-winged doves are the main game bird species. The early September season provides the best success. Along with the Cocopah Indian Reservation to the south, hunters interested in pursuing whitewings should consider these two reservations in the Yuma area.

Gambel's quail are found in the heavy brush lining waterways and desert washes. Quail also use the edges of agricultural fields. Limited waterfowl hunting is available in occasionally flooded fields and along the canals.

Bag and possession limits use California law as a guideline. Dove hunters are allowed 10 birds per day, in aggregation, of both species and 20 in possession. Quail hunters may take 10 Gambel's per day with 10 in possession. An annual hunting permit costs $25.

Nearest available services are in Yuma.

COCOPAH INDIAN RESERVATION

6,000 acres
County 15th and Avenue G
Somerton, AZ 85305
520-627-2102; Contact Gary Oliver
520-627-8857 Tribal Police (licensing agent)
Species available: White-winged & mourning dove, Gambel's quail, ducks, and geese

The Cocopah Indian Reservation lies on the eastern bank of the Colorado River and provides hunting opportunities on one-third of its 6,000 acres. Hunting areas are split 50/50 between creosote bush low desert and agricultural fields. The reservation is five miles west of Somerton, midway between Yuma and the border city of San Luis. The reservation is bordered across the river to the west by Mexico.

Agricultural crops include wheat, barley, Sudan grass seed, safflower, and corn.

The reservation offers one of the few premier opportunities remaining for large concentrations of white-winged dove. The surrounding agricultural lands are planted in, among other things, 10,000 acres of citrus groves that mimic the once great mesquite bosch dove nesting "factories." Gary Oliver, the reservation hunt manager tells me that there are many more whitewings than mourning doves.

Gambel's quail are found in the heavy brush lining the river and are occasionally intercepted feeding in the agricultural fields. Oliver also told me that there are some limited opportunities for waterfowl along the reservation's irrigation canals. Geese are occasionally seen in the fields. Seasons run concurrent with Arizona. An annual hunting permit cost $20.

Nearest available services are in Yuma.

CHEMEHUEVI INDIAN TRIBE RESERVATION

30,000 acres
Conservation Department
P.O. Box 1976
Havasu Lake, CA 92363
619-858-5322
Guides list available upon request
Species available: Mourning & white-winged dove, Gambel's quail, ducks, and
geese

The Chemehuevi Indian Tribe Reservation does not fall within the boundaries of the state of Arizona, but a listing of huntable Colorado River Indian reservations would not be complete without it.

Half of the reservation's 30,000 acres are open to hunting. Currently, the tribe is expanding its agricultural areas, so they were not able to give me a specific answer for the number of acres in fields. Their intention is to plant crops to boost the number of doves using the reservation. Mourning dove hunting can be excellent, however, whitewing numbers are low.

Much of the hunting areas currently available are natural desert. Gambel's quail are found along the washes and in heavy riparian cover alongside water. Quail hunting is rated as good to very good.

Most of the tribe's Colorado River access borders on the Havasu National Wildlife Refuge. This puts ample populations of waterfowl in the area but limits the reservation's waterfowl hunting area. Serious waterfowlers can expect opportunities to take ducks as well as snows and Canadas over water with decoys in the limited areas left open for waterfowl hunting.

The tribe follows California guidelines in establishing their bag limits and seasons. Current annual permits are: dove hunting $20, waterfowl hunting $ 20, and quail $25. Permits are available through the conservation office listed above, at Havasu Resorts 619-858-4578 and at the Havasu Landing Resort and Casino 619-858-4593.

Nearest services are in Lake Havasu City, Arizona.

NATIONAL WILDLIFE REFUGES

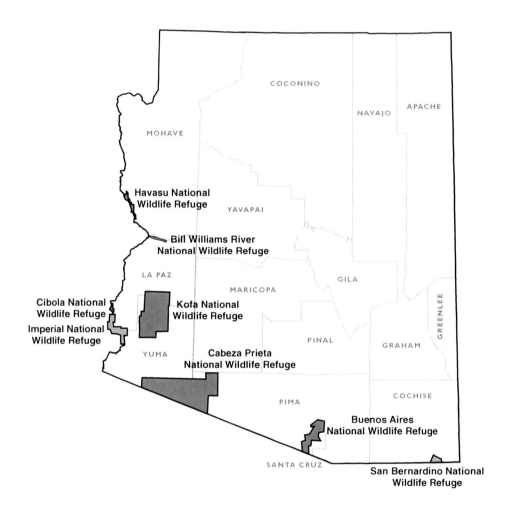

National and State Wildlife Refuges

ALAMO LAKE WILDLIFE AREA

No facilities on site
Contact Number: A.G.F.D. 520-342-0091
Location: **Region 4**

Alamo Lake Wildlife Area, which includes Alamo Lake and the surrounding lands, is managed by the Arizona Game and Fish Department. Alamo Lake State Park is on the wildlife area and is run as a public recreation area. The park is leased from the Game and Fish Department.

Alamo Lake and the surrounding wildlife area are open to hunting. Recreational facilities on the park, such as picnic areas and boat launching ramps, are closed to shooting within one-quarter mile. Hunters accessing the lake through the state park need to abide by the rules and restrictions of the park.

Alamo Lake has good populations of ducks. Occasional flocks of both Canada and snow geese use the north end of the lake as a loafing area and feed on grass along the shoreline. Waterfowl hunters also have good success along the Bill Williams River where it flows into the north end of the lake. Gambel's quail hunters find good numbers of birds along the lake shoreline, the river course, and the adjoining hills.

ALLEN SEVERSON MEMORIAL WILDLIFE AREA (PINTAIL LAKE)

370 acres; no facilities on site
Contact Number: USFS 520-368-5111
Location: **Region 1**

Water for the Allen Severson Memorial Wildlife Area is provided by treated wastewater from the city of Show Low, Arizona. In a three-way cooperative effort between the Apache-Sitgreaves National Forest, the Arizona Game and Fish Department, and the city of Show Low, unwanted wastewater was used to create the most productive waterfowl breeding area ever recorded in North America. In the summer of 1982, the area produced 2750 ducklings, the highest per-acre density of ducklings on record.

The unit has two water areas. Pintail Lake is within the northernmost fenced enclosure of 250 acres. The lake has 50 acres of water broken down into three ponds with 14 nesting islands. The south marsh varies from 15 to 50 acres of flooded meadow. Elevation is 6,300 feet.

The wildlife area is open to hunting during the season. Nearest services are in Show Low, Arizona.

ARLINGTON WILDLIFE AREA

13,020 acres; no facilities
Arizona Game and Fish Department Headquarters
7200 E. University, Mesa, AZ 85207
602-981-9400
Location: **Region 6**

Arlington Wildlife Area is found in the Gila River bottoms, a consistent waterfowl producer for Arizona duck hunters. Several ponds are found along the river channel. Thick with salt cedars, access can be difficult. The river channel itself has some gravel bars and open water backwaters. Canada geese are seen sporadically. For more information, contact the Arizona Game & Fish Department.

BASE AND MERIDIAN WILDLIFE AREA

198 acres; no facilities
Arizona Game and Fish Department
7200 E. University, Mesa, AZ 85207
602-981-9400
Location: **Region 6**

The Base & Meridian Wildlife Area is located at the confluence of the Salt and Gila Rivers. It is adjacent to the Phoenix metropolitan basin and restricted to shotgun only. Some waterfowl and upland bird hunting is available. For more information, contact the Arizona Game & Fish Department.

BECKER LAKE WILDLIFE AREA

Acreage not available; no facilities
Arizona Game & Fish Department
HC 66, Box 57201, Pinetop, AZ 85935
520-367-4281
Location: **Region 1**

Becker Lake is open to hunting in season. Amenities are found in Springerville 1.5 miles to the south.

BILL WILLIAMS RIVER NATIONAL WILDLIFE REFUGE

105 acres, no facilities
60911 Highway 95, Parker, AZ 85344
520-667-4144
Location: **Region 4**

Bill Williams River National Wildlife Refuge has extensive riparian and open water areas containing waterfowl, all of which are closed to hunting. The land south of the Planet Ranch Road on the refuge's southern border is open to hunting mourning dove, white-winged dove, and Gambel's quail in season. Nontoxic shot is required.

Nearest services are in Parker, Arizona.

BOG HOLE WILDLIFE AREA

200 acres; no facilities on site
Contact numbers: USFS 520-378-0311
                  AGFD 520-628-5376
Location: **Region 5**

The Bog Hole Wildlife Area sits at the top of the San Rafael Valley just below the road through Canelo Pass. All of the surrounding land is Mearns' quail habitat, in the public domain and open to hunting, so the only pertinent draw for hunters is the six acre pond that provides habitat for Mexican ducks and other waterfowl species. Water is at a premium in the San Rafael Valley, which during the later part of the season can see fair numbers of ducks.

Nearest services are in Sonoita.

BUENOS AIRES NATIONAL WILDLIFE REFUGE

115,000 acres; no facilities on site
P.O. Box 109, Sasabee, AZ 85633
Contact number: 502-823-4251
Location: **Region 5**

Buenos Aires National Wildlife Refuge was created in 1985 from ranchland. Cattle were removed and no grazing has been permitted for 10 years on refuge property. The refuge was created for the reintroduction of masked bobwhite quail. Refuge grasslands are being managed in an effort to reestablish the species, which disappeared from north of the border before the turn of the century. Much controversy has focused on the management of the refuge with strong divergent opinions being held by several factions.

The refuge is open to hunting in some areas, but closed to all quail hunting. That would leave dove and waterfowl hunting. Both, though listed as open, are moot points because the refuge water sources have been allowed to dry up with the new grasslands management. Contact the address or phone number listed above for more information.

Nearest services are in Nogales or Tucson.

Cabeza Prieta National Wildlife Refuge

860,000 acres; no facilities on site
1611 N. 2nd Avenue, Ajo, AZ 85321
Contact number: 520-387-6483
Location: **Region 4**

Cabeza Prieta National Wildlife Refuge is open only to the hunting of desert bighorn sheep through the Arizona Game and Fish Department. Upland bird and waterfowl hunting is prohibited.

Chevelon Canyon Wildlife Area

No acreage available; no facilities on site
Arizona Fish & Game Dept., Region 1 Headquarters
HC 66 PO Box 57201, Pinetop, AZ 85935
Contact number: 520-367-4281
Location: **Region 1**

Cibola National Wildlife Refuge

16,667 acres
Route 2, Box 138
Cibola, AZ 85328
Contact number: 928-857-3253
Location: **Region 4**

Most of the Canada geese in Arizona are found on Cibola. During an average year, 18,000 to 20,000 Canada geese use the refuge. In farm unit 1 near the refuge headquarters, an 1,800-acre closed area is devoted to crops for feeding and holding the goose and sandhill crane populations.

Three areas in the southern two-thirds of the refuge are open to limited hunting, including a monitored hunting area with numbered, staked goose fields. I have hunted the staked fields and it was not for me, but some hunters I've talked with enjoyed the staked field hunting program. They appreciated the restrictions that were in place to control sky busting. Hunters who want another option might consider hunting from a boat on the old river channel or hunting the fields on the island, both of which are found on farm unit 3.

Hunt success statistics are in line with Colorado River target rates for Canada geese harvest. During the 94/95 season, the refuge managers reported that 1,345 hunters took 512 birds for an average kill of .4 birds per hunter day.

Nearest services are in Blythe, California.

IMPERIAL NATIONAL WILDLIFE REFUGE

25,765 acres
P.O. Box 72217, Martinez Lake, AZ 85365
Contact number: 928-783-3371
Location: **Region 4**

Imperial National Wildlife Refuge covers 30 miles of the Colorado River in the southwest corner of the state, just north of Yuma. Elevation is about 200 feet above sea level. Hunting is allowed on most of the refuge including the river and the many small lakes and backwaters that run along its course. Road access is limited to the southern end of the refuge, and many of the hunting areas are only reached by boat from the main river channel.

The refuge is an important waterfowl hunting area. In addition, hunting is available for Gambel's quail and white-winged and mourning dove. The refuge has a brochure available on hunting that contains current rules and a map. Contact the address above for a copy.

JACQUES MARSH WILDLIFE AREA

130 acres; no facilities on site
Contact number: United States Forest Service 520-368-5111
Location: **Region 1**

Like the Allen Severson Memorial Wildlife Area, treated wastewater was used to create Jacques Marsh Wildlife Area. Seven ponds with 18 nesting islands, totaling 93 acres, were constructed to provide habitat for waterfowl. Elevation is 6,600 feet. Seasonally, large numbers of waterfowl can be found on the area.

The wildlife area is open to hunting. Nearest services are two miles south in Pinetop-Lakeside.

KOFA NATIONAL WILDLIFE REFUGE

660,000 acres
356 West 1st Street, P.O. Box 6290, Yuma, AZ 85364
Contact number: 520-783-7861
Location: **Region 4**

Kofa National wildlife area was established primarily to protect the area's desert Byron sheep. Quail hunting is also allowed on the refuge. The area is remote and wild and those traveling there need to be prepared for any potential problems. A brochure is available from the headquarters titled "Hunting on KOFA." It contains a map and list of hunting regulations.

Nearest services are available in Yuma.

Luna Lake Wildlife Area

Acreage not available; no facilities on site
HC 66 PO Box 57201, Pinetop, AZ 85935
Contact number: 520-367-4281
Location: **Region 1**

Luna Lake is located just east of Alpine on the New Mexico border. The lake supports a fair number of waterfowl. Contact the Arizona Game & Fish Department for more information.

Mittry Lake Wildlife Area

3,575 acres; no facilities on site
Contact numbers: United States Bureau of Reclamation 520-726-6300
　　　　　　　　 Arizona Game And Fish Department 520-342-0091
　　　　　　　　 Bureau of Land Management (928) 317-3200
Location: **Region 4**

Mittry Lake is a flooded back water off the main channel of the Colorado River. Actual water surface varies from the possible maximum high of 1,312 acres to the listed average of 388 acres. Elevation is 185 feet above sea level. Bulrush and cattail choke the marsh area and create excellent habitat for waterfowl hunting. Gambel's quail as well as mourning and white-winged dove hunting are also found on the wildlife area.
　　Nearest services are in Yuma.

Painted Rock Wildlife Area

Acreage not available
Arizona Game & Fish Dept., Region 4 Headquarters
9140 E. County 10½ Street, Yuma, AZ 85365
Contact number: 602-942-3000
Location: **Region 4**

Painted Rock Wildlife Area is northwest of Gila Bend. Painted Rock Lake is filled by runoff and irrigation water. Water depth and surface acre size varies according to available precipitation, but during wet years a tremendous flooded area backs up behind Painted Rock Dam. Due to agricultural runoff, pesticides and fertilizer residues have contaminated the lake and rendered the fish unsafe to eat. The flooded lake basin can hold large numbers of waterfowl and is a worthwhile destination for those hunters with boats and equipment. For more information contact the Arizona Game & Fish Department.

POWERS BUTTE WILDLIFE AREA

1,120 acres; no facilities on site
Arizona Game & Fish Dept., Region 6 Headquarters
7200 E. University, Mesa, AZ 85207
Contact number: 602-981-9400
Location: **Region 6**

Powers Butte Wildlife Area, located 7 miles to the west of the Robbins Butte Wildlife Area, is managed for doves. During the early season, it is open for Juniors Only dove hunting. Contact the Arizona Game & Fish Dept. for more information.

ROBBINS BUTTE WILDLIFE AREA

1,440 acres; no Facilities on site
Contact number: Arizona Game and Fish 520-981-9400
Location: **Region 6**

Robbins Butte is located to the west of the Phoenix Basin on the Gila River. It is managed by the Arizona Game and Fish Department principally for mourning and white-winged dove. Gambel's quail also benefit from the department's efforts.
The area is open to hunting, with the exception that the posted areas around department housing is closed to hunting with firearms. Some roads are closed to motor vehicles. Hours are from one hour before sunrise to one hour after sunset. No overnight camping or fires are allowed. Contact the department for more information.
Nearest services are in Buckeye.

ROOSEVELT LAKE WILDLIFE AREA

22,550 acres; no facilities on site
Contact numbers: Arizona Game and Fish Department 520-981-9400
Location: **Region 6**

Roosevelt Lake is one of three places in Arizona where Canada geese can be consistently found. The other two are Cibola National Wildlife Refuge and the San Carlos Lake/Gila River area of the San Carlos Apache Indian reservation. Over one thousand Canada geese can be found on Roosevelt Lake during the latter part of the hunting season. Portions of the lake are closed to entry to provide a resting area for the birds. Hunting is permitted outside of the closed area. Consult the hunting proclamation or contact the Arizona Game and Fish Department at the phone number above for closed zone boundaries as well as season and bag information.

San Bernardino National Wildlife Refuge

3,640 acres
RR1, Box 228 R, Douglas, AZ 85607
Contact number: 520-364-2104
Location: **Region 5**

San Bernadino National Wildlife Refuge is located in the extreme southeast corner of the state. This refuge protects natural cienegas that are one of the last remaining habitat for rare desert fish. The area is surrounded by extensive holdings of state trust lands that cover most of the San Bernadino Valley. All of the state trust land is open to hunting and offers both Gambel's and scaled quail, so there is no particularly strong draw to seek out the limited area on the refuge that is open to hunting.

Those interested in hunting the refuge should contact the address listed above. A map is available that delineates the 45% of the refuge open to hunting and shows the single hunter access road located to the north of the refuge on Geronimo Trail. Mourning and white-winged dove and quail are legal game on the refuge.

Nearest services are in Douglas.

Santa Rita Experimental Range

Acreage not available
Arizona Game & Fish Dept., Region 5 Headquarters
555 N. Greasewood, Tucson, AZ 85745
Contact number: 520-628-5376
Location: **Region 5**

This large grassland area is found on the northwest slope of the Santa Rita Mountain Range, south of Tucson, Arizona. The experimental range is a popular quail hunting destination for Tucson bird hunters. For more information, contact the Arizona Game and Fish Department.

Three Bar Wildlife Area

38,897 acres; no facilities on site
Arizona Game & Fish Dept., Region 6 Headquarters
7200 E. University, Mesa, AZ 85207
Contact number: 602-891-9400
Location: **Region 6**

Three Bar Wildlife Area is a research area maintained by the Arizona Game and Fish Department. It sits on the side of the Four Peaks area in the Mazatzal Mountains northeast of the Phoenix metropolitan area. Three Bar is a popular quail hunting area that is closed to grazing and contains some pristine Arizona upland grass cover. Contact the Arizona Game and Fish Department for more information.

TOPOCK MARSH/HAVASU NATIONAL WILDLIFE REFUGE

44,371 acres
P.O.Box 3009, Needles, CA 92363
Contact number: 520-326-3853
Location: **Region 4**

Big sections of open water marsh provide one of the largest waterfowl habitat areas left on the Colorado River. Topock Marsh is used by both Canada geese and snow geese. Hunting is allowed in the northern part of the refuge. Waterfowl, doves and quail are legal game. Contact the refuge headquarters at the address above for current rules and a map. Nearest services are in Bullhead City, and Needles, California.

WILLCOX PLAYA WILDLIFE AREA

555 acres; no facilities on site
Contact number: Arizona Game and Fish Department 520-628-5376
Location: **Region 5**

Willcox Playa Wildlife Area sits in the Sulfur Springs Valley just south of Willcox. The wildlife area is located at 4,100 feet elevation, on the 37,000-acre Willcox Playa and is the roosting area for approximately 6,000 sandhill cranes each winter. The playa is a shallow pan that fills with several inches of water and provides habitat for cranes and other waterfowl.

The area falls within an overall, playa wide, closer that runs from the first day of waterfowl season through the end of February. This effectively eliminates any bird hunting on the wildlife area.

ARIZONA'S NATIONAL FORESTS

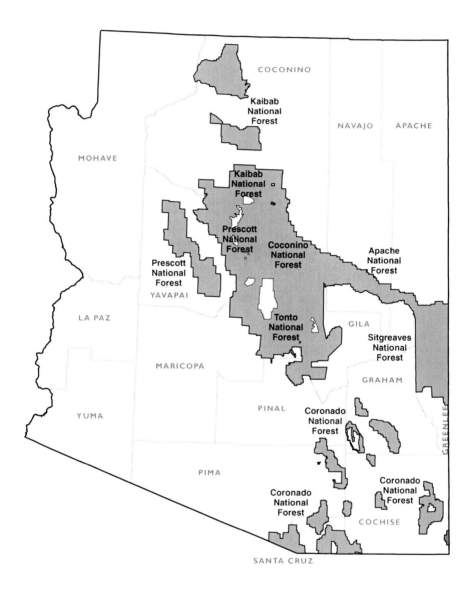

Federal and State Lands Access

NATIONAL FORESTS HEADQUARTERS

Arizona's six national forests encompass 11,369,153 acres of land, 15 percent of the state. Each national forest has a detailed map of its holdings available for a moderate fee. Contact the respective offices at the addresses listed below. In addition, national forest maps are available at map retailers throughout the state.

USDA Forest Service Regional Headquarters
    333 Broadway S.E.
    Albuquerque, NM 87102
    520-842-3292
Apache Sitgreaves National Forest – 2,003,525acres
    P.O. Box 640
    Springerville, AZ 85938
    928-333-4301
Coconino National Forest – 1,821,495 acres
    1824 S. Thompson
    Flagstaff, AZ 86004
    928-527-3600
Coronado National Forest – 1,780,196 acres
    300 W. Congress
    Tucson, AZ 85701
    520-388-8300
Kaibab National Forest – 1,557,274 acres
    800 South 6th
    Williams, AZ 86046
    928-635-8200
Prescott National Forest – 1,237,061 acres
    344 South Cortez St.
    Prescott, AZ 86303
    928-443-8000
Tonto National Forest – 2,969,602 acres
    2324 E. McDowell Rd.
    Phoenix, AZ 85010
    602-225-5200

ARIZONA'S **BLM** MAP SERIES

OVERTON 1975 T	LITTLEFIELD 1975 P	FREDONIA 1975 P	GLEN CANYON DAM 1980 P ●	KAYENTA	ROCK POINT
LAKE MEAD 1979 T ●	MOUNT TRUMBULL 1978 P	GRAND CANYON 1978 P	TUBA CITY	PINON	CANYON DE CHELLY
BOULDER CITY 1978 P ■ ●	PEACH SPRINGS 1979 P	VALLE 1983 T	CAMERON	POLACCA	CANADO
DAVIS DAM 1979 P	VALENTINE 1979 P	WILLIAMS 1990 T	FLAGSTAFF 1985 T	WINSLOW 1984 T	SANDERS 1973 P
NEEDLES ■ 1978 P	BAGDAD 1979 T ●	PRESCOTT 1987 T ●	SEDONA 1982 5 ■ ●	HOLBROOK 1982 T	SAINT JOHNS 1983 T
PARKER 1978 P ●	ALAMO LAKE 1979 T ■ ●	BRADSHAW MTNS. 1984 T ●	PAYSON 1983 T	SHOW LOW	SPRINGERVILLE 1984 T ●
BLYTHE 1978 P ■	SALOME 1975 P	PHOENIX NORTH 1979 P ■ ●	THEODORE ROOSEVELT LAKE 1982 T ●	SENECA	NUTRIOSO 1984 T
TRIGO MTNS. 1988 T	LITTLE HORN MTNS. 1982 T	PHOENIX SOUTH 1984 T ●	MESA 1979 P ●	GLOBE 1979 P	CLIFTON 1984 T
YUMA 1979 P	DATELAND 1982 T	GILA BEND 1982 T ●	CASA GRANDE 1979 P ■ ●	MAMMOTH 1978 P ■	SAFFORD 1973 P
TINAJAS ALTAS MTNS. 1984 T	CABEZA PRIETA MTNS. 1982 T	AJO 1982 T ●	SILVER BELL MTNS. 1977 P ●	TUCSON 1979 P ● ■	WILLCOX 1978 P ●
		LUKEVILLE 1983 T	SELLS 1979 P ■ ●	FORT HUACHUCA 1979 P ●	CHIRICAHUA PEAK 1979 P ● ■
			ATASCOSA MTNS. 1979 P	NOGALES 1979 P	DOUGLAS 1977 P

T Topographic Maps
P Planimetric Maps
/ Base Map not available

Out of Print

■ Minerals
● Surface

Bureau of Land Management

The Bureau of Land Management controls huge tracts of land in Arizona—16% of the state to be exact. Holdings are found statewide, but the bulk of BLM property is in the northwestern Arizona strip country and the low deserts in the western third of the state. BLM property is open to hunting, and some excellent quail hunting is found in these areas.

For maps and current information contact the addresses below. BLM maps are also available through retailers statewide.

Bureau of Land Management
Main Office
1 N. Central Ave.
Phoenix, AZ 85004
602-417-9200

Safford Field Office
711 14th Avenue
Safford, AZ 85546
928-348-4400 / Fax 928-348-4450

Lake Havasu Field Office
2610 Sweetwater Avenue
Lake Havasu City, AZ 86406
928-505-1200 / Fax 928-505-1208

Kingman Field Office
2755 Mission Boulevard
Kingman, AZ 86401
928-718-3700 / Fax 928-718-3761

Yuma Field Office
2555 E. Gila Ridge Road
Yuma, AZ 85365
928-317-3200 / Fax 928-317-3250

Lower Sonoran Field Office
21605 North 7th Avenue
Phoenix, AZ 85027
623-580-5500 / Fax 623-580-5580

Hassyampa Field Office
21605 North 7th Avenue
Phoenix, AZ 85027
623-580-5500 / Fax 623-580-5580

Tucson Field Office
12661 East Broadway
Tucson, AZ 85748
520-258-7200 / Fax 520-258-7238

Grand Canyon/
Parashant National Monument
345 East Riverside Drive
Sr. George, Utah 84770-6714
435-688-3200 / Fax 435-688-3528

Arizona Strip Field Office
345 East Riverside Drive
Sr. George, Utah 84770-6714
435-688-3200 / Fax 435-688-3528

Arizona BLM Wilderness Areas
Maps Available

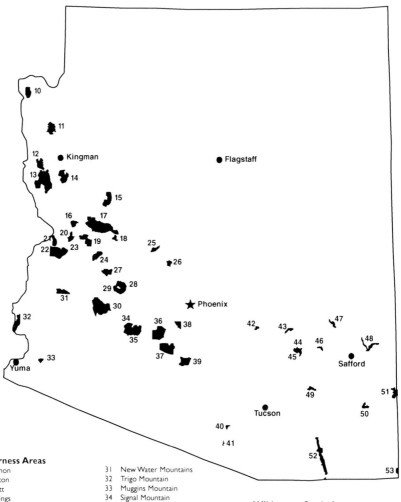

BLM Wilderness Areas

10	Mount Vernon	31	New Water Mountains
11	Mount Tipton	32	Trigo Mountain
12	Mount Nutt	33	Muggins Mountain
13	Warm Springs	34	Signal Mountain
14	Wabayuma Peak	35	Woolsey Peak
15	Upper Burro Creek	36	North Maricopa Mountains
16	Aubrey Peak	37	South Maricopa Mountains
17	Arrastra Mountain	38	Sierra Estrella
18	Tres Alamos	39	Table Top
19	Rawhide Mountains	40	Coyote Mountains
20	Swansea	41	Baboquivari Peak
21	Gibraltar Mountain	42	White Canyon
23	East Cactus Plain	43	Needle's Eye
24	Harcuvar Mountains	44	Aravaipa Canyon
25	Hassayampa River Canyon	45	Aravaipa Additions
26	Hells Canyon	46	North Santa Teresa
27	Harquahala Mountains	47	Fishhooks
28	Hummingbird Springs	49	Redfield Canyon
29	Big Horn Mountains	50	Dos Cabezas Mountains
30	Eagletail Mountains	51	Peloncillo Mountains

Wilderness Study Areas
22 Cactus Plain
53 Baker Canyon

Riparian National Conservation Areas
48 Gila Box
52 San Pedro

STATE TRUST LANDS

Arizona's State Trust lands encompass 13% of the state. Lands held in state trust are not managed or mandated for public access and recreation. They are managed to provide income for the state to benefit school systems. Trust lands are leased for grazing, agriculture, mineral use and other commercial ventures until they can be hypothetically sold.

This doesn't mean that the lands are going to be sold anytime soon. The trust mandate is to manage the land in such a way that it generates the most income. Some lands are occasionally sold, but they are generally in fill parcels that have risen in value because they nudge the edges of growing urban areas.

All state trust land is closed to entry to anyone without a valid permit. Persons holding valid hunting or fishing licenses are considered permittees. The exact language is "Properly licensed hunters lawfully taking wildlife are considered permittees for the purpose of trespassing on state land, and are therefore allowed access." See Arizona Game and Fish Proclamation R12-4-110 for more information.

To reach the State Trust Land Department contact the office listed below.

Arizona State Land Department
1616 West Adams
Phoenix, AZ 85007
602-542-4621

BUREAU OF RECLAMATION

The Colorado River is managed by the Bureau of Reclamation. This important waterfowl corridor provides much of the duck hunting and most of the goose hunting in the state. The bureau offers a map that breaks down ownership and managing agencies of the land along the Colorado River and also lists addresses and phone numbers of those agencies. A copy is available by contacting the bureau at the address below.

Bureau of Reclamation
P. O. Box 61470
Boulder City, NV 89006-1470
702-293-8415

Private Land Access

AN EXPLANATION OF ARIZONA'S TRESPASSING LAWS

No trespassing signs are an uncommon occurrence in Arizona, though as the state's population grows I see more and more. When land is taken out of cattle grazing, the next thing to go is generally hunting. Folks come from out of state, and when they unpack the moving boxes at their new ranchette, they discover that some one threw in the sign. I guess they figure that if it looked good on the fence back in "Old East Anywhere," it will look as good here.

The exact wording in the 95/96 Arizona Game and Fish Proclamation reads, "You must have written or verbal permission from private property owners for use of their legally posted private lands for any purpose including crossing these lands by foot or vehicle to get to public and state trust lands not accessible by public means."

The definition of "legally posted private lands" is lands that have been signed at all reasonable access points. The gist of it is, if you see a sign, any sign, the land is posted. Some states require a sign every so many feet that is signed by the owner or owner's agent. That is not the case in Arizona.

Some state trust land is posted with no trespassing signs, but as I mentioned in that section, those persons holding valid hunting and fishing licenses and engaged in those activities are considered permittees and are allowed access.

If a hunter is approached in the field and informed that he is on private ground and asked to leave, and the hunter is, in fact, in the wrong, he must leave. There are some people who have been granted grazing, mining or commercial use permits from the State Trust Land Department, and they try to use them to close the land to all access. This they cannot do unless they have been granted a special closure from the State Trust Land Department. Any land involved in this type of closure is required to be posted with special notices that explain the closure and when it will open again. Closures may be granted for up to 30 days.

A definition of the term "ranch" might be appropriate here. In most states the word ranch implies a large section of deeded land controlled by a private party that can be closed to hunting in its entirety. The majority of Arizona ranches are made up of mostly leased ground. A 10,000-acre cattle ranch might in reality have only 20 or 30 acres of actual deeded ground. Specifically, the land with improvements like the ranch headquarters, line shacks and developed water sites. The rest of the property is owned by State Trust, BLM or National Forest and only the grazing rights are leased to the ranch. When a ranch is sold, the grazing leases transfer with the ranch like a liquor license transfers with a restaurant.

While the vast majority of ranchers are honorable, open and friendly to hunters, occasionally someone will try to misrepresent the facts and tell a person they are trespassing and will have to leave. The best course of action a hunter can take is to know before the fact where the lines are and stay on the right side of them. When questioned, produce a map and ask for a clarification of your position. Maybe the mistake was made by you. If it wasn't, get the individual's name and license plate number and let them know that there are laws protecting hunter access in the field. See if that cools their resolve. If it doesn't, report the incident to the Game and Fish Department

A little calm and courtesy go a long way in these situations. To a rancher working from before dawn to after dusk, we hunters all look alike. He may have just spent the morning patching bullet holes in the bottom of a now-dry metal water tank. He's going to be hauling water until it fills up again. The holes were undoubtedly put there by some son of a bitch with a gun.

When you enter a ranch, stop in and say hello. Let them know who you are and that they don't have to worry about damage to their livelihood while you are hunting on their leases.

Equipment Checklists

Quail Hunting Equipment

____ Shoulder strap style hunting vest

____ Dog whistle

____ Swiss army knife in belt sheath

____ Hat

____ Shooting gloves

____ Short dog lead with belt clip (one lead per dog)

____ Snake chaps/gaiters/boots

____ Waterproof pullover shell/lightweight poncho

____ Handkerchief

____ Sunglasses/shooting glasses/ear protection

____ Lip balm/sunscreen

____ Small AA Mag-lite

____ Bird knife with gut hook

____ Quail call

____ Cactus spine pulling kit (needlenosed pliers & forceps)

____ Removable shotgun sling

____ Canteen belt

____ Additional water containers (optional)

____ Small white margarine cup for watering dogs

____ 5.5 oz. can of gourmet cat food (1 per dog per day)

____ Small sheet of folded thick-mil plastic sheet (to feed dogs on)

____ Baggie of energy treats for dogs (honey and bread sandwich cubes)

____ Short check-cord (optional)

____ One roll Vet-rap (dog first aid)

____ Small pair of binoculars (optional)

____ Bird mounting kit (optional)

____ Small camera (optional)

____ Compass (optional)

DOVE HUNTING EQUIPMENT

____ Bird bucket (for birds and empty shells)

____ Shooting stool (optional)

____ Hat

____ Sunglasses/shooting glasses/ear protection

____ Water bucket for dog/s

____ Drinking water for hunter

____ Lip balm/sunscreen

____ Handkerchief

____ Swiss army knife in belt sheath

____ Short dog lead with belt clip

____ Jaegar dog lead (tie-out cable)

____ Dog whistle

____ Cactus spine pulling kit (needlenosed pliers & forceps)

____ Shooting gloves

____ Snake chaps/gaiters/boots

____ One roll Vet-rap

____ Plastic trash bag (for policing shooting area, cleaning birds, empty shells)

____ Small binoculars (optional)

____ Bird mounting kit (optional)

____ Small camera (optional)

VEHICLE EMERGENCY GEAR

____ First aid kit

____ Five gallons of drinkable water

____ Food

____ Spare tire/s

____ Hi-lift jack

____ Shovel

____ Axe

____ Leather work gloves

____ Tools/spare parts/emergency kit

____ Air compressor/compressed air cylinder

____ Sleeping bag/s

____ Matches/lighter

Dog Supplies

____ Kennel crates

____ Dog first aid kit

____ Water container (five gallon with spigot)

____ Bucket for watering dogs

____ Dog food/bucket for feeding

____ Tie-out cables/chain gang

____ Leashes

____ Record of vaccinations

____ Certificate of good health

____ Large covered plastic tub (for soaking hot dogs)

____ Bells/beeper collars

____ Pump sprayer (type used for insecticides)
For use with water only: to wet down dogs, clean up after finding cow pies, and spraying out after kennel crate accidents (also good for hunters as a portable shower).

Hunting Supplies

____ License and hunt proclamation

____ Maps

____ Guns

____ Spare choke tubes

____ Gun cleaning kit

____ Shotgun shells

____ Binoculars

____ Game shears

____ Ice chest/s

____ Cook gear/ stove / matches

____ Flashlights

____ Compass

____ Knife

____ Sleeping bag/s

HUNTING CLOTHES

____ Underwear

____ Inner socks

____ Outer socks

____ T shirts

____ Long sleeve canvas/ chamois shirt

____ Brush pants

____ Hi top leather boots

____ Hat

____ Bandana

____ Shooting gloves

____ Sun glasses/ shooting glasses, ear protection

____ Polar Fleece

____ Shell Jacket

____ Snake gear / chaps /gaiters / boots

____ Rain gear

____ Chest waders / hip waders / rubber boots

DOG FIRST AID KIT

____ Vetrap Bandaging Tape in assorted widths

____ Gauze

____ Johnson and Johnson Waterproof Tape

____ 12 fl oz aerosol can of saline (for contact lens) to clean debris from wounds

____ Panolog ointment

____ Benadryl (for insect and snake bite)

____ Aspirin

____ Nolvasan Otic Cleansing solution (for cleaning ears)

____ Opticlear (eyewash)

____ Wound-kote spray wound dressing

____ Cut-Heal medication

____ Hydrocortisone Cream

____ Wound powder

____ Styptic Pencils

____ Ear, Nose, Throat Med-Check light

____ Thermometer

____ 3 inch and 6 inch tweezers

____ Canine nail cutter
____ Disposable razors
____ Assorted scissors
____ Rubber tubing (for tourniquet)
____ Several cotton socks
____ Tarp or sheet plastic (For carrying a bleeding dog in a vehicle)
____ Wood dowel (for holding a dog's mouth open while pulling cactus or quills)
____ Wire muzzle
____ Book: "A Field Guide: Dog First Aid" by Randy Acker, D.V.M. and Jim Fergus
____ Note pad and pencil

The Future of Upland Hunting in Arizona

Many of the men I hunt with or have contact with through bird dogs are older. They lament the loss of the "old days," and I admit a certain uncomfortableness with those conversations. I'm left not knowing what to say. Where does a hunter go in a world that is eclipsing?

I grew up on Jack O'Connor. My mother ran a small military base library; the book stacks were her principal child care provider. Jack and I spent a lot of time together. When I was 12, the base was shut down and the library disbanded. My world was taken from the shelves and put into boxes, never to be seen by me again. I feel safe in assuming that the statutes of limitations have expired when I tell you that, to my mother's credit, she violated the librarian's creed and held back a book. Clandestinely, she removed all traces of its lawful ownership. On the walk home after leaving the library one evening, she produced something from her bag and returned my favorite book to me.

O'Connor's *The Art of Hunting Big Game in North America* had a new identity, and a new clear celluloid cover to protect it for all perpetuity from the destruction of time and the ravages of change.

I was raised in southern California before municipal sterilization removed the last vestiges of the hunted from the hunter. Most hunting and any discharge of firearms was against the law, but a youngster with a passion had certain circumvention rights. There were still tattered remnants of cover left. In a vacuum, even small opportunities can sustain a fire if the core temperature is hot enough to begin with. I beared witness, so I can claim a certain right of survivorship. I have seen something go away.

It took a decade: all the wild places that I knew vanished and rematerialized as housing tracts and industrial parks connected by arteries and veins of asphalt with people flowing everywhere. Too many people.

The quality of Arizona bird hunting should hold well into the future. Gambel's especially, because there is so much available habitat for them. Scaled quail to a more limited degree. Their range is restricted to the southeast quadrant of the state where the large valleys hold much private ground that will become desirable to developers.

Mearns' also have a built-in buffer in that they live on mostly national forest ground. Unfortunately, that part of the state has become a desirable address. Of the Mearns' ground that isn't forest service, much will be lost to custom homes in the next couple of decades. Already hunter access is becoming a problem when new homeowners decide to lock off the bottoms of the canyons. The little guys have become a "destination bird," and most visiting shooters want a couple to mount. They have been hammered pretty hard, and with three years of poor summer rains, the population is down. These days they are pretty hard to find.

The glory days of whitewings are gone. Unless farming shifts from cotton back to wheat, that isn't going to change. But oh, the stories told by those who were here then. I wish I could have seen it.

Mourning doves are an Arizona staple and will continue to be. Let me take this opportunity to thank our neighbors to the north for all the mourning doves their respective states raise up and send Arizona's way. We appreciate it.

Most doves are hunted over agricultural fields (private land) and, as the state's population grows, those fields will sprout tract homes. Tract houses breed municipalities, and the next thing to happen is the restriction of shooting within city limits. Hunters will have to continue chasing the outside edges of the growing urban areas to find huntable ground.

The city of Marana, west of Tucson, recently closed almost 80 square miles of historic dove hunting ground to shooting, including popular shooting areas along the Santa Cruz River. I asked Marana Chief of Police Dave Smith why he instituted the closure. He said that it was the old story of the few ruining it for the many. He cited complaints from area farmers and ranchers such as: open gates, shot equipment, shot cattle, gasoline siphoned and stolen from storage tanks, and homeowner complaints regarding dove hunters shooting within a quarter mile of occupied dwellings. He explained that with his department's limited available resources, he didn't have the manpower to put out that many brush fires.

Arizona's saving grace is public access. Eighty-five percent of the state is held in public ownership or Indian reservation. Most of that is open to hunting. Barring some kind of statewide legislative prohibition, there will be a place to hunt. Near the large urban population centers, crowds can be a problem and hunters in those areas have to do some driving to get to fresh ground.

The overriding factor governing Arizona's bird numbers is rain. Dendrologists (those who study rain patterns through tree rings) cite that Arizona has been in an overall drought cycle since the 1930s. The average dry cycle lasts 40+ years, the average wet 60+. If they're right, that means we're due.

Arizona gets its precipitation from three sources. Fall and winter storms carry moisture from the gulf of Alaska that tracks, with the jet stream, from the northwest. Most of these storms stay high and deposit their rain across the northern tier of states. Summer (July though September) monsoon rains from the southeast are pulled out of the Gulf of Mexico. This rain pattern helps our Mearns' quail. Then there is the wild card weather pattern that forms when the warm El Niño current comes up the West Coast from the tropics, delighting saltwater fishermen and deluging the Southwest with rain. An El Niño means quail. Maybe this is the year.

The previous century in Arizona held untold numbers of quail. As we approach the year 2000 the land, though somewhat altered, is still here. All we need is the moisture. If we had 3 to 4 years of rains...

In *Game in the Desert Revisited*, O'Connor mentions seeing 10,000 Gambel's quail in one day of hunting during the 1932 season and seeing "birds, literally by the thousands" during 10 days of hunting in 1937. I have heard other accounts of men who hunted the "good years" during the '50s, '60s, and early '70s. They tell stories of hillsides lifting up and flying away. I once saw a covey of 500 valley quail lift off a hillside in Baja Norte. I saw it. I know it can happen.

Gauges of measurement are relative. O'Connor's was 10,000 quail in one day. A friend has told me that his standard of a good year was seeing 1,000 quail on a four-hour loop. That would have been as late as the 1970s. In present time, I would guess I average six to eight coveys on a three-hour January hunt. At 35 birds a covey, that is somewhere around 250 birds, but then there are those days when the extraordinary happens. I will have a dozen days next season when I see 15 or more coveys. There will probably be that many days or more, when the scenting conditions work and the dogs go from point to point to point—the kind of day where I have to root my boot through the brush to get the bird to fly and I miss easy straightaways because I got rattled waiting so long for the bird to appear. Next season, once or twice, two, then three, then four coveys will stack up as the dogs push a wash. I'll see the birds running in front and run for the high ground on the side of the wash and guess right and have 150 Gambel's flush across the front of me as they scramble for the safety of the other side of the hill.

O'Connor, in his introduction to *Game in the Desert Revisited* (January 1, 1977) wrote, "There is still pretty good quail shooting. But on the whole, a visit to Arizona leaves me depressed and unhappy. Seeing Arizona as it is today is a bit like encountering an old sweetheart in a bordello."

It would be hard to have seen what it was then and not feel a loss. Be that as it may, Arizona is still one of the last, best places for a bird shooter. I still have the book my mother gave me. The celluloid is a little dinged and frayed, it has a bit of a yellow cast, but the idea and the ideal of Arizona that the book gave to me is still captured in its pages. It's still here and waiting.

A long time friend of too many steep canyons once stopped short of the crest of a ridge we had been climbing. He had not been excited about climbing it three washes back. Earlier, when he saw my vacant stare fixed on the high ground above the drainage, he tried a polite social cue. He mentioned that the dogs were looking tired.

As I stood on the ridgeline and looked out over country I had never seen, he shouted from the downslope behind. Between breaths, he made reference to the possibility of a genetic connection between myself and the dogs. Then he shouted that I wasn't fooling him. "You just want to see what's on the other side." I never understood, until he said it, how right he was.

I really love this place. I hope this book helps you to see a part of it.

I wish I was going with you.

Good hunting, and keep those dogs watered.

Traveling with Dog and Gun

Regulations for taking dogs and firearms on a plane vary from airline to airline. Listed below are some basic guidelines, but it will be necessary for you to ask about specific policies when you make your reservation.

Insurance is available for both animals and firearms. Check with your airline for costs and limits.

Dogs

1. Your dog will have to be checked as baggage. Most airlines charge an extra fee per dog (usually around $50).

2. You will need a travel kennel for each dog accompanying you. Kennels are available at most pet supply stores and sometimes at the airport. It is best to familiarize your dog with the kennel 2-3 weeks prior to the trip so that he will be comfortable. Your dog must be able to stand up, turn around, and lie in a comfortable position. There must be absorbent material in the bottom of the kennel (a towel or black-and-white newspaper is acceptable). Two empty dishes for food and water must be accessible from the outside. Also, don't forget to label your dog's kennel with your name, address, phone number, and final destination. It is necessary to attach certification that the animal has been fed and watered within four hours of departure time. Label the kennel with signs stating "Live Animal" and "This Side Up" with letters at least one inch high.

3. You will need a certificate of health from your veterinarian, including proof of rabies vaccination. Tranquilizers are not recommended because high altitude can cause dangerous effects. If you must sedate your dog, be sure to discuss it with your vet first.

4. Federal regulations exist regarding safe temperatures for transport of your dog.
   - Animals will not be accepted if the temperature is below 10°F at any point in transit.
   - If the temperature at your destination is below 45°F, a certificate of acclimation stating that your dog is used to low temperatures will be necessary. This is available from your vet.
   - Temperatures above 85°F can be dangerous for animals in transit. Many airlines will not accept dogs if the temperature at any transit point is more than 85°.

Temperatures in South Dakota during fall may vary widely. It is a good idea to check with the reservation desk regarding current temperatures and make your reservations accordingly. If you run into difficulty transporting your dog, remember these regulations are for your dog's safety.

Guns and Ammunition

1. Firearms and ammunition must be checked as baggage and declared by the passenger. You will be required to fill out a declaration form stating that you are aware of the federal penalties for traveling with a loaded firearm and that your gun is unloaded.

2. Guns must be packed, unloaded, in a hard-sided crushproof container with a lock specifically designed for firearm air transport. If you do not already have a case, they are usually available at the airport. Call your airline for details about dimensions. If your gun does not arrive on the baggage carousel, you may be required to claim it at a special counter in the baggage claim area.

3. Ammunition must be left in the manufacturer's original packaging and securely packed in a wood or metal container separate from the firearm. Most cities in South Dakota have sporting goods stores that carry a large variety of ammunition. It might be easier to purchase shells at your destination rather than traveling with them. If you use a rare or special type of ammo, you can pre-ship it through a service like UPS.

Conditioning of Hunting Dogs

Dogs, like people, must be in top physical condition to hunt day after day. As for any athlete, proper food and exercise is the key to good health. The best performing dogs are those that are in training year-round.

Many hunting dog owners are not willing or able to devote enough time to exercising their dog throughout the year. Even if you are pressed for time, you should start working your dog regularly at least four or five weeks before hunting season. You and your dog will start getting into shape and have more stamina throughout the season.

Proper feeding of a hunting dog is important and a good grade of dog food certainly helps. Feeding once a day is sufficient, but I feed my dogs smaller amounts of moistened food twice a day. If they are working hard, animals should be given all the moistened food they want.

A dog should not be fed just prior to a workout, so feed them early in the morning before going hunting. I don't subscribe to the old adage, "A hungry dog fights best." I believe I hunt better and harder after having a good breakfast and so do my dogs. I recommend that red meat be added to the dog's diet during hunting season. It increases the palatability of the food and encourages the dog to eat more, which in turn will increase nutritional intake and energy reserves.

The benefits of a well-trained dog for bird hunting are many. Considerable time and money is required to maintain hunting dogs, but in the long run, it will add a new dimension to your life. Keep your dogs in good physical condition; they expect it of you.

- Exercise your dog all year long if possible.
- Exercise your dog at least one month before hunting season.
- Feed a good grade of dog food that is high in protein.
- Do not let your dog get overweight (an obese dog in the field can collapse quickly due to lack of conditioning).
- When transporting dogs, make sure your vehicle is well ventilated. Don't smoke around your dog in close quarters.
- Carry ample supplies of water in the field and in the vehicle.
- Dogs should be watered often which helps with stamina and scenting ability.
- Dog boots and tummy savers are useful when hunting in prickly pear country or stubble fields.
- Let dogs rest occasionally.
- Give your dogs a small nutritional treat from time to time (they deserve it).
- In the field, dogs come first. See to any needs immediately (thorns, burrs, cuts, etc.).
- Feed, care for, and make your dogs comfortable before you take care of yourself.

Preparing a Bird for Mounting in the Field

The art of taxidermy has made considerable advances in recent years. This is especially true in the realm of bird taxidermy. How you take care of your birds in the field determines the finished quality of your mounts. This crucial step is out of the control of the taxidermist. However, with a modicum of preparation, you can proceed confidently when you are holding a freshly taken bird destined for the book shelf.

Start by putting together a small kit to be carried with you in the field. Use a small plastic container, such as a plastic traveler's soap box. Throw in some cotton balls, a few wooden toothpicks, a dozen or so folded sheets of toilet paper, and a pair of panty hose.

After shooting a bird, examine it closely. First, look for pin feathers. If there are any present, you will notice them on the head directly behind the beak or bill and on the main side coverts below the bird's wing. If there are even a few pinfeathers, the specimen may not be worth mounting. By all means, save it and let your taxidermist make the decision. However, it wouldn't hurt to examine additional birds to find one with better plumage. The taxidermist can always use extra birds for spare parts.

The next step is to check for any bleeding wounds in order to prevent the taxidermist from having to wash the bird before mounting. Plug any visible wounds with cotton. Use a toothpick as a probe to push the cotton into the holes. Now pack the mouth and nostrils, remembering that the body is a reservoir of fluids that can drain down the neck. Make a note or take a photo of any brightly colored soft tissue parts (unfeathered areas) for the taxidermist's reference later. Fold several sheets of toilet paper and lay them between the wings and the body. Should the body bleed, this will protect the undersides of the wings from being soiled. Slide the bird head first into the nylon stocking. Remember that the feathers lay like shingles: they slide forward into the stocking smoothly, but will ruffle if you pull the bird back out the same end. The taxidermist will remove it by cutting a hole in the material at the toe and sliding the bird forward. When the specimen is all the way down, knot the nylon behind its tail. Now you are ready to slide the next one in behind it.

Place the wrapped bird in an empty game vest pocket, allow it to cool, and protect it from getting wet. When you return to your vehicle, place the bird in a cool spot. At home, put it in a plastic bag to prevent freezer burn, and freeze it solid. You can safely wait several months before dropping it off at the taxidermist.

For the traveling hunter, there is the option of next-day air shipping. Provided that you can find a place to freeze the birds overnight, even a hunter on the other side of the nation can get birds to his taxidermist in good shape. Wrap the frozen birds, nylons and all, in disposable diapers. Line a shipping box with wadded newspapers. Place the birds in the middle with dry ice. Dry ice is available in some major supermarkets. Call your taxidermist to be sure someone will be there, and then ship the parcel next-day air. Be sure to contact them the next day so that a search can be instituted in the event that the parcel did not arrive.

Mounted birds are a beautiful memory of your days in the field. With just a little bit of advance preparation, you can be assured of a top-quality mount.

ARIZONA TAXIDERMISTS SPECIALIZING IN BIRDS

Southern Ariizona

Crane Taxidermy
10630 E. Catalina Hgy
Tucson, AZ   520-749-1211
www.cranetaxidermy.com

Central Arizona

R and R Taxidermy
320 E. 10th Dr.
Mesa, AZ 85210
480-694-6359
www.randrtaxidermy.com

Northern Arizona

Verde Valley Taxidermy
593 S. Oasis Road
Camp Verde, AZ 86322
928-567-6471

Field Preparation of Game Birds for the Table

The two most important tools for preparing birds in the field for the table are game sheers and a knife with a gut hook.

During early season, when temperatures are in the 70° to 90° mark, I draw my birds immediately or shortly after I leave the field. You can draw your birds by several methods.

I make a cut with my sheers at the end of the breast, making a small entry hole into the body cavity. I then take my gut hook, insert it into the cavity and pull out the intestines and other body parts.

The other method I use is to take my sheers and cut up the center of the bird's back, splitting the bird in two. Then you can use your gut hook and knife to clean out the intestines and other body parts.

I like to place my birds in a cooler during the hot early season. When the temperatures are cooler (below 55°), I store my birds in either a burlap or net bag. This type of bag allows air to circulate around the birds.

I like to hang my birds before cleaning and freezing. I hang my birds in a room where the temperature is less than 60° F. I have found that two to three days hanging time is best for the smaller birds (i.e., huns, grouse, woodcock). I hang my larger birds (pheasants, ducks) from four to five days. Hanging birds is a matter of individual preference. My friend, Datus Proper, hangs his birds for a much longer period of time than I do. I suggest that you experiment and then pick a hanging time that suits your tastes.

When the temperature is over 60°F, I clean my birds and freeze them immediately. We wrap our birds in cling wrap, place them in a ziplock bag, and then mark the bag with the type of bird and the date.

Information on Hunting and Maps

LICENSES

Arizona Game and Fish Department Headquarters
5000 W. Carefree Highway
Phoenix, AZ 85023
Phone 602-942-3000
www.gf.state.az.us

VACATION INFORMATION

Arizona Office of Tourism
1100 West Washington Street
Phoenix, AZ 85007
Phone 602-364-3700 / Fax 602-364-3701
1-866-275-5816
www.azot.gov

MAPS AND PUBLICATIONS

There are several maps and publications designed to aid the hunter. Following is a list of those maps, their publishers and their cost.

NATIONAL FORESTS

USDA Forest Service Regional Headquarters
333 Broadway SE
S. W. Albuquerque, NM 87102
505-842-3198

OTHER AGENCIES

Bureau of Land Management Main Office
1 N. Central Ave.
Phoenix, AZ 85004
602-417-9600

Index

Index

NOTES

NOTES

NOTES

NOTES

NOTES